BRAIN
TRICKS

BRAIN TRICKS

TRICKS

How to Cope with the Dark Side of Your Brain...
and Win the *Ultimate* Mind Game

David L. Weiner

Prometheus Books • Buffalo, New York

Published 1993 by Prometheus Books

97 96 95 94 93   5 4 3 2 1

Library of Congress Cataloging-in-Publication Data

Weiner, David L.
    Brain tricks : how to cope with the dark side of your brain . . . and win the ultimate game / David L. Weiner.
        p.   cm.
    ISBN 0-87975-829-5 (cloth)
    1. Thought and thinking. 2. Human information processing. 3. Brain. 4. Self-actualization (Psychology). I. Title.
BF441.W445   1993
153.4—dc20   93-3901
                                                                        CIP

Printed in the United States of America on acid-free paper.

"To understanding and the greater application of common sense."

—Ilyich Barkeloff
A village in the Urals, Russia

Contents

THE ANSWERS

Acknowledgments

Although I have spent much of my life doing a great deal of business writing, it is something else all together to write for the general public and on a subject that, up to now, has been uncharted.

Every one of the tens of dozens of books I have read or skimmed about the brain or the mind has either been clinical, describing what little we do know about these two subjects, or obtuse. Early on, I learned that in order to examine the mental aspects of the brain with pure rationality, it was necessary for me to strip myself of every shred of basic belief so that my own brain became the research laboratory. My readings and observations of others became the affirmation.

Before I began this book in 1979, an old friend of mine, Paul Smith, told me, "David, it's dangerous to tinker with your mind. You might not be able to put back together what you undo."

I never forgot that warning and often felt some fear about where the process of writing this book would lead. Because at the beginning, I didn't know what the ending would be. In fact, I didn't know until four months before I finished it, when the "Answers" section just seemed to pour out. That experience reminded me of what vaudeville comedian Eddie Cantor used to say, "It took me twenty-five years to become an overnight success."

What I found I needed most during the writing of this book was encouragement. After all, I felt I had no business writing a book like this, even though I knew it would take someone without credentials to do it.

The people I would like to acknowledge here are those who took the time to read the manuscript along the way and to give me their honest comments about its direction.

Heather McCune, a trade magazine editor, read what I thought was the finished manuscript almost five years ago. She volunteered to manage it for me, but in the end we all agreed that while the book had a message, it wasn't focused enough. And so I worked on.

Barry Berish, a close friend of mine, who at this writing is chief executive officer of the American Brands division handling Jim Beam and other distilled spirits, read the beginnings of the manuscript in the early 1980s, around a pool at the Sheraton Maui Hotel in Hawaii. Much of the book was written at the hotel during vacations. Barry pointed out that the book could be important in the business world and encouraged me to continue over a ten-year period.

Bob Cox, who literally shoved me into my own business in the early 1960s, and his wife, Phyllis, helped me mold a couple of their favorite characters into the book.

Others who encouraged me through the middle and final stages of this book included Rebecca Claus; Marion Townson; Bill Freer; Jane Storey; Dave Olssen; Larry and Dolores Dore; David Cohn; Muriel and Harold Levie; Howard and Rita Levitetz; Phil and Simon Garb; my ex-wives, Phyllis Weiner and Barbara Gould; and my sons, Barry and Andy.

Kathleen Keenan came to my rescue the final year, submitting the manuscript to publisher and agent alike, and who used the rejections to help me find a new direction for the book that gives it both a message and a category. She also suggested some important edits. Bonnie Borgstrom, who had read the manuscript previously, was the first to read the new "Answers" section and told me, "It looks like you really found them."

To Eric Barinhotz, I owe the idea of the "points" found at the end of each chapter, and to Roger Axtell, the author of *Gestures* and other books about the business and social customs of nations throughout the world, I owe guidance in finding a position for the book and an elementary understanding of the publishing business.

To my secretary and friend for over twenty-five years, Donna Czukla, I owe gratitude for her quiet encouragement during the entire time the book was in process and in rearranging the order of the final manuscript. Finally, my thanks to Jan Greene for making my diskettes presentable and for handling the endless edits I gave her week after week.

David L. Weiner, February 1993

Preface

The Process of Realizing
the Trickery of the Brain

If someone had told me only a few years ago that my brain was tricking me, that I was the victim of its genetic programs and its flaws, I would have passed it off as another nutty idea in those pamphlets that zealots try to hand to you in airports.

I am a relatively normal guy. I was brought up in a religious household, went to college, married, had kids, worked hard, the whole nine yards. Two divorces later, however, it became obvious that despite the normality of what I thought my life should be, something was wrong. I spent some time seeing psychiatrists and psychologists. I read Krishnamurti and other Eastern philosophers; they appeared to me to be close to something. I read just about every self-help book that looked like it might have some answers. After years of effort, nothing clicked. I had no idea about who I was, why I was, or why I thought and acted like I did.

Then I went to an EST seminar. It was sweeping the country at the time. It was supposedly a mind-awakening process that involved two day-and-night weekends and was put together by Werner Erhard, who it later turned out, never got what he managed to communicate to others. EST was a hodge-podge of mental exercises, the final night of which we were supposed to get "it." What "it" turned out to be, for me, was that we have tapes in our brain that are programmed to play whenever someone or something presses a starting button.

It was a small beginning, a little door of insight that can only

11

be experienced, once you've gone through all those exercises they put you through.

After that, I started reading some books about the brain. There was one written by Carl Sagan called *The Dragons of Eden,* with a subtitle, *Speculations on the Evolution of Human Intelligence.* This book was another turning point for me.

Sagan described how our DNA, our genetic thread, so to speak, is composed of four letters that emanate from the binary code used in computers. What follows is one paragraph (minus his mathematical equations) from this book describing the coding for DNA:

> If there are approximately six letters in an average word, the information content of a human chromosome corresponds to about five hundred million words. If there are about three hundred words on an ordinary page of printed type, this corresponds to about two million pages. If a typical book contains five hundred such pages, the information content of a single human chromosome corresponds to some four thousand volumes. It is clear, then, that the sequence of rungs on our DNA ladders represents an enormous library of information. It is equally clear that so rich a library is required to specify as exquisitely constructed and intricately functioning an object as a human being.

It took me a while to get beyond this paragraph.

Sagan is saying that in every cell in our body we have a strand of DNA that when encoded would take up 4,000 volumes. I found this fact absolutely mind boggling. I started flipping pages to see if anywhere he would say something like, "Gee whiz, can you believe this?" He didn't.

He then described the computer-like nature of the brain, how it works on a binary system that is again, the foundation of computer programming. He pointed out that our brains have about one hundred billion neurons or nerve cells, each of which "has between 1,000 and 10,000 synapses or links with adjacent neurons." He then pointed out: "If each synapse (or connection) responds by a single yes-or-no answer to an elementary question, as is true of the switching elements in electronic computers, the maximum number of yes/no answers or bits of information that the brain could contain is about 10 trillion bits."

Again I looked for a "Gee whiz, can you believe this stuff" type of comment, but found none.

So I started saying to myself: what are we, some kind of robot? Who could design a genetic system with all those letters on it and on a strand of DNA so small that it is invisible to our most powerful microscopes.

For the next year or so, I started reading in earnest every book I could understand about the brain. I recall reading a special issue on the brain in *Scientific American,* and taking weeks trying to comprehend its most technical aspects.

What amazed me more than anything is that as much as we know about the brain today, it is still in many respects a total mystery. As of this writing in 1993, we don't know how we think . . . what the actual physical process of it is, and we don't know how our memory works.

When I first learned this, I spent weeks asking friends and business acquaintances if they were aware that the functioning of the brain is primarily a mystery and that our scientists really don't know what makes us think or how we remember things. Without exception, this was news to everyone. So I decided to write a book that would communicate this basic ignorance of the brain to people. The original premise was that if we didn't know how we thought, then how could we be certain that anything we "knew" was correct. If our most brilliant and famous scientists were stumped by the brain, why didn't they just come out and tell us, "Folks, it's really true, when it comes to the big issues of life, we just don't know jack." My goal was to expose this.

Now, among the things I have mastered in my life is technical writing. I can dig into a technical subject, learn it, then communicate it in language that virtually anyone can understand. For example, back in 1963, I wrote a manual called *Understanding the World of Sewerage.* It was written for aldermen and other city officials who had to vote on different types of sewage treatment systems. I assigned the copyright to the clay pipe company who hired me. Today, almost thirty years later, people manage to dig up my telephone number to learn where they can get a copy.

So I'm a writer and a pretty fast one. When I began this book, the words came fast. But I noticed that two or three weeks later, when I would pick up the manuscript to review it, it sounded like gibberish. And so I would start over. And over and over. I began to suspect that my brain didn't like what I was writing, since I was decidedly critical of it, and it was doing whatever it could to sabotage the effort.

Then one day I saw the movie *My Dinner with Andre* and got the idea of using two characters in each chapter to explore the subject matter. It worked. The ideas emerged, but it was still a slow process, because I realized that the only way I could get rational, objective information about the implications of our collective ignorance about the brain was to rid myself of my own beliefs. I didn't want to color anything if I could help it.

The actual writing of this book has spanned about twelve years. It wasn't until the eighth year, however, that I realized that the brain is full of trickery in order to get us to do its bidding, that the brain has an independence of its own. This altered the general scheme of the book. Now, in addition to communicating our general ignorance, which our brains like to mask, I began to see and describe the brain as both ally and foe. It's not always our friend. It doesn't always do its best for us. For example, in pressure situations it will often make us freeze up. If we're playing golf and we need a three-foot putt to win, it doesn't work to help us. It doesn't automatically calm us down, make us precisely remember what the stroke is supposed to be. It doesn't guide us mechanically through the motion and so forth. More often than not, unless our brains have the propensity to withstand pressure, we blow it. In that kind of situation, our brains are definitely not our friends.

As I continued writing the book and rearranging the chapters, I found that my own life was changing as a result. It turned out that I was going through another process that had the scattershot nature of EST but which resulted in a number of positive changes in my own personality. Today, I know who I am. I was never Mr. Calm, for example, and still am not. *But now I know why I'm not, I accept it and can control it better.* I still become upset when faced with certain traumas, but the upsets never last very long and they are not as deep as they used to be. I have found that my basic contentment level is up two or three notches. My lows aren't as low as they used to be and my highs are much higher.

There is a great comfort level in knowing that your brain is a programmed, independent instrument that is trying to trick you into doing its bidding. It is programmed, for example, to make us want to reproduce, to have children. We don't know why we are supposed to have children, since the brain doesn't come preprogrammed with our purpose precisely defined. But it gives us a predisposition to think of a purpose and so we think that one of our purposes is to have kids. And so we have them. But if we recognize that the drive to have children is a brain trick, we're not going to go totally crazy if we don't have them.

If you know that your brain is programmed to make you distrustful of those who are different from yourself—something that was useful when humankind lived in caves—you can understand your feelings of bigotry toward other ethnic groups as another brain trick. It's easier to get over these unthinking hatreds.

If you know your brain is programmed to push you toward the highest possible power level you're capable of, you won't feel as bad when you fail at something. This power thrust translates into our specific level in a family or environmental pecking order.

The primologists saw this clearly with gorillas, orangutans, chimpanzees, and baboons, when they studied them for years in the wild. It is nature's way to maintain family and herd discipline. The same pecking order still manifests itself today in some Bedouin tribes. Everyone in the family has a place in the pecking order, and when they walk somewhere, they walk in that order. Most of us don't live in the wilderness and a pecking order is no longer essential in our social lives. But the brain is still tricking us in the same way. As one result, we may feel envy when someone we know moves up to a better job or home. But if we also know it's a brain trick, the envy is easier to take and with a little focus, get rid of.

This book is a process. The chapters build upon each other to help you trick your own brain into allowing you to see it for what it is in your head. And so you've got to read them in order. If you are religious, it doesn't meddle with that belief. If anything, it might strengthen it. The book may or may not help you with your mind set, but if you are looking for some answers, you might just find them.

The other day, a friend and business associate of mine was upset because her daughter announced her marriage. She wanted a small wedding in a hotel. My friend wanted a larger wedding. She wanted to invite her friends and, if nothing else, to have the wedding ceremony in her home. Her daughter felt that her father, now divorced from her mother, would be uncomfortable attending the wedding if it were held in the family home. And so my friend spent an entire weekend in rage. She told me the story when I came to work on a Monday. After listening for half an hour, including a description of how the father hadn't done a "damned thing financially," I told her, "Your brain is working you over, it's tricking you. It wants you to have power over this situation. Your daughter's brain has somehow been programmed to long for her father. Her brain couldn't care less about what he did or didn't do with money. She is also programmed to want the wedding her way. For Christ's sake, realize it and cheer up." By the next day she had.

The first chapter of this book is a necessary nitty-gritty explanation of the wonders of the brain. It is based on fact. The chapters on science, economics, and the genome are also based on fact. Other chapters on purpose, religion, sex, and so forth are based on both fact and speculation. The speculation comes from the introspection I developed by divorcing myself from core beliefs.

While I can now write about the brain and its trickery without the benefit of characters, I have left them in the book because they make for easier reading. At the end of each chapter, however, I have included "the point" of the chapter to clarify and reinforce what the characters, many of whom repeat themselves in subsequent chapters, have said.

The last section is entitled "The Answers." There you will find very specific information about how and why our brains trick us, the programs involved, and what we can do to trick our brains back. This section will be most helpful to you if you go through "The Process" chapters first. In other words, please don't read the "Answers" section until you've read the "Process" chapters. The answers will be far more useful to you.

The Process

1

The Brain

It was not yet 7:30 A.M. on a warm Sunday morning in August. Dr. Roy Sanders and his brother Ed had already been on the road for half an hour, heading to their mother's farm some ninety miles from their home in Madison, Wisconsin. Their mother, almost eighty and a widow for five years, was in poor health, but insisted on living on the farm alone.

"I wonder if Al McCoy has been out to see mother yet?" Ed said.

"I'm sure he has," Roy replied. "I called him late last night and described her symptoms. Al said it sounded like a side effect from some arthritis medication he had been giving her and that he would be there first thing this morning. And when Al says 'first thing' it's usually before seven."

Roy, 44, was a neuroresearcher at the University of Wisconsin. He discovered early on that he was fascinated by the study of the brain and relished his moments in the laboratory studying brain function and its genetic origin. Neuropsychology had become his passion and he had published several innovative papers in the field.

Ed, three years younger, owned a small insurance agency in Madison. He had dropped out of college after his freshman year and, in a family of academics, was forced continually to nourish a self-esteem that had suffered at their hands.

The two brothers drove in silence for some moments, Ed behind the wheel. Roy, who was lean and tall, was slumped in his seat watching the rolling hills of Dade County's moraine countryside.

Ed glanced in Roy's direction and said, "I saw another article

19

quoting you last week. Something about the memory of a minnow, or something or other." Roy laughed.

"You're almost right. Actually, it was an Aplysia, a sea snail. That's what we're reduced to studying when it comes to memory."

"What do you mean?"

"I mean that despite the dozens of years people like me have been studying the actual anatomy of memory, we don't know a whole lot more today than when we started."

"You're kidding."

"No, I'm not kidding. Take this scenery along the drive, for instance. I cannot even tell you the actual physical process that takes place when something as simple as this scenery gets inputted into our brains. We have some ideas, but nothing more than that."

"But what about all those papers you've written?"

"I have written papers on memory, but they all focused on the little we do know. I'm embarrassed to tell you that *Scientific American* recently used a special issue titled 'Anatomy of Memory' as an inducement for new subscribers. What was embarrassing was that it was only eleven pages long. Of course," he said grinning at Ed, "none of my papers were included."

"Would your papers have added anything?"

"Nothing of significance." They laughed.

"You don't really want to talk about any of this, do you?" Roy asked.

"Hey, it's a good way to kill some time. Go ahead. So tell me what else we don't know about the brain that's important."

"Okay, you asked for it. Well, not only do we not know much about memory, we hardly know anything at all about how we think . . . the actual physical process of it. For example, what is going on in my brain precisely at this moment as I reach into my memory for knowledge that I want to pass onto you? How do I synthesize that knowledge into thoughts and then communicate them to you? Now, we know where some of that process takes place, but the actual physical totality of it is still beyond us. And I might add, despite everything that has been published about the brain, it's still, for the most part, a great mystery. Probably the last mystery that science needs to conquer about life on earth."

"I thought we had most of that figured out."

"A common assumption. The truth is, we are only just at the

tip of the iceberg. We have considerable knowledge about the physical anatomy of the brain, its cellular make up, the connective devices, how the brain controls many of our physical functions. But when it comes to the mental processes, we just don't know. A colleague at another university, in one of his published papers, referred to it as a mysterious black box that we at least know is ticking."

"I don't understand why most people don't know this."

"Well, let me quickly give you Brain Anatomy 101 in a nutshell and maybe you can understand the problem."

"Okay, shoot."

"Let's start with the fact that the brain has 100 billion nerve cells called neurons. Each of these has a number of branches that connect to other neurons. One reasonable estimate is that we have something like 1,000 trillion brain connections, probably more. It's tough to count in those numbers. But interestingly, one of my colleagues has estimated that if you were able to string out all your brain connections in a straight line, it would circle the earth about ten times. And even more mind boggling is the fact that in order for the brain to have its neuronal structure in place by birth, brain cells have to multiply and form connections at the average rate of 250,000 cells per *minute* during the nine-month gestation period in the womb. Can you imagine that?"

"I don't think so."

"Now to get into something even more mind blowing, all those connections had to be preprogrammed in the genes of a fertilized egg in the uterus, an egg that isn't even large enough to be visible to the naked eye and that also contains the programming for every other area of the body. Then, as the brain develops in the fetus, those 1,000 trillion connections begin to connect up as if some unseen hand were orchestrating it. Some researchers I know who have zeroed in on this one process, the development of the brain in the fetus . . . become simply overwhelmed at the mystery of the phenomenon. They say that it's like they were observing some supernatural or God force within us supervising a chemical construction process that is far beyond our current intellectual capability to grasp."

"This can give you religion," Ed groaned.

"There's a serious side to that. One of my colleagues became so crazed out with the work he was doing, the wonder of it all, that he converted to Catholicism. For other brain researchers it has done the opposite. I'm one of them. The mystery and wonder of it began to transcend any religious and philosophical concepts I believed in. I now simply look at the brain and its development in awe, without the slightest amount of comprehension of what things are really all about."

"And you're a scientist, Roy. What are dummies like me supposed to think?"

"Come on. Get off that. In terms of comprehending the mysteries of the brain, we're practically equals, believe it or not."

"I like that part."

"Do you want me to go on?" Roy asked.

"Go ahead. This is fascinating."

"Another interesting fact is that the brain works much like a computer, which is composed of hundreds of millions or even billions of single on-off circuits. Computer people call it the binary system. No matter how complicated a computer appears, it all boils down to coding that allows or disallows these billions of switches to turn either on or off. Chip designers concern themselves with designing switching mechanisms called transistors that open or close when specific electric charges are later introduced."

"Now you're talking, Roy. Computers, I can comprehend."

"That's right, you are into them. Well, okay. The brain's neuron cells are designed to function in much the same way. They can only fire what we call an excitatory or inhibitory impulse, which is very similar to the computer's on-off process. To fire those impulses, each one—every single one of those 100 billion neuron cells—actually contains tens of thousands of molecules that chemically create the electrical firing system that transmits those impulses. Under the microscope, each neuron looks like a factory unto itself. But the point is that the brain works very much like a computer, and even though it's incredibly more complicated, it is a programmed instrument that carries us through our everyday lives."

"I don't understand."

"What I'm saying is that you and I are programmed. Our brains are programmed and so are we."

"What do you mean programmed? We're certainly not programmed like some damned computer," Ed said with agitation.

"You asked me for a few interesting facts to lift you from the boredom of this drive, so I'm reciting them."

"All right, go ahead, I'll grit my teeth," Ed said, half jokingly.

"Okay, try objectively to observe your reaction to my comment that we are programmed, Ed. Then try to absorb the fact that one of the tricks the brain plays on us is that it masks the very basic, real-life nature of our lives. It actually fools around with us, plays games, in a sense. For instance, it doesn't let us think much about our brain wiring and the programs it creates. The brain turns our consciousness away from it to more ordinary things like work, sex, and football scores. There's something almost fiendish about it. So we have to exert our rational thought process to get beyond the emotions and other feelings the brain tricks us with, to make us forget what is taking place in our head at any given moment. Do you get my meaning?"

"Not really."

"Let me put it this way. Here, I'm putting my hand out and wiggling my thumb. Now where did the commands to my thumb emanate?"

"In your brain," Ed replied, beginning to calm down.

"Exactly. I made a conscious decision to wiggle my thumb. Now, we know where most of our motor functions are located in the brain." He paused thoughtfully and then said slowly, *"What we're having trouble figuring out is the thought process that caused me to make a decision and then commanded my thumb to wiggle.* Where did that thought process come from? Where was it triggered? Where was it absorbed? What exactly happened when the thought commanded the thumb to wiggle? Beyond that, which is a lot *not* to know, we do actually know a lot. It was right about here, for example, that the neuron cells fired that led to my thumb wiggling." Roy pointed to an area on top of his head, slightly in front and left of center.

"The neurons involved there," Roy continued, "fired impulses that raced in microseconds through parts of my nervous system to the thumb muscles causing it to wiggle just the way my commanding thought wanted it to. The relatively insignificant process of wiggling my thumb is enormously complicated, involving billions, perhaps trillions, of chemical reactions inside my body. We have that basic wiring process pretty well figured out. But do you agree that wiggling my thumb happened via the brain, and that it wasn't some act of God?"

"Yes, I agree. There's nothing to disagree with. But what does this have to do with your statement that the brain is tricking us?"

"Hold on, I'll get there. But first, do you agree that what we have in the brain is some sophisticated wiring that can allow me to wiggle my thumb or you to steer the car, move your head, scratch your foot, what have you?"

"That makes sense. Sure."

"So there can't be much argument that anything we do physically—walk, run, twist our heads, smile, sneeze, and the like—is controlled by brain functions. That in fact our brain is programmed to allow these movements to happen."

"I knew you'd get to programming again."

"But do you *disagree* that the brain is programmed to make this thumb move when I rationally command it to do so through a network of neural wiring, the connections in place, ready to be activated by chemically created electricity?"

"I guess not. In that context, programming is as good a word as any."

"Then you'd also have to agree that the subconscious control of physical movement such as heart beat, stomach contractions, and other internal organ function is also programmed by the brain. And I might add that the brain controls through its multitude of programs, tens of millions of chemical adjustments that keep the body functioning without any of us being aware of them. How many of us are really consciously aware of our hearts beating or our lungs breathing? You'd have to agree that this was all preprogrammed in the brain by whoever or whatever created us, because it's all functioning at birth. Obstetricians only deliver humans, they don't design their brains."

"I'd have to agree, yes."

"All right. Going one step further, do you have any objection to the statement that when a baby emerges from the womb, he or she is programmed to do certain things to survive such as suckle and breathe and swallow at the same time—which by the way he or she can't do after the first year of life—and that baby animals, insects, and other living things with brains are also programmed at birth to do certain things to survive?"

"I have no objection to that statement."

"Would you also say that human babies as well as their parents are programmed to feel a deep, abiding love for each other during the hours following birth? Would you also agree that this love is Nature's way of making certain that the baby is provided for and has a much better chance of surviving?"

"I'm sorry, Roy, I don't see how you can say *love* is something that is programmed."

"Do you believe love emanates from the brain, Ed?"

"I never thought about it, but I imagine so."

"It can't come from the heart or liver, can it, or from any other bodily organ? We can transplant or excise most of these vital organs, yet love isn't affected. So like every other emotion we experience, love emanates from the brain."

"Well, okay, but there are certain feelings that do seem to be coming from my heart or my gut."

"But you do understand, Ed, that every feeling, physical as well as emotional, a burn on the hand or intense envy is sensed in the brain. Sever certain nerves between the brain and your arm and you can feel no burn on your hand. Take specific drugs and you can alter your emotions, including envy, love, hate, and so forth. These drugs act on the brain."

"So where are you going with this?"

"What I'm getting at is that if an emotion like love is located in the brain and can be altered there, then it is wired in. And if it's wired in, then the capacity for love, other emotions, and rationality is all programmed, at least for what we might call a normal brain. True, that capacity for love and most other emotions can be affected significantly or even *created* by environmental conditioning and socialization. But the conditioning only works on brain wiring connections that have a potential to exist or already exist but need to be triggered for the first time by some experience. Our total emotional and intellectual brain programming thus remains in a state of flux. It can be ever changing. But how we are programmed in our brains at any moment in time is what we are programmed to be as thinking humans at that moment."

"I don't know, Roy. Aren't you making humans out to be robotic computers? We are far more than that. We have a spirit, a divinity, an awareness that doesn't jibe with these theories."

"Look Ed, you are again experiencing how the brain tricks you into not wanting to know exactly what it's doing. What I have talked about isn't just theory. We do know how the brain works. We know its cell structure and its neural firing systems. We know the programmed nature it appears to have. Most of what we don't know centers around the mental processes that take place *after* the cells fire up—how we think. Scientifically, we've been able to find no spirit, no soul, no outer psychic forces. We humans simply appear to be animals with an enlarged cerebral cortex that allows us to think and be creative. Without that ability we are no better than animals. Come to the hospital sometime and see what people become when they suffer brain damage that destroys most of their mental faculties."

"I've seen people with brain damage."

"Most people have, but they look at it as another sickness. Their brains keep them from seeing what is really going on: the total control their brains have over every physical and mental aspect of their lives. The result is that all these great new facts about the brain are being uncovered and yet most humans continue to think they are something above and beyond their brains. Most of us continue to believe in theories about the spirit and the soul because we were taught or guided to believe in them. When we were sitting out there in caves and on the desert these theories made some sense. But a lot of time has passed. Today we have fantastic laboratories and other facilities for brain research, but most of our new-found knowledge goes for naught because we aren't listening to what little we are learning. Our brains aren't letting us pay attention. It's a real struggle. Most of us still have at least one foot back there in the caves and desert believing in hand-me-down, ancient and medieval concepts."

"Christ, you've really changed."

"Sure I've changed." Roy responded, somewhat irritated. "What we are learning I've attempted to apply to my emotions as well as to my rational thought process. I view humans as nothing more than enlightened, creative animals, who, while intellectually capable of reaching unknown heights, still possess powerful, animalistic, emotional drives that cause misery and death and may perhaps lead to the complete extermination of all life on Earth. What most of us don't want to realize is that if the brain is a mystery then so is everything else a mystery. If we can't comprehend *how* we comprehend, then what does make sense for sure?"

"A bit of philosophy."

"Why not? There is a new philosophy to be derived from our studies of the brain. Some are already pursuing it."

The two brothers rode in silence for a few moments, each contemplating the magnitude of the conversation. Then Ed volunteered, "I got a little excited there, didn't I Roy?"

"You got excited. I got excited. It still beats listening to a religious service on the radio."

"Okay, one last question?"

"Go ahead."

"What do you think our biggest problem is with the brain, today?"

"That's easy. The problem is not inside the brain, but outside of it, namely, our inability to understand that most of the powerful emotional drives we have—the drives that create conflict within ourselves and in society—come from what many call our 'old brain.' This term refers to the hypothalamus and limbic system, where our raw animal emotions are stored and over which supposedly evolved our cerebral cortex, which houses our intellect. Our ability to reason, which comes from the cerebral cortex, very often comes in conflict with drives from that old limbic system, what some have called the 'dark side' of the brain. Sometimes we'll recognize those conflicts, say a feeling of sexual jealousy or hatred, or the fright that our reason doesn't want to feel during moments when they make no sense. We simply take for granted these old limbic drives and the confusion they create as a basic human condition. There are many recognized authorities who believe that many of our more basic human drives, such as power, the awe of authority, the social pecking order, territoriality, ritualism, and so forth are the result of limbic system programming."

"And how is it that all this is such a big problem?" Ed interrupted.

"Because most humans aren't taught to recognize these raw drives as purely genetic and animalistic. If we were, we'd have a better chance of putting them in a perspective that would allow us to determine if we really needed to follow them. Many of us have emotional drives that our reason doesn't want. We'd like to be able to ignore or get around them. Some of us find our own special ways for doing so. But the problem that most individuals throughout the world have is that we haven't pinpointed most of these drives as animalistic and outdated. And the brain itself doesn't cooperate in telling us about them. As a result, we just let old brain drives push us around. And, as a result, the world is filled with mayhem, violence, and inequity."

"That's a big problem."

"That's a problem, Ed."

Ed reached over and turned on the radio.

"Maybe we can find some quiet music."

"Suits me," Roy said.

"Maybe we can talk more about this on the way home."

"Do me a favor, Ed, just turn up the music."

THE POINT

Our brains, it turns out, are very humble instruments. They would like us to believe that something else "out there" is controlling us: a soul force, a mind force, a God force, or simply the force of our own wills, whatever that is.

The brain appears programmed to mask its role in our lives, as Dr. Roy Sanders pointed out. It's as if it doesn't want us to know that it's up there, controlling us with computer-like techniques. The discovery of the binary system and the development of computers should have helped us to recognize this fact. After all, we know that many of the images we see on television come out of a computer. And as complicated as those images may seem, they are all based on brilliantly coordinated computer switching mechanisms that are either turned on or off—switches turned on or turned off. In essence, that's all a computer really is. And that's all we've discovered the very basic operating system of the brain to be. Neurons firing or not firing.

If somebody asked us who we are as human beings, probably the last thing we would ever say is, "Well, as far as we know, we are a chemical miracle of some kind with a computer-like brain as our control mechanism." And yet, that's really what we all are in the very essence of our being.

Even more unsettling is the fact that while we know the brain works with on-off switching mechanisms, we haven't figured out the software that stores our memory and allows us to think. The brain imaging devices that neuroresearchers use these days show that as we think and feel emotion, there is something like a lightning storm going on in our brains. So we know it's all happening there.

Most of us read newspaper articles about the brain or see them reported on public television. It's not as if we don't know what's going on. But the genetic masking mechanism with which we appear to be programmed is obviously a very strong one. *It doesn't let anything really sink in.* An hour after reading this, you probably won't give it a second thought.

But in order to prepare ourselves to begin tricking our brains back, we have to begin thinking about the brain as a computer during the traumatic moments of our lives.

Let's go on.

2

Life Is a Lottery

Elsa Dixon, 34, a psychologist, sat comfortably in a chaise lounge on the sun deck of her New York City apartment building. Next to her was her husband, Alexander, 36, a fashion designer. It was Saturday afternoon and a hot, muggy day. The sun deck, located on the top floor of their Manhattan high-rise, was relatively uncrowded. Elsa and Alexander had staked out a corner for themselves that would catch the sun for most of the afternoon.

"I wonder where everyone is," Alexander said, looking up from the magazine he was reading.

"I'm not sure, but I would suspect that there are a lot of people off visiting their kids at camp," Elsa replied.

"You're probably right. I thought the sun deck would be loaded by now."

"Thank God it isn't."

"Amen."

They sat in silence for a while, oblivious to the sounds of the city all around them. Then Alexander spoke. "You know, Elsa, I'm sitting here reading this article describing the incidence of a specific gum disease among teenagers—it's really frightful. Once you encounter it, you can pretty well kiss your teeth goodbye. And yet nobody knows how you get it. One day you wake up, look in your mouth, and that's all she wrote. Now what does that tell you?"

"It tells me not to look in my mouth unless I am prepared for bad news."

"No, come on Elsa, what does that really tell you?"

"I don't know, Alexander, what does that *really* tell me?"

"It should tell you that life is damned chancy."

"Oh, shit."

"No, I mean it, Elsa. There you are, the odds of getting this thing, they say, are about 300,000 to 1. You look in your mouth and you've got this disease. What that says to me is that this is one very solid example of how chancy life really is."

"Are we getting into one of your weird conversations again, Alexander?"

"Well, hell, we have nothing else to do."

"For Christ's sake, Alexander, it's 98 degrees in the shade, the humidity is so high that my sunglasses won't unfog, and you want to get into something weird again. All week long I see crazies. On my day off I don't need your weird discussions."

"But what's so bizarre about chance? Just what is so strange about how life is really a lottery?"

"Oh sure, I talk about that everyday with my Aunt Tillie. It's an obsession with me."

"Come on, Elsa. You had a paper published in some journal that touched on it. Just after we were married."

"I don't remember that."

"It had to do with psychism and predestination. It was a great piece of writing."

"Oh, you're right. Now I remember it. Flattery always jogs my memory. Something somebody said on TV about how our lives are totally guided by unseen forces got me mad and I wrote it in one day. It was a short paper."

"So it was short. You were into the subject at one time, so let's talk about it now."

"You're sure you wouldn't rather talk about the Mets?"

"No. I'm sitting next to an expert. So let's talk about how chance affects our lives."

"Some expert," she shrugged. "Off the top of my head, it was a two-page article, and it didn't have that much to do with chance."

"But it was a good article, and as far as I'm concerned that makes you an expert."

"I'm simply amazed how you manipulate me with flattery, and even more amazed at how well it works. All right, where do you want to start?"

"I don't know. Wherever you want to start."

"You're really helpful, Alexander."

"Come on."

"Give me a few seconds to think."

Elsa stared up at the clear sky for a few moments. Then she began.

"Let's start with the ejaculation."

"I knew it. Not only an interesting start, but a dirty one. Amazing, Elsa, how in your serious moments you always revert to character."

"Alexander, get off it. Let me start on this. I do have a couple of thoughts."

"Go ahead, press on."

"All right. When you get right down to it, just the mere fact that we are born as we are is a matter of incredible chance. I mean, visualize this. A bed, Alexander, and in it your mother and father are doing it . . ."

"Hold it, Elsa. That's a simply marvelous visualization. That is a wonderful thing to behold in one's imagination. Mom and Dad . . . doing it. You are a definite sicko. Continue . . . this is a fascinating beginning."

"Well, there they are, doing it. No children as yet. Your parents were married as I recall for about three years before you were conceived, so let's guess that they had done it 600 times. This was intercourse number 601."

"Hold it," Alexander interrupted. "I can't imagine my mother and father doing it 600 times during their entire marriage. Once, twice, maybe."

Elsa stared blandly at Alexander.

"Okay, okay, I'll get off it. You must admit, however, that this *is* a bit weird."

"If you'll just let me stick to the subject."

"Go. Speak."

"Thank you. Here they are this night doing it and it turns out to be the night you were conceived. So the odds of you being born at all start out at 601 to 1. And that doesn't include all the times your father might have masturbated."

Elsa paused.

"I'm not saying anything. Heaven forbid. Please proceed."

"All right, let's go back to the ejaculation that created you."

"By all means."

"That ejaculation after the lovemaking contained somewhere between 100 million and 500 million sperm cells. For right now, let's be conservative and call it 100 million. We now have 100 million of your father's sperm cells swimming up your mother's vagina while simultaneously fighting various acids and substances that are trying to kill them all off. As a matter of fact most of them are indeed killed off. By the time the remaining sperm cells have reached the egg, there are only about 50,000 left. So the odds of you, Alexander, as a sperm cell even getting close to your mother's egg were only 1 in 200."

"How does that relate to the 601 to 1 odds you recited before? In other words, what are the cumulative odds at this point in your sick example?"

"I'm not a mathematician. I am just reciting facts here. You compute the cumulative odds."

"Forget it."

"Okay. There are now approximately 50,000 of your father's sperm cells surrounding that egg, all wanting to get in."

"Pardon me, Elsa. Is this all medical fact?"

"This is medical fact, Alexander. You can check it in the library."

"Never mind, I believe you."

"Thank you. Now, talk about life being a lottery. Only *one* of those 50,000 sperm cells, yours, is accepted by the egg. At the instant of entrance, a membrane is created around the egg that keeps all the other sperm cells out."

"I am in there alone."

"By yourself. The other 50,000 sperm cells simply die, as did the original 100 million minus one. You are the winner. Forget the prior odds. Just the mere fact that you got inside the egg was a minimum 100 million to 1 shot, maybe as high as 500 million to 1, just from that single ejaculation that night."

"You're saying, Elsa, that any other sperm cell would have created a different me."

"Absolutely. No two sperm cells are identical. Just for starters, each sperm cell carries either a female or male chromosome. It's the sperm cell that determines sex, not the egg. So the sperm cell that created you, Alexander, might have just beat out the sperm cell that might have made you a woman. Perhaps by microseconds."

"It could have been that close, huh? Me, a woman."

"Or another man, different than what you are. Look at some of the incredible differences that can exist between fraternal twins. Those twins involve two sperm cells fertilizing two eggs. It's a fact that no two cells in our entire body are totally identical, including sperm. By the same token, no two eggs are alike. The odds of you coming into being from one specific sperm cell out of the trillions produced by your father during his lifetime combining with fertilizing one of approximately 700 eggs produced by your mother during her lifetime are beyond calculation."

"I'll tell you, Elsa, I never looked at it quite that way."

"If you want to go deeper into your own chance happening, think of the odds of your father meeting your mother, and the fact that they then courted, fell in love, and married. Any other person marrying your father or your mother might not have created any children at all. And if a child was created, it certainly would have been far different than you."

"My father and mother met in college."

"Well, look at the odds of that. What if they had each gone to different colleges or never went to college at all. In all probability they would have never met and you wouldn't be here."

"The more you go on, the more incredible I sound."

"But what I've said is only the beginning. Now look at the same odds that created both your mother and your father. The same process was followed. The chance happening of each of their mothers and fathers meeting, courting, and marrying. The hundreds of times your two pairs of grandparents had intercourse, the trillions upon trillions of sperm cells involved. If the odds were incalculable before, think of them now."

"I prefer not to, Elsa. Big numbers throw me off."

"Now keep going back 5,000, 10,000, 100,000, 500,000 years and more, even back to the primate stage and follow that same process through. The chance happening of your being here today, sitting with me on this sun deck is totally beyond comprehension. A practically infinite number of sperm cells died except the ones that counted and led to the conception that created you."

"So I suppose I should be happy."

"You are a supreme winner, Alexander, just for existing on Earth. In just your own father's ejaculation, you beat out at least 100 million other sperm cells, all swimming upstream like mad. If that doesn't make you a winner, what does?"

"So why am I usually depressed?"

"Good grief, what a question after all that. Probably because you don't know how lucky you are just to be here. If you understood that—if you could cut through all your basic mind-sets, beliefs you were taught or just absorbed—and could intellectually understand why you exist and how you came to be here, you probably wouldn't be depressed. None of us would be. We have a big problem in that we can't see the reality of our own lives within the perspective of the miraculous chance happenings that created us."

"Aha. But that leads to an even deeper question. Are we better off being a winner and going through the mess of our earthly life or being one of the trillions of losing sperm and getting some time off from this real life existence?"

"Too deep for me. Besides, it's off the subject. You asked me about the effect chance has on our lives, and if I must say so myself, sweating like the devil up here, I didn't make such a bad beginning."

"No, you didn't, Elsa. It was far more than I had ever imagined."

"Okay, so with that as a backdrop, take a look at the chance happenings of celebrities and heroes in our own lifetimes and in history. Ronald Reagan, the product of one lucky sperm cell. Henry Kissinger and Richard Nixon, both fast sperm swimmers. Julius Caesar, Jesus Christ, Moses, General Franco—big-time sperm swimmers. Cary Grant and Benedict Arnold, both lucky swimmers. We are all chance happenings with the odds of the happening multiplying from generation to generation. When you get right down to it, all of it is probably without any plan, unless there is some giant computer in the sky with a magnetic contraption that can spur certain sperm cells out of trillions to action on specific days to create some predestined outcome."

"I think that was the point I liked so much in that paper you wrote."

"You're right. It's amazing. I really haven't thought much about it since. That must have been eight or nine years ago. Oh, God, that sun is hot."

Elsa stood up, adjusted her towel on the chaise lounge, and laid down on her stomach.

"Could you rub some lotion on my back?"

"Sure enough."

Alexander picked up the suntan lotion, squeezed a big glob into his hand, and began rubbing it on Elsa's back and legs.

"Um, I love the way you do that."

"You're just lucky I won that sperm race."

"If I could have been there, I would have cheered you on."

"I would say the quarters were a little cramped for bleachers."

"You know, you're a little nuts."

Alexander put his face close to Elsa's.

"*I'm* a little nuts? After that monologue of yours, you can call *me* nuts?"

Elsa laughed.

"You know, the way you put it," Alexander continued, "with all that cold chemistry, you are throwing the notion of predestination into a cocked hat."

"Not necessarily."

"What do you mean? Those chance happenings have such infinite odds, predestination just doesn't fit any part of the picture."

"Yes, but don't forget, Alexander, life here is really anyone's guess. If nature could figure out how to pack the coding for our body structure into a sperm cell so tiny it's invisible to the naked eye and then produce millions of them a day, it can do practically anything."

"Yes, but if we take what you've said seriously, then some kind of fate or predestination for all of us seems out of the question."

"From a purely rational point of view, you're probably right. If the Creator had predestination in mind, I don't think He'd design a reproductive system involving billions of sperm cells. Rather, He would make it possible for one predestined sperm cell to be implanted in one predestined egg at some predestined point in time. And that would result in one predestined person. If He had predestination in mind, I can't imagine why He would want to design an overkill reproductive system, with billions of sperm being reproduced in the testicles every month. Unless you have some faith or belief system that includes the concept of predestination, it's hard to give it much credence."

"But it could exist," Alexander said.

"Yes, it could. There is just no rational explanation for it. That's just the process of being born. If you look at life after birth, the concept of predestination appears even more unreal. Let's get back to you again, Alexander."

"I'm ready for it."

Elsa chuckled.

"Let's talk about what happened *after* you were born. If we all believed as, say, Napoleon actually did, that everything that happens after birth is predestined, then some unseen guiding force of Nature would have led you to choose the toys you played with and determined when you decided to ride your tricycle, the times you refused to eat your pudding, who your classmates would be in kindergarten, the songs you sang in music class, the precise times you went to the bathroom each day, the people you met each day, what you watched on television each hour, the girls you dated, the food you ate at each meal of your life, the jobs you had, and what you did in Boy Scouts. When you think about all the coordination necessary to orchestrate predestination for every person on Earth past and present, you again find yourself in a mind-boggling situation. Practically everyone today has some ultimate effect on everyone else on Earth. For predestination to work in our lives everyday, someone would have to coordinate and guide what 4.5 billion people are doing every second and what happened every second during the lives of the tens of billions of people who came before us."

"Which sounds impossible," Alexander interrupted.

"And yet it is possible. That's the crazy thing about not having any important answers to life outside of faith. You can't be too sure about anything. Rationality by itself is only one more belief system, no more defensible than any strong belief in a religion or concept based on spirituality, mythology, or faith. Rationality is only an intellectual conclusion of what we coldly observe; it may not be the real world at all."

"But it is real, Elsa, from our vantage point of living in the world. I mean if you accept the fact that we are living and that we are not all illusions and so forth, then reason is the best shot we've got."

"In your opinion. In my opinion. But not in the opinion of the spiritualists and religionists who contend that there is far more beyond our own chemistry. And as we've both said before, they could be right."

Elsa and Alexander stopped talking as they looked up and watched three skywriters rather quickly spell out the name of a beer slogan.

"Would you look at that? Three of them," Alexander said.

"It's marvelous. Speaking of coordination, that is really well done. There must be something going on down at the river."

"Probably."

They watched the planes for a few more minutes and then Elsa spoke:

"All right, let's cover one more thing."

"What's that?"

"Once born, then comes the chance happening of death."

"I knew you'd finally get onto something really cheerful."

"If you think of death from a cold, rational point of view, it is as much of a lottery as is birth."

"In what way?"

"Well, the interesting thing about death is that Nature did not design humans or other living things to live in perpetuity. At least physically. We are all going to die, unpleasant as that thought might be. The only question is what element of chance will cause our deaths and when? In terms of our physical defenses, nature does not deal with an even hand. Some of us from the time we are born are more susceptible to disease and disorder than others."

"Or even in the womb," Alexander said. "Some of us die in the womb."

"Right. One brother out of four might die in that womb. Another might succumb at the age of 3 from a kidney ailment; another might live to 60 and die from cancer. The remaining brother might live to be 112 and die from pneumonia because he was caught out in the rain. While there might be environmental influences effecting the deaths, some genetic studies have shown that some of us are predisposed to an early death."

"I think I agree with that."

"There are other ways chance affects the onset of death. Some of us might drive cars for years without mishap; others are killed while taking driving lessons. Tens of millions of soldiers have been involved in wars of one sort or another. Millions were killed. Millions of others on the same battlefields were not. There is no pattern to any of it. Nature doesn't strike dead prematurely only those persons with negative personality traits. How we lead our lives in a spiritual sense also doesn't seem to matter. Hardened criminals can die of old age. A gentle priest can be ripped apart by bullets in a guerilla war or die of a heart attack at the age of 30. I mean, just look at the cold facts of life and try to put some sense into it, other than the fact that we are all just accidental happenings that exist very temporarily."

"Well, I don't think I can make any sense out of it."

"The chanciness of it all is right there for us to see. Yet our brains appear to be programmed in some way that blocks this fact out of our minds. I mean, we don't go around everyday wondering what chance happening brought us into life and what chance happening will cause us to die. If we did that, we wouldn't get very much accomplished in between."

"I can tell you that that kind of thinking would occupy my mind, without that blockage or whatever it is," Alexander interrupted.

"You're probably right," Elsa paused. "But getting back to it, the fact that the brain blocks out reality causes us to focus on ourselves. We become possessive of life. We believe we were born for some purpose. We don't think of ourselves as some random sperm cell that got in an egg, out of some 100 million others. We think we know the reasons why we were put on Earth. And if in the midst of our quest to fulfill those reasons some tragedy strikes like a cancer, we'll wonder, 'why me?' Why not someone else? Someone in jail, for example. Or some real jerk. Or someone older. Why me with this cancer? Why Mr. or Mrs. Nice Guy? What we don't realize is that being Mr. or Mrs. Nice Guy doesn't matter when it comes to sustaining life. It only matters because we'd all be a lot better off if this Earth contained more Mr. and Mrs. Nice Guys. Life would be easier, more pleasant and harmonious. But being nice doesn't assure a long life. One day we are born and one day we die. That's the long and the short of it. And if there is some computer in the sky programming all of it, then my compliments to the Design Engineer."

"So what are we supposed to think, Elsa?"

"I really don't know what we're supposed to think. We can believe in a religion that has pat answers based on faith. If that makes someone feel better, then I suppose that's a good thing to think. Or we can believe in nothing. Or we can just be curious about what is really going on. There is probably nothing we are *supposed* to think, because when it comes to figuring out what life is really all about, we haven't even reached the batter's box."

"This all means, I imagine, that I needn't worry about where we're going to have dinner tonight?"

"Good grief, Alexander, you mean you haven't made a reservation yet? This is a Saturday night."

"Are we back to the real world? Notice how quickly a chance remark brings us back to reality. Nature doesn't let us hang out there zeroing in on our limbo state very long. Among other things, it wants us to have dinner."

"Correct. And unless you get your little ass off this sun deck and down to the apartment where you can dial a telephone and make a reservation at Jimmy's, because I have a taste for ribs, you will be in damned big trouble."

"Like what kind of trouble?"

"Like I'm going to go back to the beginning of this ridiculous conversation and describe your mother and father in bed again."

"Enough said. You win. I am making my way downstairs. Notice my feet moving. Please don't talk. Make use of the quiet time while I'm gone." Alexander backed slowly away. "If Jimmy's doesn't have a table, I'll threaten to come in anyway and make a terrible scene. I will. . . ." Alexander's voice faded away as he passed through the doorway to the elevators.

Elsa smiled, looked up, and saw the beer slogan in the sky begin to fade away.

THE POINT

Who and what we are is simply a matter of luck. The random accident of our birth could have placed us with billionaire parents or in a public housing project, or as aborigines in the back hills of Australia.

The genetics that were involved with our egg could have made us virtuoso musicians, marvelously coordinated athletes, brilliant chess players, or unwieldly klutzes.

As young children, we might have had parents who were wonderful guardians or child abusers. If we were gifted genetically in some way, music for example, we might have had parents who recognized that talent and nurtured it. Or we might have been sold by young, peasant Chinese parents into a Philippine brothel, with no chance of ever expressing our talent.

As young adults, we might have found ourselves working as forklift drivers in a factory, supporting three kids and without any hope of bettering ourselves, perhaps because we didn't have the basic smarts or because we were afflicted with a genetic depressive state that made it difficult to get through the day. Or, we might have had very high genetic capability, with the I.Q. and the inherent motivation to get into medical school, become a cardiologist, and be comfortably wealthy. Then again, maybe we had the genetic coordination and the conditioning from guardians that allowed us to make the tennis finals at Wimbledon. Or maybe we were one out of hundreds of thousands of young actors who had precisely the right looks and energy level to be picked for a part in a TV soap opera.

It's all luck, all of it: from conception to the conditioning we had during our upbringing, to the breaks we had in later life. Certainly we can take credit for making the most of the breaks that come our way. We can also take credit for keeping our heads down and working hard regardless of the luck we have. But it's the breaks that are crucial: without the right ones, we might not be alive.

If we understood what luck is, if we had any comprehension of its substance and could control it, we wouldn't see millionaire baseball players crossing themselves at bat, or a family praying for a son to pass the bar. The good luck charm manufacturers would be out of business and superstitions would vanish.

Our brains, however, mask all of this. They want us to believe that there may be predestination out there, that there is something important going on. So we end up blaming ourselves for things that are absolutely not our fault, because our brains allow us to be misled by the so-called experts who encourage us to believe that we control our own destinies. Tell that to a stricken child born in a public housing project addicted to the same crack cocaine as its mother.

Life is indeed a lottery. As Oscar Hammerstein wrote in the song "Some Enchanted Evening" from the play *South Pacific,* "Who can explain it, who can tell you why, fools give you reasons, wise men never try." That sums it up. If in this life your luck has been bad, then maybe you'll do better in the next one, if there is a next one. In the meantime, do the best you can with what you have. Maybe some needed break, some whim of fate, will still come your way. No one can explain it.

3

What's Behind the Universe?

Carl Ullman walked into Studio A of WCRK, a public service radio station in San Francisco. He greeted his guest who was already seated in the small studio and then began reviewing the questions he would be asking. The program was taped, but it was Ullman's practice to let it air unedited. He liked the spontaneity that it added to the show.

"Unlimited Reality" was syndicated to public service radio stations where market support warranted an offbeat listenership. Consisting of one-on-one interviews with people who shared their groundbreaking ideas in psychism, consciousness, transformation, transcendentalism, and mysticism, the program was known for its innovation and dynamism. Its audience was fiercely loyal.

With a quick "go" sign to the control room, Ullman signalled his readiness to the producer, who nodded and cued the engineer to let the tape roll—another adventure into reality was about to begin.

"Welcome to 'Unlimited Reality,' " Ullman intoned through his microphone. "Today we have with us Henry Heiman, a man I met for the first time on a bus two weeks ago. Out of nowhere we struck up a conversation and immediately I became fascinated by him. Let me preface this by telling you that Henry is 46 and has no academic credentials to speak of. He hasn't written any books, he hasn't given any lectures, and this is the first broadcast he's ever participated in. Now let me tell you what he *has* done. He's given a lot of fresh thought to a number of subjects, in particular evolution. I thought you'd enjoy hearing what he has to say. With introductions out of the way, let me turn to my guest and begin with the obvious question. Henry, how did you first become interested in the subject of evolution?"

"Well, Mr. Ullman, I'm going to have to start out with an ambiguous answer and tell you that I'm not really sure. It was sort of like evolution, it happened over a long period of time." Henry chuckled, enjoying his little joke, then continued, "I read Charles Darwin's *Origin of Species* two or three times and a lot of other books on the subject and it just seemed to me that everyone was missing the point."

"What point?"

"That the process of evolution on this planet is not very important. That what we know so far doesn't mean very much."

"Can you explain that?"

"Well, it's been more than 140 years since Darwin wrote that book and it seems that a good deal of scientific research has gone into finding hard evidence linking the gorilla and man. I can't get excited about that. So we find that last link. Then what? What do we really know?"

"We'd know that Darwin's theory of a slowly evolving life process was correct. That humans did evolve through a series of life forms."

"Big deal."

"But shouldn't we be curious about that?"

"Why should we be?"

Ullman began to feel a little uneasy. In the back of his mind he was already thinking of some standby guests he could bring in tomorrow and still get the program aired on schedule. He lit a cigarette and decided to punch out a little.

"I think you are trying to say something and now might be a good time to just say it," Ullman said with a hint of impatience.

Henry stared in puzzlement at Ullman for an instant, then said, "By gosh, I think I will. Okay, then. Let's go back to the beginning of everything in the heavens, and beyond, if there ever was a beginning as we understand the word. The result of that beginning, or whatever we want to call it when whatever exists was started, is what we see around us and know about today. The number of years that have transpired between then and now is probably immeasurable, but certainly nothing we can comprehend at this moment. Our universe alone is supposedly 15 billion years old. But how long before that was something happening, something going on? Life on Earth is probably not meaningful at all in the range of total time, even if there is such a thing as total time, since we know of no beginning. How important, therefore, is it to know if there is a link between man and gorilla, considered within that perspective? The subject of evolution really covers that entire expanse of total time."

This is a little better, Ullman thought.

"How do you think it all started, Henry?"

"I haven't the vaguest idea and neither does anyone else," he harrumphed, "except for people who are led by blind belief rather than rational knowledge. The fact is that we have wound up with living organisms on Earth and we haven't been able to detect life anywhere else. For all we know, we are the only living beings anywhere.

"One thing we do know from the scientists who have developed what we earthlings consider sophisticated instruments, is that the handful of basic chemical substances found on Earth are present throughout this universe. That, of course, includes our own galaxy of about 100 billion stars. So the odds are that the same set of circumstances that produced life on Earth created it somewhere else. But it's a guess. We are all part of some happening whose very origins are still unknown. It wears you down thinking about it, which I do a lot, and that's why I like old Abbott and Costello movies."

Ullman fought to hold back a chuckle as he replied, "It's interesting, Henry, that you equate the question of life in other places with the process of evolution here on Earth."

"Well, there are a great many people who think that astronomy and space exploration are both connected with the study of evolution. We are trying to find out what has been going on out there: the whys and wherefores and hope that we'll discover other humans somewhere who have more answers than we do. Now I'm as anxious as the next fellow to communicate with other humans, wherever they may be, but I'm not sure they'd know a whole lot more than we do."

"What do you base that on, Henry?"

"The universe is big, isn't it?"

"It's big, very big."

"It's big beyond words, at least from our viewpoint. It may even be endless, whatever that means. I heard one physicist say that we will eventually learn how big the universe is because it's circular and thus can be defined once it stops expanding. I think that's ridiculous.

If the universe is circular and remains so at its final expansion point, then what's beyond that? My friends and I used to talk about this when we were 12. There are absolutely no answers. If you put together every scientific fact we know today, the sum total of them doesn't project the slightest clue as to why the universe even exists. So why would people on other planets quadrillions of miles away know any more than we do? What are they closer to? Maybe we're closer. Why would whoever orchestrated all this single out groups of people on selected planets to let them in on the secret and not tell anyone else?"

"But maybe that happened."

"Heck, anything is possible, but it would certainly make me extremely upset if that were the case."

This was definitely more like it. Henry Heiman was a real off-the-wall character, Ullman thought. His audience would like him.

"But why, Henry, would it make you angry if some other planetary people found the answer to this mystery of life or were handed the answer?"

"Because it would be unfair. Why should we on Earth have to live in the dark if the answer were available somewhere else? Now, it's conceivable that a civilization 15 million years older than we are understands that the mystery of the universe is insoluble and has systems that allow life to exist without unnecessary conflict. Or maybe it takes longer than that. Or maybe an understanding of reality is not comprehensible to anything or anyone in the universe and beyond, with a standard human brain as we know it. My personal view is that if we were able to hold a convention with all the representatives of all living beings in the universe, one of the first subjects on the agenda would be, 'What is the general idea behind the universe?' Any insight would be welcome."

"How do you think life has evolved here or anywhere, Henry?"

"Nobody knows that for sure, either. Theoretically, it all started with the 'Big Bang' 15 billion years ago, when the universe was formed. Something exploded, whether accidental or not, and the pieces of it that flew out formed the stars and whatever else there is in space, including our own planetary system. If this is true and life evolved as Darwin and others have theorized, then the coding for what took place here was on the planet from the time that bang took place, or was transported here later. Either way, the initial life organisms obviously contained programs that ultimately created all the life forms that exist today."

"In some kind of preordained pattern?"

"I would think so. We can't be an accident of Nature as some think."

"What do you mean?"

"The engineering of the human body or even the mosquito is an absolute wonder. Can the human eye, for example, be the result of some random tinkering of Nature? The lens, the cornea, the iris, the chambers, the muscle control, and, among other things, the one million or more sensory cells that send messages through additional millions of nerve fibers to the brain where in some way we are able to see an image. There are volumes of medical books devoted just to the structure and workings of the eye. It's an absolute design and engineering wonder.

"What about the inner ear, with its thousands of tiny and highly sensitive hairs that move opposite the direction of our heads to communicate to our brains a sense of motion? Who thought of that? Or the brain itself, with its trillions upon trillions of intricate connections that control millions of body functions including our thought processes. Then there is the human heart that beats 100,000 times a day, moving more than 2,000 gallons of blood through the body and tens of millions of gallons in a lifetime. Was this the result of random natural forces or preordained coding?"

Heiman paused for a brief instant.

"I know some people, Mr. Ullman, who think that given enough time a human could design another human. Maybe that will eventually be possible. But we can't do it now and we certainly couldn't have done it when we were huffing about in caves. I don't give a darn if somebody could sit under a tree for a billion years, he couldn't figure out from scratch how to make an eye. There has to be some super spectacular genius intellect somewhere that did all this and then developed the coding so it could *evolve*, believe it or not. It just wasn't enough to make an eye, which goodness knows is impressive enough. No, whoever did all this had to really dazzle us by coding the eye on a strand of DNA, which is so microscopic, it's practically beyond description. And then growing the eye, this marvel of invention from that. Who can grasp it? It's all so incomprehensible."

"Maybe humans were just plunked down here, Henry. There are some who believe it happened some 50,000 years ago in the South Pacific. What about that theory?"

"Why didn't they plunk down dogs, mice, ants, gorillas, and so forth? In terms of mechanical function and DNA construction, the world of animals, birds, and insects is very close to humans. At one time it was estimated that there were about 1.5 *million* different living things on Earth. Now the estimate is up to about 30 million. It does appear that there was some form of evolution. Whether all 30 million forms of life were preordained or whether the basic coding allowed for environmental adaptation and natural selection is just another of the mysterious questions we have to contend with. The only point I'm making is that there had to be some coded matter on whatever Earth was as it flew through space after that big bang and which ultimately resulted in the design of the eye, for example. It couldn't have been an accident."

"Does that mean there is definitely life somewhere else?"

"It's all so speculative, but one would think so, Mr. Ullman. Where did this coding come from? If the theory of the 'Big Bang' is correct, then the coding was probably on everything that came out of that explosion. When the environment becomes right, the coding begins to develop."

"In other words, if the planet Mars were pushed into Earth's exact position, life there would at some point begin to develop."

"Maybe so, maybe not. Why should this one little planet Earth be singled out to have the coding? It only makes sense that in similar environments within the universe there is also life, and it's probably close to our own life forms. But then who knows? Maybe Earth is the penal colony for some errant genes. The way living things treat each other down here, eating and killing each other, you could easily believe it. And this all goes back to my original comment. So we discover the last link between man and gorilla. Big deal. What I'd like to know is where did this whole idea of life originate and why? Whose idea was this? What's the point of it all? Not only that, what coding is still left in our genes to be developed further? What are we going to be like in 10 million years if the human species survives?"

"Those are rivetting questions, Henry."

"But obviously not rivetting enough. How many people think

about this? Why aren't we humans demanding some answers? Maybe we need a worldwide hunger strike to get someone's attention. Maybe we need constant vigils to plead for rational, clear, credible, and understandable answers about the reasons for the universe. Maybe the radio signals we send into outer space with those enormous saucers should just be a series of SOSs screaming for help. But no, we'd rather fight a war over two square miles of land. People on this planet, and probably others, live in the dark and don't even know it."

"We really don't even think about it."

"That's right. And I have a theory on that, too."

"And what is that?"

"I think the brain is designed to trick us into keeping our minds on our own earthly realities and to block out the frightening fact that we are only a planet circling in a dark, inky space. If you think about it enough, it can begin to scare you to death, detaching you from the anchors you've constructed mentally as guideposts for life."

"But we are curious, Henry, at least to some extent. We do a great deal of work on our own evolution."

"That's different. That is part of our own reality here on Earth. We remain concerned with evolution on Earth, utilizing the same form of curiosity many of us have about our genealogy. We like to know where we came from. But except for some scientists, too many of us stop when we get back to the first organisms in the slime. What happened before that we tend to block out. Where was the genetic coding that eventually resulted in a human organism 100 billion, billion, billion years ago? And before that? Or was the Maker itself created around that time. But if so, what was there before that? The scale of time is an entirely different subject."

"Are you curious about your own genealogy, Henry?"

"No, Mr. Ullman, not at all."

"But why?"

"Why should I be? What difference does it make who was having intercourse with whom five centuries ago, that ultimately resulted in my creation? Why should I be concerned about what my great-grandparents did or where they lived? It was all happenstance. My family wasn't planned by the one or more random apes who had the orgasm with the unusual sperm that contained the makings of the first Homo sapiens. No, I couldn't care less who came before me. We are all people of this planet who have milled about as humans and animals for tens of millions of years and begot this one and that one. My curiosity focuses on what was happening before there was even an Earth. What a granduncle on my mother's side did for a living doesn't interest me at all."

"So you think the study of genealogy is useless?"

"I didn't say that. It's useless for me. Researching your family tree is fine if you consider it entertainment. It has no real meaning otherwise. It is no better or worse than spending hours in front of a television set watching cartoons."

"We're running out of time, Henry. You mentioned that the scale of time is an entirely different subject. I made a note of that. Would you be willing to come back in two weeks and talk about it?"

"I wouldn't mind at all. The Union Street bus picks me up four blocks from where I live and stops in front of your building. So coming here is not inconvenient."

"I think our audience would like to hear more about your views."

"That's very kind of you to say."

"Thank you very much, Henry Heiman."

"Thank you, Mr. Ullman."

Ullman cued the music. The program ended.

THE POINT

Untold time and money are spent by evolutionists trying to determine how life evolved on Earth. In addition, there have been numerous physicists preoccupied, as Einstein was, with discovering the one equation that will encompass every form of energy we know, thus defining the underlying structure of the universe. But no one appears to be excited about the ultimate question—the question that should be asked before all others—that is, what was the *idea* behind the universe in the first place?

Until we have answered that, what difference does it make if we locate some fossil that creates a Darwinian link to our past? How much more enlightened will we really be when scientists nail down their equation or are able to explain step-by-step our earthly evolution, from those first moments in the slime to this very instant?

What appears to be clear is that our brains are tricking us into masking the mystery of the universe, obliterating it right out of our consciousness. Think about it. Here we are, floating about on an Earth that is a mere speck within a gargantuan universe, and a universe for that matter, which may be just one of many others. And all of these existing without our having the faintest clue as to why. A frightening thought, as Henry Heiman pointed out. But instead of delving deeper into it, our brains trick us into obsessing over next week's bowling league score or who will be elected Scoutmaster of our son's Boy Scout troop or even something as mundane as when to mow the lawn.

More than that, as is illustrated in the next chapter, our brains appear to trick us into defining a purpose for ourselves, to further mask the incredible mysteries surrounding us.

These brain trick programs are enormously strong. I have been aware of them for years and yet I, like everyone else, become fixated on my own problems, not the least of which is the weak topspin on my tennis backhand. Our brains simply don't want us to soar too far aloft with our thoughts, even though we might suspect we are being taken for a ride.

4

Our Purpose

The two philosophy professors, both retired from the same university, had spent a month together each summer in a cottage on Mackinac Island, on northern Lake Michigan, for the past twenty years. Alfred Hoffman now lived in upper New York state, where he devoted most of his time to writing. Andrew Hill had been living for the past seven years in India, but came back to the United States each summer to be with his old friend.

The cottage they occupied was owned by a former student of Hoffman's and was situated on a somewhat deserted beach on the western side of the island. While together, the two men divided their time between reading, writing, and talking. On those days when the weather was good, they would sit on a porch facing the beach and talk late in the day while they watched the sun begin its descent, their discussions often continuing through dinner and beyond.

The skies were practically cloudless one day and the two men sat silently on the porch watching a freighter passing southward.

"I forgot to tell you, Andrew, about an interesting paper sent to me by a former student who requested my comments. The university press is going to publish it. I thought its content might form the basis of our little discussion today."

"What was it about?"

"What he did was quite interesting. He stood in a number of shopping malls over several weekends and asked people from all walks of life what they thought the purpose of life was."

"Well, that is certainly a new twist. I imagine, Alfred, that there must have been some confusion among those interviewed. Here they

51

were, probably expecting to answer some question about their opinions of a dishwashing detergent, and they get hit with a question like that."

"But that was one of the intriguing things about the responses. The author said there was not much hesitation and no two answers were completely alike, despite the fact that this is probably the most important of all questions regarding life itself."

"Give me the gist of them."

"I have the paper right here," he said, pulling it from the side pocket of his sweater, "and I've marked just eight of them, which more or less describe the best sampling of the responses. They're all pretty short."

"Go ahead, read them."

"The first answer is this: 'We are here to do God's bidding. He put us here to see how we withstand the trials and tribulations of this life. Through His prophets, He has revealed to us what the pattern of our lives should be. Our purpose and challenge is to follow those patterns and be upstanding to ourselves, our children, our families, our friends, and our communities. In the end, we will join God as one of His children.' A basic religionist approach, I would say."

"Exactly. It would apply to most religions, where purpose and living in general are placed at the appropriate god's doorstep. What's the next one, Alfred?"

"This is another response that has a religious bent, but is somewhat more succinct. This person said: 'Our purpose here is to live our life to its fullest, to make the most of ourselves every minute, and to raise our children in God's image so that they do the same.' "

"A little more practical, but along the same line."

"I agree. Now here is one from a teenager who said: 'Our purpose in life is to learn how to do something very well, to contribute. That way we can make our parents proud of us, earn decent money, and, hopefully, afford to raise a family.' "

"Not a bad statement on purpose."

"Not at all. Here's another from a teenager: 'The purpose of life is to make money. You're not going to enjoy life very much if you don't make money. You won't have much respect if you can't buy things to make you comfortable and be important.'"

"That person is into *things,* wouldn't you say?"

"An understatement, Andrew. Now here's a surprisingly candid response from a woman coming out of a supermarket. She said: 'I think there are many purposes, like raising a family and attempting to control one's more sinful instincts for the better good. I'm not very religious, but I do believe in a God and I do believe He has a purpose for us, that will be revealed to us, someday. In the meantime, I can't believe what's happening with the price of meat. To me, that's closer to home.' "

"Marvelous. The woman is a true pragmatist."

"Now here is one, Andrew, from a local high school teacher, who by the way, teaches an excellent adult course on astronomy. He said, 'You know, I've wondered about that myself. I gaze into space, seeking out galaxies that are billions of light years away and each time we develop some new telescopic technique, we discover more galaxies beyond the ones we have already found. It appears endless. Against all of this, I can only venture that our purpose should be to live a life that is as useful as we can make it and forget why or for whom we're doing it.' "

"I like it. A wonderful perspective."

"And seeing as how you now reside in India, Andrew, I know you'll like this one. The interview was with the director of a local meditation group who is into Eastern theory. He said, 'The purpose of life is clear. To learn what we can from it. To cleanse our consciousness of its impurities. Each individual human has been doing this for a multitude of lifetimes, improving in each one, and we all will continue doing it until we have reached a state beyond nirvana. Then our spirits will soar free. The universe will then be our home.' "

"Well put, very well put. Any more?"

"There was one more I thought you'd enjoy. The author came across a homeless person, who replied to the question, if you'll excuse me, 'Who gives a shit?' "

Andrew burst out laughing. He practically fell from his chair.

"Right to the point, I'd say. I'm glad you did this, Alfred. It was most enjoyable."

"And now, I'm interested in your general reactions, Andrew. You've now spent seven years in India. Your goal, as I recall, was to get rid of every shred of structural belief, and against that context, I wonder if you've gained any new insight into our purpose, here. There's obviously worldwide disagreement as just this small sampling can attest."

"Yes, and that's why I enjoyed that last remark so much. You can't imagine the work it takes first to identify all the belief systems we humans have and then to work them out of our minds. As I've mentioned to you before, I chose India for this process simply because that country always held a mystique for me. Belief systems there are as structured as they are here and so you have to be careful not to transfer one for another.

"But, there is something about the environment there that allows one's thought processes to move into new areas. It's akin to the fact that some books for some people can only be properly absorbed when read in a library. India did that for me. I think after one more year there, I'll have the mindless mind I've been seeking, with perhaps curiosity the only singular thing left in my life."

"Which you believe will be enough?"

"I do. I'm beyond most physical passions and I'm now to the point where I can observe each and every emotion triggered in my brain. I do tend to drift off now and then into memory or some imagined future and that's still something I have to work on. That was practically a speech in response to your question about contextual purpose, but I wanted you to understand something about that context, as we sit here now. And by the way, this view still thrills me."

"It's magnificent. Being with you, here, makes it all the better."

"Thank you, Alfred. And now to your answer. Much of what you and I have done in our entire working lifetimes has had to do with the study of purpose. In a broad sense, that is what the great philosophers have tried to articulate. You find traces of this thinking going back some eight thousand years, to the start of recorded history and I'm sure it went on for tens of thousands of years before that. For all this time, the best thinkers of the world have speculated about the purpose of life. It has been a major philosophical issue, if not *the* major issue, I'm sure you agree."

"Of course."

"In general, it has been inconceivable to both ancient and modern thinkers that we humans are here on Earth without some specific purpose, even though nobody pinned a note to Adam and Eve or whoever represented the first thinking humans saying: 'Now this is what we have in mind for you,' and then recited it."

"That would have been an interesting note."

"It would have been the salvation of this planet, because then everyone on Earth would be living under one viable belief system— the one on that note—and there would be harmony. But in its absence over the centuries, we filled the vacuum with thousands of conflicting beliefs on purpose. That's why I found those responses in the paper so interesting. The Earth is 4.5 billion years old and we don't really know anything more today about our purpose than we did then, or, to be a bit more fair, in the few hundreds of thousands of years that some degree of rational thought has existed. I can't for the life of me understand why. Whether we have a purpose or not, why did Nature leave this vacuum?"

"Nature, Andrew, from our vantage point, is far from perfect. Although what it has done has been extremely impressive, to say the least."

"Exactly. That's why the vacuum is such a major contradiction when viewed against the sum of nature's achievements. Even more contradictory is this obvious predisposition the rational brain has to be ingrained with some belief system regarding purpose. I often feel that this predisposition for a basic belief is an inherited trait. A genetic program, if you will."

"Hard to prove."

"Impossible to prove, at least today. But if we observe ourselves, our inner thought processes as well as observe others, a natural, genetic predisposition for a belief as to our purpose appears more and more obvious."

"Well, it is quite possible, Andrew, and it is a contradiction, to be sure. Continue."

"The result of it, in any event, is that most humans believe it is better to believe in something, than to believe in nothing at all. The idea of a life without purpose or real meaning sounds depressing. The upshot is that as we grow up we are taught to believe in something. What we believe in for a good many years, depending on our rate of maturity, is what our parents or guardians told us to believe in."

"But the beliefs of some people do change. Yours have altered quite significantly during the past ten years, Andrew."

"Of course they can change. I'm sorry. I didn't mean to give the impression that all of us move through life with the same set of beliefs, although it would appear that quite a number of us do.

But you'll note that usually when one belief system is given up, it is replaced by an altered or totally new one. The vacuum continues to exist and must be filled."

Andrew paused for an instant.

"And it has real strength," he went on. "Look at what happens when a traumatic experience causes what has been a strong belief to weaken. We immediately look for reassurance. We'll pray or visit our ministers and pour our hearts out. Or we'll go to a psychiatrist. Or we'll pay renewed attention to what some government leader says about our destiny. Or we'll begin the process of believing in something totally new. One way or another, we'll attempt to fill the void."

"You have an interesting perspective, Andrew. I wish I had it. But the fact is I am still victimized by the religion of my youth and I must admit that it gets in the way of pure thinking. An enlightened Presbyterian still has to deal with a God figure and the sphere of cult belief that surrounds Him."

"Yes, but at least you can look at the problem. Those who are fanatic in their belief systems can't see any problem at all. They can't see things any way but their own. Curiosity about what we are doing here on Earth and for what becomes totally muffled, and in some countries, forcibly outlawed. As a matter of fact, the basic problems of the world today, in my opinion, stem from fanatics in the areas of government, religion, and social custom.

"It is impossible to argue or even discuss an issue with persons who are fanatic about their side of it. When these fanatics get into positions of power, they come into conflict with other powerful fanatics and the result is war, misery, frustration, or some other kind of unpleasantness. There doesn't appear to be any end to it. The old saw 'come let us reason together' doesn't apply to persons who can't see any side but their own. From my own perspective, the outlook for the world as a whole looks dismal under these circumstances."

"But we've had the same problem for centuries and the Earth has managed to survive."

"Yes, but we've never had such destructive power in our hands. Genghis Khan could wipe out millions of people, which he literally did as he created his empire. Fortunately he couldn't kill everybody. Today, with our nuclear warheads we could wipe out the entire planet."

"But if we don't really know our purpose here, as you've been suggesting, how awful would that be?"

"Now that's an interesting point. So the people of Earth are gone. Who would miss us? I'm not sure anyone would miss us."

"Unless you believed in a God figure. He might miss us."

"By golly, Alfred, now I know why you stick with some formalized religion. You want somebody who'll be sure to miss you."

"Or greet me."

"Perhaps so. You know, I refuse to become an evangelist for the perspective I was able to achieve for myself. . . ."

"Excuse me, Andrew, but clarify that perspective for me once again, would you?"

"Of course. I have achieved a perspective of nonbelief. In other words, there is no single belief system to which I ascribe. As I mentioned before, I believe there *is* some purpose to all of this, it couldn't have been done on a whim. I just don't know what that purpose is. Further, I don't think anyone knows. Everything so far, in my opinion, has been guesswork.

"Now if we don't know what we're supposed to be doing on Earth or what we're supposed to achieve, we should loosen up. Certainly living in society requires rules and approved forms of behavior: we must protect ourselves and our loved ones from criminals, quacks, and the ever-present fanatics. We must also make a living because that's the way the world works. But beyond that, if we don't know what it is we're supposed to be or do, why take life so seriously? Why get so upset if we lost the football game or if we got passed over for an important job or whatever. Do your best, go for it hard, if you find that fun, but for goodness sake, don't get carried away with the consequences, win or lose. The judgments we make while we're here on Earth surely can't count for very much, because in terms of anthropological time, we are hardly here at all. It is only speculative that a judgment is being made anywhere else."

"So if a man at age fifty, Andrew, gets fired from his corporate job and has no employment in prospect, his wife leaves him, his kids won't talk to him, his home is foreclosed on, he shouldn't be too upset?"

"Well, it would be remarkable if he wasn't upset. But that man doesn't necessarily have to judge himself a failure. What has he failed? Whose goals aside from specious, man-made goals didn't he reach? Unfortunately for him, he was probably into goals and purposes and so were his family and friends, and as a result he will suffer.

If the man had a nonbelief perspective, as we might call it, he would still be upset, any strong emotional shock can be upsetting, but he wouldn't suffer long."

"You sound a bit evangelical."

"Do I? I don't mean to. It's just that I'm sure the world would be better off, and so would all of us as individuals, if we got off our strong beliefs and looked at ourselves and our surroundings in the context of a mystery that has yet to be solved or its essence revealed. Perhaps I do go too far in expounding the theory and, in so doing, sound a bit evangelical. I'm going to have to watch that. For all I know, I am all wet and some fanatic I despise could be right on target. That's what's so crazy about all of this."

"It's strange, I'll admit."

"Maybe someday the puzzlement of purpose will be solved for us. We'll look up in the sky, all the people on the Earth at one time, and there will be a message describing our purpose written out in a language no one has ever seen before, but which we can all immediately understand. It would take some supernatural event like this that the people of the world could all witness simultaneously that would get us all to believe in one thing and allow us to live in harmony."

"That would be something to hope for."

"It would, indeed."

The two men remained quiet for a few moments, obviously comfortable in their silence as they gazed out over the water, the sun now close to the horizon. Then Alfred turned to Andrew and said, "How about a nap before dinner?"

"An excellent idea. Maybe some brand new purpose will come to us in a dream."

"It might at that."

They stood up, stretched, smiled at each other, then walked through the screened doorway to their bedrooms.

THE POINT

We really haven't the vaguest rational idea of what our purpose on this planet is. Many of us think we do, either through a religious faith or belief in some cult—and if we are happy with that, then let it be. But from a purely rational point of view, we are in the dark.

Philosophers have been rambling on for centuries describing in torturous detail their concepts of reality. None of them have been able to prove to any reasonable sampling of the Earth's people that their concepts are fact.

Yet we go blithely on our way, relying on experts with impressive credentials who have scoured libraries in their fields of specialization compiling mounds of data, and then subjecting us to their protestations. But what they tell us is as meaningless as the best guess of the average six-year-old. Pure and simple, they just don't know.

Andrew Hill made the point that we appear to have a brain disposition, a genetic program, for absorbing some purpose into our life's outlook. Why else would practically everyone on Earth believe in something?

It's as if some Creator, wishing to keep us in the dark for His own reasons, bestowed upon us this genetic program of purpose, holding it dear so that we'd feel more comfortable with our lives. And so we let this idea of purpose shepherd us through life, without realizing that it might be the ultimate brain trick of all.

The frightening part is that there have been crazed leaders who have emerged throughout the centuries, some of them living today, who are super communicators. They have caused their people to believe in conflicting purposes, resulting in entire societies warring with each other, leaving misery and death in their treacherous paths.

It would seem that right from the beginning, we earthlings might have been better off simply gaping at the sky in wonderment, all of us agreeing on the mystery of our lives, but understanding that in order to exist on Earth we must follow rules of behavior that allow our lives to unfold in a fulfilling and peaceful manner. It would have made our world a lot more harmonious.

5

Hope for the Future

Ed Grogan, 86, sat in his favorite chair on the porch of the Sunnyday Home for the Aged. The day was warm and clear. Grogan stared off into the distance, not paying much attention to Essie Beecroft, 82, who usually spent part of her day seated beside him.

Down the street a group of boys and girls in their early teens ambled slowly toward the home. As they passed in front, one of the young boys turned to Grogan and said: "Hey, old man, how're your hemorrhoids?" All the kids looked at Grogan and laughed. Grogan said nothing. He ignored them. The kids continued down the block.

"Sniveling little asshole," Grogan said.

"Please, Mr. Grogan, your language," Essie responded, but not with any great shock. She, in fact, was used to Grogan's language.

"That little fucker."

"Please."

"Hey, look it, if you don't like how I talk, go inside and talk to those old stiffs in there. The fact is, you don't like to talk to them any more than I do. All they do is talk about the weather and their health and what their goddamned grandkids are doing, and I don't care about that bullshit. Last night some guy who was all bent over got me in the hall and told me he was intent on pissing in my shoe. So I talked to him about it. As far as I was concerned, that was the first satisfying conversation I've had with anyone since I got here."

"Oh, Mr. Grogan."

"Don't 'Oh, Mr. Grogan' me. The only reason you like to hang around me is because I'm not like the rest of those old dodos. My mind is still as sharp as it ever was. I might have lost a little short-term memory and maybe it takes me one hell of a long time to dream up a passable sex fantasy, but other than that, I'm pretty much all there."

"My goodness, I don't know what will come out of your mouth next. But to get all wrought up because some small boy makes a smart aleck remark."

"Smart aleck, bullshit. That boy represents the future generation and even when he's grown up, he'll be bullshit."

"I don't understand how you can say that."

"Oh no? You know, about a month ago, one of our so-called giant corporate executives was quoted in the newspaper as saying that the hope of the world lies with the kids, the future generation. I guess that's been in my mind because I can't believe how anyone with any intelligence can say such a goddamned stupid thing."

"Why is that so stupid? It's been said many times before."

"For Christ's sake, woman, you aren't blind and deaf. How many generations have you seen grow up around you? At least three, right? Tell me, what's the difference between those three generations? Nothing that's important. There have been no real differences during the past two thousand years, and there may not be for the next eighty thousand. Nature is slow to change.

"Hell, I don't give a damn that some little kid asked me about my hemorrhoids. Ordinarily that would give me my best laugh of the day. What got to me was watching all those young kids and thinking to myself that when they grow up, nothing much will be changed in the overall human condition. There are still going to be a whole lot of unkind, unloving adults around. There are going to be a lot of hardened criminals who will make their life's work stealing from others.

"I saw one little boy in that crowd who had the eyes of your typical aggressive, hard-nosed businessman, who couldn't care less about the next guy or who he stabs in the back on the way up. There will be more unhappy marriage partners, divorces, and broken families. There will be kids who will grow up to be government leaders and spew out nationalistic crap that will continue to keep us all fighting with each other. Some kids will be money smart, others money dumb, some socially well off, others not, all leading to continued inequality among us. And as adults, there will continue to be jealousy, envy, ritualism and . . ."

"But that's all so negative. What about love and warmth and kindness. . . ."

"Yes, that too, and thank goodness for it. I focus on the negatives because they aggravate me so. The negatives are what create so many problems in the world. We somehow think, many of us, that we'll get a little better as each generation passes."

"But aren't we?" Mrs. Beecroft asked.

"Hell no, we aren't. Oh sure, life is a little more convenient for us. They have places like this for old people like us to go to. Good old Sunnyday Home. This is better than being part of one of those old Indian tribes that would leave the old folks behind out in the desert to be devoured by animals and vultures. At least I think this is better. After that dinner last night, I'm not so sure. We can watch TV instead of sewing cloth in our mud huts. We can crap in some degree of comfort with indoor plumbing. . . ."

"Please, Mr. Grogan."

Grogan continued as if he hadn't heard her.

"We have electricity so we can see better at night and run our little appliances. And so on and so on. Physically we have done better. We even live longer. But mentally we are still in the pits. The contradiction is in the fact that we all *think* we have done a lot better, that the world is making progress toward some undefined goal, but inwardly most of us can see how rotten the world is. That's why we look to the future generations for our hope."

"But really, when you get down to it, Mr. Grogan, what is wrong with that? Why can't we have hope in the future generations that they will make things better?"

Grogan, as was his habit when irritated, bolted up from his chair and stamped his feet. Then he whirled around, looked at Essie Beecroft, and said, "What is wrong with hope in the future generations? That's what you asked. I thought I had explained it. I will go into greater detail. Here it is." He looked her straight in the face. "*Hope in the future generations is nothing but some dumb, useless idea we human beings have fallen for. Hope itself will do nothing for us.*"

His shouting startled her. A shocked look covered her face. Then it transformed into one of bewilderment. He continued, hardly noticing her reaction.

"It's a goddamned no good belief that fools us into thinking that things will get better. 'Oh look,' we say, 'things are rotten now, but those youngsters out there, those little beauties with their bright faces and innocent minds, they'll make things better, they'll make this a better world.' What bullshit. Like I said before, what we forget is that when those youngsters grow up, the innocence will be gone. They will have matured and become the same as we are now. They'll be slammed up against the world as it is and to survive outside of a monastery, that innocence will have to go. Some of those little kids we saw walk by will even grow up to be tenants of this sick Sunnyday Home if somebody doesn't wake up before that and condemn it."

Essie was now staring intently at Grogan.

"And I'll tell you another thing that depresses me and that's watching some science-fiction movie on TV, where they show what will be taking place some five thousand years from now. What is it? The same old shit. There we are, whipping through space whopping the crap out of each other with laser guns and cannons. We are still having wars, except now it's between one planet and another. Inside the space ships we still have all the same emotions emerging between humans: jealousy, power struggles, rage, envy. It's depressing as hell. Sometimes I think the world would have a better chance if we made citizen's arrests on those writers, and put them in jail. But then I think that maybe they have the better insights. Maybe they know more than most that nothing much will change and why not make a few bucks writing about it."

Grogan looked at her.

"But that doesn't mean I like it," he continued. "The fact is we can't change things until we pull our goddamned heads out of the sand and see the problem."

"What problem, specifically, Mr. Grogan?"

"The problem of our goddamned attitudes and beliefs. You take a look at that group of kids who passed here. They are being programmed like some damned computer by their parents, their teachers, and this lousy society as a whole, just as their parents were before them and their's before them and all the way back in time."

"I'm afraid I don't get your meaning."

"What I'm saying is that we all come out of the womb dumb as hell, ready to be inputted with language, custom, culture, attitudes, biases, skills, you name it. We don't grow up in a vacuum. We become victims of our surroundings. An eight-year-old can't fight his way out of a bigoted household, neighborhood, or country. The kid picks up what he or she sees, hears, or in other ways senses. At some point in time we've got to stop feeding our kids the traditional bullshit and then maybe they'll have an easier time figuring out a life here that has more positive experiences."

"I think I see what you mean, Mr. Grogan, but I would say that those changes are easier said than done."

"Christ, who said it was easy? But it's possible if enough people would see the light. We do have the capacity for raw rationality. If we could just get the gumption to exercise it, we might better see what this world is *really* all about. Maybe we could get ourselves in a better position to change the way we think, maybe even agree more with each other, since we would see that none of us really knows enough about anything that matters to disagree."

"I'm afraid I don't understand, again."

"What I'm saying is that once we recognize that we are born with some rotten drives and then are indoctrinated with a bunch of beliefs that have no rational basis we might be better able to work on changing the way we think. Hell, look at me. When I was young I was into all the bullshit everyone else was in my little sector of the world. Every little sector seems to have some kind of indoctrinated bullshit. Man, I carved a wide swath in the business world. I went to church. At one time I even belonged to a country club. But I got over all that. I only wish I had had myself, at the age I'm at now, with what I know, as my mental trainer when I was young, instead of all the traditionalists who surrounded me at the time. I wouldn't have had to waste all the time I did being up to my neck in the crap of hand-me-down structure."

"I see, you would have had more of your years available to be as kind, sweet, gentle, and understanding as you are today."

Grogan chuckled.

"That's a good one. But hey, inside I am kind and gentle. Down deep. What erupts from my mouth is the aggravation that results from watching it all. Using lousy language makes it easier for me to resolve an inner conflict of seeing what could be in this world versus what is and being goddamned angry about it. I only wish I could see those kids walking down the street and say, 'There goes the future generation, the promise of the world.' All I can say now is 'There goes the future generation, and phooey.' "

"Would you like to go inside and have some iced tea, Mr. Grogan? It's nearing dinner hour."

"The thought of going inside this place turns my stomach."

"But we live here."

"My stomach turns a lot."

"Well, if you don't mind, I think I'll get some iced tea. I'm awfully thirsty."

"Go ahead."

"Can I bring you some out?"

"For Christ's sake, I don't want tea—a double martini maybe—but not that shitty, weak tea they serve."

"I'll see you at dinner."

"That is a generous description of the activity."

Essie Beecroft left the porch. Ed Grogan folded his arms and watched as another group of children made their way down the street toward the home.

THE POINT

We do have the capacity for rationality that could make this planet a decent place to live. The ideas, the attitudes, and the concepts of purpose that have been handed down from generation to generation as an unrelenting dogma to instill "our values" in our kids can be stopped and rethought. The "Creator," assuming there is one, fortunately, gave us the capacity to think freely, once we put our minds to it.

But until we start thinking without the anchors of our instilled beliefs and absorb everything that our scientists are uncovering about the nature of the universe and our genetics, nothing much can change. Each of our societies, our tribal groups, will continue to hand down to their children their own "values," their own belief systems, and so the hatred, misery, and mayhem will continue.

Once we begin to realize the trickery of the brain, we can start to rise above it. It's essential that we understand that a better future for our children lies not in looking backward to the traditions and beliefs of our forefathers, but in simply guiding our children to act decently toward one another. If that includes some of our older beliefs and traditions, then let those parts remain.

6

The Delusions of Maturity

Ludmilla Denisov made her way up the narrow path with some difficulty. How could such old people walk steep paths like this one, she thought.

Ludmilla, a small briefcase in hand, had just gotten off the train after a hot and dusty overnight ride from Moscow. It was just after the period of perestroika and, as a young TASS correspondent, she had received the assignment of interviewing Ilyich Barkeloff, who this week was celebrating his 110th birthday and was renowned in this area of the Urals for his energy and spry mind.

Barkeloff lived in a cottage on top of a rise about two miles from the village train station. The walk was mostly uphill and Ludmilla regretted she hadn't gone through an exercise regimen to prepare herself for the ordeal of the hike that her editor had warned her about.

After more than an hour, the path leveled out and at the end of it was a small cottage, which Ludmilla ardently hoped was Barkeloff's. The cottage was set among trees, but there was a broad, sunny clearing in the front. One of the few large trees in the clearing had a bench surrounding it and here a man who had to be Barkeloff was sitting. She recognized him from the small photo she had in her briefcase.

He certainly did not look 110, she thought to herself. More like 75, she would have guessed.

As soon as Barkeloff spotted her he rose and welcomed her warmly. They exchanged the normal courtesies about her trip, and then he asked her to sit on a wooden chair he had pulled close to the tree bench.

"So," he said, "TASS is interested in knowing what I have to say."

"Yes, they are," Ludmilla replied.

"Your letter said you wanted to interview me, but it didn't say what about."

His voice was firm and his directness surprised her.

"Primarily they wanted me to talk to you about your views on aging and whatever is related to that. According to our source notes, you have some interesting thoughts about it."

"I see, and how much time do we have?"

"I would really like to do this interview in an hour or two, if possible, Comrade Barkeloff," Ludmilla said. "There is an early evening train back to Moscow and I would like to catch it. I should get down that trail before dark."

"Of course. I'm not sure I have very much to say about the subject, anyway. Please, Ludmilla, do call me Ilyich, not Comrade Barkeloff. It will make us more quickly feel as equals."

"Equals? But I am only 27, you were born before my great-grandparents. How can we be equals?"

"We are equals as humans. I am basically still who I was at age 27. It is true I have experienced many things since then, there is more stored in my memory, but that is absolutely insignificant when measured against all there is to know. Aging is primarily a physical, bodily process that is caused by the passage of time. Except for some addition to memory, that is all that happens."

"Yes, but we do grow old."

"And how do you judge that someone is old?"

"From the way he or she looks. The body ages."

Ludmilla was beginning to feel uneasy. She had accepted this assignment reluctantly, believing it would be totally boring talking to some sputtering 110-year-old antique. But now, she was beginning to feel challenged.

"Ah, but don't you see, Ludmilla, that we must look beyond skin and bone in perceiving anyone. We must look directly to the brain, which is the repository of all thought, emotion, and spirit— that is, unless you are playing soccer, then physique becomes important. The condition of one's skin and body only creates an image. A person is what his brain is."

"An interesting thought, Ilyich."

"Good." Ilyich smiled widely. "So now let's pretend we have glass heads and it is our brains talking to each other. We will be better able to communicate as just two people on a mountain without the barriers of age, time, and custom."

Ludmilla decided that she had to interview this man as she would any authority and get his age off her mind. She could report her own initial reservations in doing this interview in the article, to add interest and insight into Ilyich's comments. "How long have you been living here?" she asked rather tentatively.

"About 35 years," responded Ilyich. "I spent most of my life before that in the foreign service, traveling around the world. I somehow managed to survive all the ridiculous conflicts and bloodshed. My objective was to get through this process of life because I am only curious about the process itself. I watch it. I enjoy it. It is great entertainment once you can step back and see it all unfold."

"But you must have had an exciting life, seeing and doing the things you did. Why would you want to live out your years in this remote place?"

"Because people live longer here, as you know. When you walked through the village, Ludmilla, you no doubt noticed the older age of many of the inhabitants. We've had scientists by the dozens from many parts of the world working here with their instruments attempting to figure out why that is. They've reached no conclusion. An American journal once reported that it is due to our consumption of yogurt. I myself am unable to eat it. It makes my eyes water. Only a small number of people here actually do eat it. The phenomenon is also obviously not due to the water. If it was, we'd be exporting it all over the world. No, it is something else that helps our bodies fend off all that wants to attack them and shorten the life process. Some say it is lack of stress, a living with a sense of harmony. But whatever it is, it doesn't work all the time. Young people still die here, but the odds are better."

"Those odds have seemed to work in your favor, Ilyich."

"Yes, so far. I have lived much longer than I ever expected to— not that a long life is necessarily important. But it has given me more time to think, to attempt to pierce some of life's very basic mysteries."

"And which mysteries have you pierced?"

"None yet."

Ludmilla chuckled and said, "And why don't you think it may not be important to have a long life?"

"All I know is what I can sense, and I sense that, once born, we humans are guided through to adulthood by some chemistry of the genes. Through intercourse and fertilization we attempt to pass those genes on to a new generation. Then we age and die. The process has some variance between individuals, but the general thrust is identical for everyone. Now within that context, how important is the length of our lives?"

"But we are not living our lives in that narrow context, Ilyich. We live day by day with love and pain and all the other experiences. Why should we want to shorten our lives?"

"I don't think we should want to shorten our lives purposely. The question is: Is a long life important? For me as an individual it is, since I am finding it an enjoyable experience. As an overall concept, I am just not sure how long the average life should be, although at this very instant we have only limited choice. It depends on the battle that goes on within our bodies."

"You mean the battle against sickness?"

"Yes, exactly. We can only do so much to remain healthy, to live longer through rational action and thought. Cancers invade, heart muscles weaken, important organs fail. We can only control the battle to a very limited extent. If we manage to keep humans on this planet for another five hundred years, this battle within the body will undoubtedly change. Artificial hearts and other organs will keep the body alive longer and the brain active. The question then will become how old can a brain be and still function? And can we regenerate the brain? Will it be possible for our brains to live for a thousand years, for example, in a body composed of wonderfully functioning artificial organs and limbs. Keep in mind, Ludmilla, that the only objective of our physical body is to serve the brain and keep it alive."

"One moment please. I always thought the brain was interactive with the body, that one served the other."

"They do," Barkeloff replied, "but the brain is the essential organ. It controls everything the body and mind does. The body must serve it totally." Barkeloff hesitated and stared at Ludmilla. "Forgive me, you must be hungry." He smiled warmly at the young reporter. "Sometimes I ramble on. Let me fix you something to eat."

He stood up and walked inside his cottage. Ludmilla could hear him puttering about. The man was a wonder, she felt. Here he was, 110 years old with a mind that was alive and a body as supple as her 67-year-old grandfather's. He soon returned with a plate of assorted cheeses, fruit, and bread. They ate in silence for a while looking out on the beautiful landscape surrounding the cottage.

"This is wonderful, Ilyich." She was beginning to feel very close to this man. She wondered if she could ever be good friends with a person this old.

"What are you thinking?" Barkeloff asked.

"I like you. I was wondering if it would be possible for me to have a friend who is someone your age."

"Why not? If your worldview is compatible with mine. For the most part, the young place too much importance on age. They are taught to respect their elders. They should really be shown the importance of respecting everyone if we are all going to live together with some degree of civility. As I said before, in terms of the unknowns of life, what we learn as we grow older is practically nothing. I do not, for example, know any more than you do about why we have two ears instead of four. Your guess is as good as mine as to what's beyond the stars. Yes, I have had many more experiences than you have, but I haven't necessarily learned from them. You cannot look at me and say: 'Look at that old man. He must be wise.' I don't know how wise I've become. It could very well be that I was wiser at the age of 27 than I am today. At some point in life, our brains mature. By that I mean when we reach the point of rational, independent action. Some achieve this at age 12 or earlier, others not until their twenties or later. Whenever we reach it, we deserve to become an equal in society, without regard to age. We should become as one with one another. Under that concept, age would be no barrier in our becoming close friends."

"But how can anyone become capable of what you call rational, independent action at age 12?"

"It happens. Don't forget that Alexander the Great was an accomplished general at the age of 15. Many of our great historical figures accomplished wondrous things in their teens. They had to, since life expectancy didn't go much beyond 30. Women were married and bore children upon the onset of menstruation, age 12 or under. No one told them they were too young to bear those children. Once it began, they were on their own, exerting rational, independent action."

"So what is your point?" Ludmilla asked.

"The point is that today age has become a ridiculous barrier between young and old. It is a useless human attitude, a program of thought that should be neutralized. I, for example, feel you are my absolute equal. If you felt the same way, we could spend time together and enjoy it. We could exchange thoughts and ideas. I would not be condescending. I would not bore you with my experiences. They are worthless. What is past is past. We would talk about today, the future, our surroundings. This is the way the world should work."

"Do you have children?"

"Yes," Ilyich replied.

"Would those children not become a barrier? They would be old enough to be my great-grandparents."

"I would not talk about my children, or their children. I do not consider them trophies. I would not brag of their accomplishments. They are not my legacy to the world. I had intercourse, they were born, and I helped raise them. I enjoyed the experience of watching them grow and mature, and the experiences of their families. I had other experiences I enjoyed equally well."

"But you appear to be an exception, Ilyich, which I imagine is why TASS sent me all this distance to talk to you," Ludmilla said. "Of course I do view old people from the perspective of the young. With only rare exception I feel the barrier of separation you described. I also feel that I have more knowledge and intelligence than many older people I meet, but at the same time I have a feeling that there is some *wisdom* among the old that I do not have. This point is reinforced by many older persons. There is an implication that wisdom is something one acquires through age. You appear to be a rare person in that your worldview, as you put it, is not even slightly condescending toward the young."

"Well, there are many others like me. You just haven't met them or you were preconditioned to believe as you do. On the other hand, what you say is generally true. Many people, as they grow old, will become condescending and use their age as a badge of merit. They will say, 'Look, I have lived many more years than you. Believe me, I know.' Sometimes they do know and sometimes they don't, just like a person of any age. Simply having more experiences, more knowledge, more memories doesn't assure that one has more wisdom. I have met some very wise and mature people, Ludmilla, who are younger than you. Wisdom appears to come from more than the mere element of age."

Ludmilla thought for a moment.

"I just don't know. What about the ability to grow, to change? Doesn't that diminish as one grows older? Doesn't one become more set in one's ways?"

"Not if one is open to the world. It is up to the individual. I know many very young people with closed minds, Ludmilla. Furthermore, we are forever susceptible to change through emotional trauma. A woman of 70 is raped in the park, for example. It will be a long time before she might walk in the park, any park, again, if ever."

"What is amazing, Ilyich, is that I never thought of old people in quite this light. There is definitely a barrier, a program of sorts as you say."

"The thing to remember is that we are all humans no matter what our age. Our bodies grow old, but our brains continue to function. I can still raise my hand on cue. I can count as high as you can. I can communicate. True, time might pass more quickly for me, for the passage of time does seem to accelerate as one grows older. And true, my short-term memory might not be as good as yours. But when you can't remember much, you enjoy the present more. It wouldn't bother me to lose all of my memory, except the essentials—how to read, for example. But all in all, the similarities between young and old make the differences inconsequential."

"That, of course, would not apply in the case of parents. Parents and their children cannot be equals."

"Why not? When the parenting is done, the equality should begin. It is better for everyone. It is, in fact, more fun. Too many parents remain parents all their lives. They want to take responsibility for their children, even when those children reach the age of adulthood. This is not right. Parents should welcome their children into adulthood, accept them for who they've become; tell them what they tried to do as parents; listen to what the children, who are now adults, think they did right or wrong; accept the opinions; hug and kiss each other; and become friends and equals."

"Another interesting point. My parents are still my parents, constantly advising me what to do. They are certainly not my friends," Ludmilla said.

"That is unfortunate. What can they tell you to do now? You are 27. They have done their work. Maybe it was good work, maybe it wasn't. Parents are not licensed. As a child, you have to be lucky to emerge with parents who can do the job well with love and understanding. But when the parenting is done, it's time to find a new occupation. One can still give advice to one's children when asked, but that advice may be no better or worse than advice received from other friends. There is a good deal more contentment that can be achieved on the part of parents and children when the children are old enough for a feeling of equality to emerge. It is much more enjoyable. Yet it is so hard to do. The old feelings of authority and identity remain. But the children must fight through them as adults and look at their parents as people to whom they owe nothing but perhaps love, affection, and care if the relationship is at the time a good one. If it is not a good one, no obligation should remain. This in itself would make more parents understand that what they did in raising children was a parenting experience that ends when the children are adults. The former children should now only be loved, if that love still exists, and treated as equals."

Ludmilla put down her note pad and looked once more at Barkeloff.

"I don't know what more to ask."

"Then the interview is over."

"But there is so much more I would like to talk to you about. On the other hand, I would like you to show me your cottage and some of the beauty of this area before I leave."

"A good idea. Come, we'll start with the cottage, then there is a beautiful little trail that leads to an area overlooking the village. You will love it."

Barkeloff rose, took Ludmilla's hand, and led her toward the cottage.

THE POINT

One of the hardest jobs we have is to position ourselves as an equal in relation to those around us. We will use practically any excuse to imply or actually wield power over someone else. The genetic propensity is there and being older is the easiest excuse to use. But when we imply or wield power, we cause conflict that results in separation, a barrier to raising our levels of contentment.

By seeing this genetic propensity for power as a brain trick, we can begin to fight back simply by admitting it to ourselves. The result can be a great relief, not only for ourselves, but for those we have victimized, particularly our children. If we are lucky, the vacuum can be filled with a deep respect, which is so much more powerful as an influence than the raw power it replaced.

As Ilyich advised Ludmilla, we need to look beyond the condition of our bodies to our brains. They are the instruments that are communicating with one another. Some are older, some younger. But in light of the tremendous complexities our brains already possess at birth, age as we know it on Earth isn't really the big deal we make it out to be.

7

Our Propensities for
Mental and Physical Violence

Rabbi Stanley Harris sat in the ambulance with the victim who had just been stabbed. She was a rather attractive woman in her mid-thirties. He noticed the wound was high up on the chest and wondered how serious it was. As if reading his mind, the two paramedics who were working on her told him she would probably live.

One of them extended his hand to the rabbi:

"My name is Dick Stanley, rabbi. How did this happen?"

"I'm not sure, Mr. Stanley. I was walking near the bar when I heard a scream from inside so I ran in. The woman was on the floor. People in there were holding the man they said did it—her boyfriend. They said she started flirting with some other man and her boyfriend became enraged and stabbed her. I did what I could for her until you fellows came."

"You know, we see this kind of thing every night," Stanley said. "We get used to it because it's what we do for a living. But I'll be damned if I can understand it. It appears you men of God aren't doing a very good job," Stanley said, with genuine irritation.

"That's very true, Mr. Stanley," the rabbi said, calmly. "We haven't been very successful in convincing people to lead peaceful and harmonious lives."

Stanley turned back to listen to his partner, who was conversing on the ambulance's radio with an emergency room doctor. Then he once again faced the rabbi, who had guessed Stanley to be in his late twenties.

"You know, rabbi," Stanley wondered out loud, "after seeing all this heartache and violence, is it even possible that the people of this world can ever lead a peaceful life? I mean, is it realistic to think we can get rid of this kind of violence?" He pointed toward the girl.

"I'm not at all sure."

"That's encouraging," he said sarcastically, "coming from a religious man."

"There's quite a limit as to what we can do, considering the state of the world as it is today."

"What about God?"

"What about Him?"

"Don't you think He's concerned about all the violence and mayhem that takes place down here?"

"I really wonder, Mr. Stanley. I was a chaplain during the Korean War. It was an absolute whirlpool of violence. People trying to kill or maim other people however they could. It was as if God was on a vacation somewhere. I used to have the strangest thought that He was in Miami Beach wolfing down corned beef sandwiches and I was his paid employee doing the work. It annoyed me. What was He doing there and what was I doing in Korea? He had the supernatural power, all I could do was talk and pray. I felt as if I were caught up in some great lie. I would rationalize why some boy was dying as I held his hand. How could I tell him he just got caught up in some nonsensical mess and didn't luck out? That's what I really thought."

"Are you a real rabbi?"

"Yes I am. I don't have a pulpit. I work for the Jewish Board of Education here. Why do you ask?"

"It just sounds a little strange for a rabbi to envision his God eating corned beef sandwiches in Miami Beach."

"I suppose it is strange. Once I did have a pulpit, about twenty years ago, and I mentioned that in a sermon. My contract was up later that year and it was never renewed. In our negotiations, the board kept mentioning the 'Corned Beef Incident.' They made a big issue of it. The departure didn't really bother me; I was young, in my early thirties. I couldn't stand the structure of a congregation, anyway. I felt that my basic job was analyzing what God meant us to do in this world, and not figuring out how to raise money for another new but unnecessary building."

The ambulance was making its way carefully through the streets. The siren would whine only at intersections or when the driver was changing lanes to avoid traffic.

"How much longer before we get to the hospital?" the rabbi asked.

"About five minutes. We've been instructed to take her to Northwest Hospital. There's a doctor on duty there who is an expert on this kind of wound. He's the one my partner's been talking to."

"That's good."

"You certainly have different ideas, Rabbi Harris. How would you explain this kind of violence?"

"Well, I think that part is simple enough. First of all, I disagree with most of my colleagues in the ministry in that I don't believe in the divinity of the human being. Somebody gave us the label of being divine, above animals, and that has caused nothing but confusion. Humans are, in fact, animals.

"As we evolved from higher animal forms," the rabbi continued, "our brains didn't transform into some marvelous brand new instrument. We just grew more cells that helped us think rationally. In other words, our basic animal rage center was never exorcised. It's still there, supposedly in or near the brain stem or limbic system according to neuroresearchers whose latest works and findings I find compelling reading."

The rabbi pointed toward the rear part of his head.

"For the rage center to go into action, it has to be triggered by something. You don't see animals in a continuous state of rage. That rage has to be triggered. Hit a lion on his head with a club and he is going to get mad and attack you. Or steal his mate's food or try to harm his young and he'll attack. Only once in a while will you find lions or tigers or elephants or dogs who are mad most of the time. They are the psychotics of the animal kingdom. Just get in their line of sight or smell and watch out.

"When it comes to triggered rage, there are definite similarities between higher animals and humans because we operate with practically identical rage centers. The big difference is that animals don't come in conflict with the human concept of morality. What they do they do by instinct. In humans those same instincts come in conflict with our rationality, our thought processes, and in essence with the morality of the Ten Commandments, which form the basis for civilized living wherever humans are civilized."

"Yes, but not everyone is Jewish."

"I know. But whether civilized people got their initial principles of behavior from Moses and his colleagues or thought things through themselves, it doesn't make much difference. To live together peacefully, we have to follow these commandments or variations of them. They evolved naturally from rational human thought. And this caused a conflict that plagues humans. On the one hand, we still have our animal brains, which harbor a number of negative programs that, once triggered, can cause physical harm or mental trauma to others: sinful action, if you will. On the other hand, we have the capacity for logical thought, which we can utilize in an attempt to control those animal-like programs and act with civility.

"In other words, when somebody takes a poke at a tiger, it is instinctively going to attack. When somebody takes a poke at a human, the person attacked is theoretically supposed to think rationally, which will neutralize that same instinct the tiger had and allow the victim to turn the other cheek. What many consider the inherent evil within us is nothing more than that old animal brain wiring, which we are supposed to control rationally. Some of us can do it better than others, while some can't control it at all. The control mechanism in the brain isn't there or possibly it isn't strong enough. And that's the rub."

The ambulance pulled up to Northwest Hospital and Stanley and the other paramedic gently transferred the injured woman to a section of the hospital's emergency area, where she was examined. The rabbi sat in the waiting room. Momentarily the paramedics reappeared and Stanley told the rabbi that the doctors had taken the woman into surgery.

"I'm off duty now and I'd really enjoy talking to you some more," Stanley said. "Care to join me in a cup of coffee?"

"Fine with me," the rabbi replied. "Do they serve beer here?"

"I think I can scare one up."

"I can use it."

Stanley led the rabbi to a deserted staff room, left for a few minutes and reappeared with two cans of beer.

"I didn't know rabbis drank beer," Stanley said.

"They do."

"I don't know why, but it just sort of seems out of character."

"Rabbis, like most other ministers, can drink alcoholic beverages.

There's nothing wrong with anyone drinking as long as you don't harm anyone or anything, either physically or with mental abuse. I suppose that's really the bottom line when it comes to the use of any artificial substance that alters your state of mind. There is nothing terrific about reality. A substance that can ease the tension of it now and then can be useful. It's the abuse that may follow which is harmful. If we can see rationally that alcohol aggravates abusive situations, we should then follow any path to stop the abuse. If it isn't harmful, if we don't become irrational or addicted, I don't see anything wrong with it."

"But we can become addicted to either alcohol or other drugs."

"It does appear, according to a number of studies, that some of us have a genetic propensity for addiction. It's a chemical process. The brain is chemical, and alcohol, as one powerful drug, acts on the chemistry of the brain to alter its perceptions and responses. The question then is should all alcohol be prohibited because some of us are unable to use it in moderation? I don't know the answer."

"Well, we're in the same boat on that one. I drink a little myself. But there are nights when I see some terrible things caused by alcohol or drugs and I wonder which way I would go if they put the thing to a vote again."

"It's an interesting issue."

"And you're an interesting fellow, rabbi. You wouldn't mind if I asked you a couple of questions that are sort of personal?"

"No, go ahead. If they're too personal I'll tell you."

"Have you ever cheated at anything, rabbi?"

The rabbi smiled and leaned back in his chair. He was of medium build, age 50, and with facial features that looked more Nordic than Semitic.

"Churchmen, be they rabbis, ministers, priests, whatever, are in the same predicament as other human beings. We have the animal brain still within us, with all the drives geared to self-preservation and self-gratification. Going through a seminary and becoming ordained doesn't make those drives disappear. We remain subject to the same conflicts as others. The difference is that we are supposed to control those drives better than others. That is what the process of seminary training is supposed to help us do. Some of us do control these drives better than most, and some of us don't.

"I believe that in general when a man of God is unable to control an instinctive drive that is contrary to his religious or cultural beliefs, he feels a good deal more guilt than other persons because he's been heavily trained to follow a righteous path, to set an example for others. When the guilt becomes overwhelming, the usual result is that he'll resign from his ministry. Those who don't resign and can't handle conflicting drives usually become ineffective."

"What about hunting then?" Stanley asked eagerly. "Have you ever done it? Have you ever shot an animal?"

"Well, there you've struck on something. It bears on the entire subject of violence. Humans are basically carnivorous: we eat other animals. There is violence in that, whether we pull the trigger ourselves or we allow others to do the killing for us. If we were truly divine creatures of God, then He should have given us a digestive system that would allow us to live without killing of any sort, including the uprooting of corn and beans and such, which for all we know, have souls of their own.

"In other words, we have to destroy to live and there is confusion in that fact. I, personally, have never shot an animal, yet I love corned beef and strip steaks. I also wear leather belts and other items made from animals. That makes me a hunter by proxy. Beyond that, I freely kill flies, mosquitoes, and other insects when they bother me. Killing a fly is as much a violent act as shooting a deer, yet I don't feel any guilt at all in killing that fly. Shooting a deer would overwhelm me with guilt. There is no rational sense to that, unless one is prepared to accept the fact that all humans have drives for physical violence that differ only in depth. In other words, there is no such thing as a totally nonviolent human, churchmen included."

"But if violence is a basic human condition, rabbi, where do you draw the line?"

"In terms of what?"

"In terms of what you can kill and what you can't."

"If we could look at the problem without emotion, we could say that we are stuck with our human design, which I personally think has some terrible defects. We have a problem with it, one of which is our instinctive tendency for physical violence. As a starting point, we could agree that killing each other is not a good thing to do, but we all don't believe that, even though it has been preached for centuries.

"As we sit here this minute, hundreds, perhaps thousands, of humans are being killed by other humans. If we could find a way to stop this killing once and for all, then we would have a platform to begin looking at what else we shouldn't kill. How can we say that killing deer or squirrels is wrong if we are still killing each other? We could never get the point across."

"Because of that instinctive tendency?"

"Yes, and it also goes beyond physical violence. We practice mental violence on each other as well. When our rage center is triggered by something somebody else does or says, we might not physically hurt them, but we can create terrible mental trauma by what we say or do. All of us have experienced the feeling of rage. We want to lash out, to hurt in some way, in order to release it. We feel this tremendous drive to inflict punishment when we maliciously say things to hurt others and cause a definite pain. That, quite frankly, should be as unlawful as a malicious physical pain. Mental rage is a human condition and aside from disciplined control, which not everyone can develop, there are no universally established formulas for dealing with it. The best we can do is to transcend our basic rage reactions by learning to recognize them. But that takes enormous time and effort and the methodologies are controversial. There is no agreement on the best way to go about it."

"Give me an example, rabbi."

"Well, let's go back to that incident in the bar tonight. Let's say that the man was in love with the woman or he was linked to her in some other way that made him possessive and dependent on her. Let's further suppose she did begin flirting with another man in his presence. Something clicked in his brain and he felt tremendous jealousy. Perhaps she then started kissing or touching that other man. Her boyfriend's jealousy turned into rage. He was afflicted physically by that feeling. If he were a trained guru, he might have allowed the woman to have her space to do what she was doing. He also might have asked her to stop, because it was causing him emotional upset. The woman might have stopped if she, too, were trained to transcend the emotions she was feeling, in consideration of her boyfriend.

"In a more peaceful time and place they would discuss their mutual emotional programming and determine if they were compatible together. If they decided they were, they would continue their relationship. If not, they would separate. Believe it or not, doing something as simple as that can require years of training because there are emotional responses that are extremely difficult to modify. For some, I don't think it can be done at all. The capacity for physical or mental violence will always be there, ready to be triggered. Our rational selves become its victims."

"So in the meantime, we live with the problems."

"We live with the problems, Mr. Stanley, because there is nothing else we can do."

"The world is confusing."

"It is all quite puzzling to say the least."

The surgeon who operated on the woman walked into the room the two men were sharing and reported that she'd be just fine in a few days. The ironic thing, he said, is that the woman was asking for her boyfriend.

"Can you believe it?" Stanley asked.

"I can believe it," the rabbi said. "Deep down we all accept acts of physical and mental violence because we know we are all capable of them."

The surgeon excused himself. He had others waiting.

"What do you mean by that, rabbi? Are you saying that we condone violence."

"No, I said that somewhere deep down we accept it as a human condition. It's part of the program of our lives. We accept without overwhelming surprise the fact that that man stabbed his girlfriend, and so did she. We don't condone it, because unless that fellow gets some clever lawyer, he'll end up in prison.

"Maybe I'm not making myself clear. Look, we all feel in some way that there is a potential for physical or mental violence within us. Even the greatest of transcendentalists would become filled with rage if he watched helplessly while a group of psychotics were gang raping or torturing his mother. There is, in other words, some combination of circumstances that can trigger violent reactions in any human being who possesses a functioning, aware brain."

"Well, rabbi, you do have a point when you say that we accept violence. It's a primary component of most of the cartoons my kids watch on television. One character is usually chasing or zapping another. Many of the most popular movies produced today are filled with the worst forms of violence. It's as if we have some curiosity about it."

"That's a good point and I'm sure in your work you see that

curiosity manifested practically everyday. Something violent occurs and people gather around."

"They sure do."

"Or there will be some cheering when a fight breaks out between two athletic teams. Some psychotherapists believe that we find a release for our inherent violent tendencies when we see it acted out for us. Even if it's a grand argument in a soap opera or stage play. That might be true. I don't know. And nobody else really knows for sure. The brain remains wrapped in mystery."

"So what's the answer to it all?"

"I think the ultimate answer to violence will come only when we understand the brain. If we could definitely pinpoint the brain processes that incite us to violence and then chemically or electrically adjust them in some way, that would probably solve the problem, or at least allow us to view our lives and how we are supposed to live them in a more logical way."

"But I thought you said that scientists know where the rage center is in the brain."

"They have a good idea of its whereabouts. But there is no technique as yet for random adjustment. Not very long ago, I don't know if you saw it, one of the network TV shows covered the story of a man who abused his wife terribly, yet outside the home he was a kind and gentle man. But once he sighted his wife, something triggered his rage center and he would become violent. He was finally arrested. During a medical examination, the doctors found that he had a tumor in his brain; it was touching on the limbic system. They removed it. After the operation the violent reactions triggered by the sight of his wife ceased. On seeing this evidence, the judge handling the case dropped all charges against the man. I thought this was an interesting insight into how we might eventually treat crime and violence not only medically but judicially. It may be the very thing humankind needs most."

"Can I give you a lift home, rabbi?"

"No, thank you. Coincidentally, I only live a few blocks from here; I'll walk, if you don't mind. I could use the fresh air."

"I don't mind at all. It was nice meeting you, even though the circumstances weren't exactly pleasant."

"It was nice meeting you, Mr. Stanley. Goodnight."

The rabbi walked down the hall to the elevator.

THE POINT

Many of us sit and watch the evening news with its usual sequence of violent incidents and wonder how it all could be happening. After all, we have passed through centuries of civilization that should have taught us that humans can resolve conflicts without violence.

This form of brain trickery has been our own doing. Religionists, philosophers, and others have convinced us that humankind is above animals, that there is a special divinity unique to us.

But the difference in the genetics between a human and a chimpanzee is less than one percent. It is little wonder, then, that within the close quarters humans live relative to chimpanzees, that the violence continues among us unabated. In World War II alone, we managed to wipe out 60 million of our own species. On the streets of Washington, D.C., in 1992, and in other cities and communities in this nation and around the world, murder continued to run rampant. We are carnivores and carnivores kill.

Humans can communicate with one another verbally and one would think this might have helped the problem. But it's only made things worse.

The things we say to each other can be as violent as a physical blow to the head. Verbal communication can also be the cause of physical violence: the ability to articulate has not been enough to convince those who are more prone to physical violence of the need to control it. Nor has the threat of prison, a brain trick we play on ourselves.

While we haven't as yet located the "criminal gene," there should be little doubt that the program of violence itself is genetic. The animals tell us that as we see them hunt and defend themselves, we were once out there in the caves with them. The *depth* of our propensity for violence differs between us, as it does with animals, and it crosses all lines—ethnic, income, and sexual. Some of us grow up in the worst poverty, with violence all around us, and become ministers, while a brother or sister becomes a sinister drug dealer. Others of us grow up in the best of circumstances only to become serial killers. We know all this, but we like to hide it from ourselves, a classic self-imposed brain trick.

As one result, we think it's quite normal for the nations of the world to spend trillions of dollars each year on law enforcement and on defense against each other. The thought of a serum or an adjustment of the DNA to root the program of violence out of our lives altogether is considered anathema. Yet this is probably what we'll end up doing, assuming we don't kill ourselves off before we figure out how to do the job without destroying the basic "human condition" of which we are so fond.

8

The Brain as Machine

This was the second year that Elliott Simmons and Art Meyer had been traveling the country. According to their original plan, they had one more year before returning to their professional careers, before they would end their "step out trip," as they liked to call it.

Simmons, 44, a bachelor, had been an English teacher at a small college in Springfield, Missouri. Meyer, 47, also single, had worked in a Springfield bank, doubling as a loan officer and manager of the bank's computer department. He had a minor in Greek classics, a master's degree in business, and at one time had considered a career in education. The two men had been close friends for many years.

It was Simmons who had suggested that they take three years out of their lives and travel the country using their savings and picking up odd jobs to support themselves along the way.

"What have we got to lose?" he would implore Meyer. "We're single. We have no family to worry about. We're going nowhere in our careers. We'll undoubtedly have jobs when we get back. Let's meet a lot of people. For Christ's sake, let's get out of this rut we're in and enjoy ourselves."

For months Simmons kept after Meyer: "We can see some theater, go to the libraries and museums, learn new things. We can have great, deep discussions. It will be fun."

Finally one day Meyer said, "Okay, three years it is. On one condition. If I think it isn't working, I'm coming back."

Off they went on their great "step-out" adventure. They traveled primarily by bus and learned that they could stay in one place from three weeks to two months, depending on the size and throb of the community, before becoming bored and moving on. They learned that their best means of supplemental support was working as waiters in better ethnic restaurants where their charm and sense of urgency had the proprietors begging them to stay on. They roomed together in transient hotels where they were usually able to negotiate a very affordable weekly rate. Most of their meals were taken in the restaurants where they worked.

They had now made one complete circle of the areas in which they were most interested and had returned to Chicago for the second time. It was July and it was hot and muggy. They were staying in one of the transient hotels located on the city's near north side, right off the lake. They found jobs as waiters at a popular, cozy Italian restaurant near their hotel. It opened an outside veranda during the summer months. It was early Sunday afternoon and the men didn't have to report for work until 5:00. They were walking along Chicago's lakefront.

"It's another four-star day," Elliott said, "look at all those sailboats out there."

"I don't like sailboats," Art replied. "I was on one once and got seasick as the devil. I looked in the mirror and I actually was green. You do turn green when you're seasick. I thought when people said that, it was a joke. So now green is my least favorite color and I don't like sailboats."

"But they are pretty to look at."

"They are for me only when I squint my eyes and they become a blur, sort of impressionistic. I can tell you one more thing about sailboats."

"What?"

"I don't like the role of sailboat commander."

"What do you mean?"

"Well, sailboats do something to people when they become the boat commander, even if it's a one-man dinghy. Maybe it's just me, but it seems that people transform. They actually believe they are in command of something and then they act like it."

"Good God, Art, they *are* in command of something, the damned boat."

"I understand that. And I can see how silly my thinking is. But emotionally I can't handle an everyday Joe transforming into Sinbad the Sailor because he's commanding a boat."

"Maybe you just don't like the concept of authority."

"You could be right. I really don't like being subservient to anyone. Maybe there's a connection."

"Who knows?"

"Yeah, who knows?"

Approaching a bridge that spanned a waterway leading to one of the harbors for Chicago's boaters, they leisurely walked over it, stopping once to watch two small power boats make their way slowly out to the lake. When they got to the other side, Art said, "It could be that knowledge itself is slowly becoming obsolete as a concept. By that I mean the knowledge that each of us has."

"This sounds fascinating," Elliott said, feigning a yawn.

"Well, I agree the subject isn't rivetting, but it could be interesting, despite your yawn."

"Then press on and I'll try to mask any yawn that may emerge," Elliott said, attempting to hide his interest in the subject. He had found his casual talks with Art on off-beat subjects to be the best part of their travels.

"Okay. With that magnanimous gesture let's start with the thought that when you really look at things, authority is almost always connected with knowledge of some sort. Wouldn't you agree?"

Elliott looked at Art quizzically. "Well, yes, I think that is probably true as a general statement, if you are looking for a serious answer."

"I am."

"Of course, there are some exceptions," Elliott said. "In monarchies, for example, it isn't a matter of knowledge that puts one in authority, but the fact that one was born into a royal family. I suppose that also applies to families and other units of wealth and power when one simply inherits or is thrust into authority. What are we trying to get at here?"

"It's something I've thought about from time to time," Art answered, "and the sailboat commander concept reminded me of it again. We are now in a new age of computers, something that authority figures like Thomas Jefferson never had to think about. We appear to be barely on the edge of it, despite the roller coaster nature of the industry. And when it begins to hit full force, say in five, ten, or twenty years, it could give us a new perspective on knowledge, which, in turn, could change many of our other attitudes on authority and how we view people in such positions."

"How so?"

"Well, to begin with, the big time computers we already have make our brain *limitations* more obvious. Big-city newspapers, for example, store every article they've ever written on special reference software. By pushing a few buttons, you can retrieve on screen the text of some obscure story written in 1942 about Japanese general Tojo, or the winner of a golf tournament that took place on a specific date in 1952. Oh sure, you can look up the same thing in some library, but that takes time. A computer can recall the same thing in seconds, about the same amount of time it takes you and me to bring up in our own minds what happened of any significance in those years. Tell me, what happened in 1966? Anything."

Elliott thought a few seconds.

"To tell you the truth, I can't think of one thing."

"But a computer can flash in front of you, almost instantaneously, practically everything of importance that happened that year in hundreds of different categories. Now don't get me wrong, I don't know enough to make any direct comparison between the brain and a computer, except for the storage of knowledge. The brain is much more limited in this respect than a computer. Humans have to work strenuously to become knowledgeable in a subject that requires any depth. It takes years of study to become a doctor, for example, and that's after spending many years learning to read and write and become otherwise literate.

"The average brain is *very slow* on the intake, then it needs continued activity or refresher courses to maintain the knowledge it has absorbed. So just because someone spends years going through all that book work or study doesn't mean you have to look at him or her with awe. They did it and that's nice because we can use doctors, as well as lawyers and accountants.

"You see what I mean?" Art gestured widely with his hands as he continued. "If you can look at knowledge as a storage base of data and the brain as the memory bank, then that gives us a different perspective on authority. In other words we can say, 'Oh, there is Dr. Levin.' Now who he is is Sid Levin who went through all that trouble to absorb into his brain everything one needs to know to be a doctor. He was able to do it because his brain was in other ways also up to the job. So today he is Sid Levin with a brain model that allows him to be a doctor. That is very nice for Sid and for his patients because brain models like his are extremely useful, but that doesn't make him any better than the rest of us. He is an equal with us on Earth as a human being, but with a brain model that is good for us."

"Are you sure you aren't allowing a few sour grapes to seep out, Art?"

"I don't get you."

"Well, the fact that you never got very far in your banking career; the fact that you probably resented others being promoted over you into positions of authority—doesn't this little discussion have a sour grapes basis?"

"Oh, that's wonderful, Elliott. Just the kind of thing I like to hear on a Sunday. I couldn't stand authority when I was eight. The difference today is that I have thought about it a lot to determine why I have this attitude, which no doubt contributed to the mediocrity of my business career, of which you so generously reminded me just now."

"I apologize."

"Never mind," Art said with a touch of frustration.

"So what are you talking about?" Elliott asked.

"The knowledge we are able to stuff into our brains and the specious aura of authority it creates, that's what I'm *really* talking about, you who always suspects ulterior motives, even in casual conversation."

Elliott looked a little sheepish.

"All right, I said I was sorry. So let's get back on the subject. You and I have talked many times that every brain is not equal in capacity. Some people can absorb knowledge faster than others. And still others can store it longer than others."

"Yes, but that only strengthens my point," Art said. "So what if you have some genius or whatever who can absorb and remember everything in a quarter of the time it takes you and me. So what? How far does that get you? Why does that make you better? How many people do you know who are trained and skilled to be a doctor, lawyer, accountant, mathematician, engineer, sculptor, historian, marketer, carpenter, plumber, and geologist, *all in one?*

"No one," Art answered his own question. "And why? Because the brain is terribly limited. No matter how brilliant your brain makes you appear, you still have to focus on the special spectrums of knowledge you need for a primary vocation and avocations and then absorb, store, and maintain it all in depth. You can't be a Leonardo, a genius in every area in which geniuses exist on this Earth. And if you end up being successful in one thing you do, or even in a dozen things you do, that's very nice and that's all. It's not worth admiration, only acceptance of the fact that that's what happened."

"But people like to succeed, to identify, to be admired. They like to take pride in all the things they know, even if one of those things is knowing how to do a good polka. That's what makes the world tick. Why knock it?"

"I'm not knocking it Elliott. I'm just saying let's not sit there in some goddamned awe about the knowledge somebody absorbed. Let's put it into perspective."

"Well, right now I'm in awe of that woman over there eating an ice cream bar. Let's get one," Elliott said with enthusiasm.

"Who's paying?"

"My God, you're cheap."

"I'm not cheap," Art replied. "I just like to keep track of my cash flow. It's knowledge I picked up during my mediocre career at the bank."

Elliott grinned at Art as they walked to a nearby concession stand and got their ice cream bars. Elliott paid.

"You get the next one, Art."

"Money, I've never seen a man who was so much into money."

"Then how come I don't have very much?"

"Because you don't like the concept of money. That's one of the reasons we get along so well."

"Well, at least we agree on that."

They sauntered back to the path that followed the lakefront.

"You know," Art continued, "I really believe that just talking about knowledge as a subject unto itself sort of points out what a charade life can be. For example, the knowledge that creates the authority that so many people go cuckoo over is a direct function of memory. If the brain had no mechanism for memory, we would live, but as little more than trees. We would be born, grow, and one day we would die. At the end, we really wouldn't *know* anything as we commonly use the word. Memory is what allows us to know things beyond instinctive reaction and to function as intelligent, rational human beings. It is a critical element in the knowledge/authority equation, yet we don't know very much about it."

"We know that it is there."

"Yes, but we don't know very much about where in our brain it exists or how it functions. Scientists are still in the dark about it. I heard a group of them on the radio talking about it when we were doing dishes in Des Moines."

"Yes, I think I remember that."

"One of the scientists talked about people with excellent memory mechanisms, who can recall facts and bits of trivia much better than others, yet they can't synthesize the facts; they can't apply their greater fingertip knowledge to problems of everyday life. Their memory-recall brain function is either genetically better than yours or mine, or they constantly read encyclopedias and other reference stuff and use exercises to hone their memories. But many of them don't know how to apply that knowledge to anything that is really useful, such as making money if they are into that, or making a good decision when they are in a conflict of some kind.

"All those memories, including experience factors, are at their fingertips, but the brain process that can bring it all together and create a solid judgment or decision might not be up to snuff. It's disheartening to hear what these scientists *don't* know. One thing they don't know for sure is how that synthesizing process works, what happens in the brain as facts are relayed to its rational, thinking center by its memory and our other senses. In other words, they don't know how we rationally perceive and think. They don't know that."

"You're saying that we are simply at the mercy of whatever our various brain processes happen to be," Elliott shrugged.

"Exactly. I am what I am and you are what you are precisely because of what our brains are able to do. If we don't know how our thought processes develop, then we can't physically adjust them, like we can adjust a machine with a screwdriver. We do the best with what we have, but we can't go to a human organ store and say, 'Look, I'm not happy with my brain. I love baseball, but my brain doesn't allow me to hit a curve ball, even though my memory tells me what to expect when I see one thrown. As a result, I cannot be a major league baseball player, which is what I want to be. Please replace my brain with model 4115-660-A.'"

"We can't do that."

"No, we can't do that, at least for the present. But someday it may be possible. So now we're back to the point again. In light of what we know about knowledge and the brain we shouldn't be in awe of anybody. What are we in awe of? His brain? Take it out of his skull and put it on the table and what are you looking at? A sickly gray looking mass of billions of cells that is so damned complex according to the brain scientists, we're not even close to trying to understand it. But then maybe when we do, we'll be able to improve it, yours and mine included. I could be president of that shitty little bank yet."

"How about some popcorn?"

"Man, Elliott, have you got a tapeworm today or something?"

"I'm not that hungry. I just want you to buy it. I feel out of balance after buying the ice cream bars."

"Maybe, Elliott, it's time for you to send away for brain model 3216-554-WH. It has generous virtues."

"Buy the popcorn."

Chicago's lakefront has concession stands about a half mile apart and they walked to one that was nearby, where Art bought two boxes of popcorn.

"It's too salty," Art said. "They must be pushing the soft drinks today."

"You're just unhappy because you bought."

"I'm trying to be gracious."

"That's out of character for you and you know it."

They both laughed.

"You know what's so strange," Art continued, "is that we think we have such control over our lives, yet I can't remember what we did two Sundays ago. Can you?"

"Is it important that we know?"

"Probably not. That's probably why we can't remember it. But neither you nor I had any say-so about it. It's as if the brain is a living organism unto itself. *It* decides for us what we should remember and what we shouldn't. We can go to a class or read a book and learn memory tricks, but they only go so far. The fact is, when you think about it, our memory function *is primarily out of our control.* Knowing what we did two Sundays ago isn't important, but we didn't necessarily make that judgment. Some automatic mechanism in our brains did and had to exercise some judgment of its own in doing so. It's like there is another person in there calling the shots."

"Is that bad, Art?"

"Hell, I don't know, but I would suspect it is. Who is really in charge, when you get right down to it? All things considered, I would rather be in control of my own memory than have some mysterious controller handle it."

"Why?"

"Because it would make my life easier. There are things I read, for example, that I want to remember. When I worked for the bank, I would read a lot of trade journals and there were facts in articles I read that would have been in my best interests to remember. I would say to myself, 'This is good, I am going to remember this.' Three or four months later when that information would have been of value to me, I couldn't recall it.

"In other words, what I want to remember I can't always control. On the other hand, there have been things I've wanted to forget that I couldn't. Some years ago, I was deeply in love with a woman. She left me for somebody else—another guy who worked in the bank. It killed me. I wanted to forget about her and that whole situation. She was happier with this other fellow, and I still had my whole life in front of me. But I couldn't stop remembering. I was miserable for two or three years. Even today, just talking about it, I feel some negative emotional responses. That's what I mean. What I did two Sundays ago I might want to remember but can't. What happened eight years ago I don't want to remember but do. The point is, I would rather be in control of my own memory so I can remember what I want to remember and forget what I want to forget. Come to think of it, if we could all do that, life would be a lot more peaceful and gentle for us and I think we could be better human beings for it."

"Now that *is* an interesting point," Elliott responded. "Some other thing in our brain makes our memory decisions for us. Like it knows what's good for us. But it isn't always good for us."

"It is odd, isn't it Elliott? When you really listen to what these big-time scientists are saying, you realize that there is so much within us that is totally out of our control, even though we like to think we are in rational control of ourselves. We just don't like to recognize the fact, for instance, that our brain is like some big, independent and powerful authority figure controlling on its own the functioning and synchronization of every organ in our body, whether we are awake or asleep. And that this same 'Mr. Big' also controls our emotional drives, which can sometimes make us daffy. Beyond that it controls what we do and don't remember. It can make us wonder who or what is up there and what is it up to? It can also make us wonder why we as humans aren't allowed to understand the brain's design and then be able to adjust it . . . to be more comfortable, since we are the ones who are stuck with the damned thing."

Elliott grinned. "You're right. We just don't really think much about all of that."

They stopped for a few minutes to watch a father and his small son struggle with a kite they were attempting to get up in the air. There wasn't much wind. Then they resumed their walk.

"Getting back to what we were talking about before," Art said, "the brain models. About a year before you and I decided on this long trip, I attended a computer seminar for banking managers. Later I had lunch with the instructor. This guy lived computers day and night. He said that he had developed a program that he thought could make anyone a successful bank executive; he just had to figure out a way to implant that software into the human brain. He wasn't really serious, but sometime after listening to that radio show, an idea came to my uncharted mind. What about brain cassettes, I thought.

"My God, if scientists could ever figure out where our memory and knowledge synthesizing base was in the brain and could develop chemical/electronic chips or cassettes to replace or fit in with the appropriate brain cells, it would solve many of our problems."

"Interesting, Art. I'm not sure it's that farfetched. My brain is currently allowing me to recall an article I read not very long ago about how the firing systems on some of our fighter planes are now guided by the movements of the pilot's eyes. They are working on something that will be even faster, that will react in accordance with what the pilot is *thinking*. 'Biochips' I think they called them in the article. Maybe this kind of super-secret Pentagon research could lead to your brain cassettes or chips or whatever."

"Nobody today can say it can't be done," Art said. "Our scientists don't seem to have all the big answers yet. That makes anything possible, including brain cassettes. If we had them and, say, you wanted to be a doctor, instead of going through all those years of gut-wrenching study and practice, you just go to a Brain Center and ask for brain cassette DO-159-UR."

"What's the UR for?"

"Urology. For Christ's sake, man, you have to have a specialty."

Elliott stopped, looked at Art, and burst out laughing. He had a deep, staccato laugh.

"You know, I like the idea. I would walk into that Brain Center supermarket tomorrow and order cassette TN-418-WI."

"What does that stand for?"

"Tennis Aptitude, Wimbledon Class. Of course, I don't have the body and coordination for it."

"But under this concept, it might not make any difference," Art said. "You would at least have the brain program to compete and so you might be a darn good tennis player in terms of being able to hit the ball, anticipate, and so on. Just because you order a Wimbledon Class cassette option probably doesn't mean you can actually get to Wimbledon. That would screw everything up. But it does mean that you'll be able to play in some tournaments and not look like a complete fool."

"So what we're saying here is that with these cassettes you aren't assured that you will be successful."

"I'm not sure," Art said, looking somewhat puzzled at the thought. "When you think it through, it becomes clearer that all we'd be doing is giving more people the mental disposition to do well. Other brain and physical faculties may not be up to making them a consistent winner in the area the cassette covers. But maybe *that* could be handled by other cassettes." He paused. "Who knows? For the time being we'll assume that there may be no guarantees of absolute success but only of improvement, with something involving a lot of physical effort."

"I'll buy it."

"So, you have the possibility with this concept of having the mental capability of being practically anything you want to be just by going into a store and ordering a cassette and having it installed. Say you want to be a lawyer specializing in corporate bond issues. You simply order cassette LAW-768-CB and there you are. We could build into the program the experience factors of the nation's best corporate bond lawyers. So no matter what situation you are up against, the cassette will automatically feed to your mind the best options, just as if you had earned a law degree and then spent twenty-five years in actual practice. You could have all that right away."

"Which may not guarantee you're going to make a lot of money."

"Yes . . . well, there may be other things about you that potential clients won't like."

Again Art looked puzzled, trying to think the idea through. "Body odor, maybe. Or specific personality traits. Or, on the other hand, we might put into that chip or cassette a program on personal habits, including buying clothes . . . you know, three-piece striped suits. It would give you just the right taste in buying corporate outfits." Art paused a few seconds. "Yes, exactly." He sounded more confident now. "In service-oriented professions where physical prowess doesn't count . . . we're assuming right now that such cassettes couldn't totally handle something that was mostly physical . . . we could put almost everything into the program that would make you as good as anyone else. As a matter of fact, if all corporate bond lawyers had the same cassette, nobody would have to worry about who would be the best lawyer to consult. They would all be in the ball park. All would look well groomed and act authoritative, and reflect to you instant credibility. I don't know, maybe that thought is a possibility—or it would be after a few drinks."

"You know, Art, if it worked, this theory, regardless of how farfetched it is, could put teachers out of business."

"I suppose it might. But don't worry about it; this whole thing, if it's ever possible, has to be at least two hundred years away, if not more. That's a guess, of course, a Sunday afternoon shot in the dark," Art said.

"That's a relief, even if it is a guess."

They smiled at each other and ambled over to a park bench where they sat down.

"Do you see what this thought does with the perspective of knowledge, authority, identity, and position—all those things?" Art continued. "So the guy's a doctor or a lawyer or a corporate big wheel, so what? Anyone could go to a Brain Center and be that. So he's a diplomat. Big deal. All he bought was cassette DIP-467-LA."

"What does that stand for?" Elliott asked, smiling.

"Diplomat Specializing in Latin American affairs. Now just let our minds roam on this. The Brain Center would keep that cassette right up to date to the last minute. The instant it is installed, our person knows exactly what has been happening in Latin America, from its full history to what took place there yesterday morning.

It would also have built in a knowledge of Spanish, including several dialects. So what we have here is instant diplomat. We could now say to ourselves, 'So there is Jim Bixby, a diplomat. Now isn't that nice for him.' It would make it much easier not to look in awe at some guy who is a brilliant expert in Latin American affairs. Under the principle of brain cassettes you could be anything you want to be and you wouldn't be out to impress anybody because no one would be impressed anyway. They could all do what you did if that's what they wanted to do."

"You have one big problem in all this, Art."

"What's that?"

"Who controls who gets what cassette? You might have a jillion requests for the corporate raider tape or airline pilot tape, but none for menial labor."

"That's true. We probably wouldn't have enough people requesting garbage collector tapes. We'd have to think of a system." Art looked pensive.

"Hey, wait a minute," Elliott said excitedly. "This cassette thing could take all the boredom out of menial labor. Take that garbage collector cassette. As part of the program there would be tremendous happiness built in. Instead of being an ordinary garbage collector, you would be an *ecstatic* garbage collector. You would be instantly programmed to enjoy the outdoors; the smell of fetid garbage is what you'd long for each day as you set out for work. The satisfaction of taking care of a basic human need—ridding society of its waste matter—would give you tremendous fulfillment. Look at it that way."

"I like it, Elliott. What we'd do is set up some centralized system for these brain cassettes. We'd have people apply for them based on preference. If we could accommodate them, fine. We might even have waiting lists. But if someone wanted instant employment, an instant profession, they would take what's available. But no matter what they took, there would be gratification. As soon as the installers were through getting that cassette into your brain, you would be happy with your newly found profession, no matter what it was."

The men rose from the bench and started walking again down the wide, asphalt pathway that bordered the lakefront.

"You know, Art, I was going to ask you what you would think about going over to that concession stand just ahead of us and ordering a hot dog."

"Oh, no."

"But this loony concept has me so excited I've almost lost my appetite, so forget the hot dog."

"Well, that's a miracle right there."

"The whole thing is so farfetched and yet there is something very real about it," Elliott said.

"The realism comes from the fact that what we're talking about may be ultimately possible. Maybe not with cassettes or chips, but with some system whose concept has yet to be touched on."

They walked for a few minutes in silence, lost in their own thoughts.

Art touched Elliott's elbow and said: "You know, this thing could also work with relationships."

"What do you mean?" Elliott asked.

"Say you're going with somebody of the opposite sex, maybe even getting married. You walk into the Brain Center and get 'His' and 'Hers' matching relationship cassettes. What they would do is make matching adjustments so you are more compatible."

"I don't get you."

"Well, in the first place, one program built into both cassettes would make a person more considerate of the other person's needs. Then there might be a choice of options. If the woman wants the man to be courtly, maybe there is a courtly option. You know, he stands up when she comes to the table, pulls out her chair, opens doors, throws his coat over puddles, and so on. Of course, he'd have to be willing to go for it. But the nice thing about it is that once he has that cassette option, he would love what he is doing because the love for it and for her would be built in."

"I see," Elliott said. "That could have possibilities."

"Damned right it could. Maybe he needs someone he can communicate with honestly, someone to whom he can say exactly what is on his mind at all times with complete and full understanding and acceptance on the part of his mate. Maybe that option could be available. In other words, he could say, 'I don't really like the fact that your mother insists on sleeping on a cot in our room tonight, dear. That doesn't mean that I mind her visits. I just don't like where she likes to sleep when she visits. And I still love you. Now if you don't mind, I'm going in the living room and sleep on the couch.' And she would say, 'I'm happy you communicated that. I understand it. My mother has a strange quirk. She needs to sleep on a cot in my room. I accept it. I also accept your quirks. Try to have a good night's sleep on the couch.' Or maybe the guy loves football, and in order to accommodate the relationship, she gets the football option on the cassette and then loves the game as much as he does. If the designers could ever come up with enough options this concept could possibly eliminate divorce."

"That's one hell of a thought, Art. It might even be better if we could rent the cassettes. For a great date. Or a weekend away. Having a nice time would be guaranteed even if you go skiing and it starts to rain like hell. We would have a built-in rain option that would make you happy whether you were skiing or shut indoors as the slopes melt."

"Of course, this is all getting off our original thought that the basic function of the brain cassette program would be instant, credible knowledge."

"You're right. We were beginning to talk there like a couple of real promoters ready to make a killing."

"A basic human tendency, I'm afraid. We're rarely satisfied with one good thing, one success in something. Even one reasonably good idea. Most of us have this tendency to keep going for more."

"Hell," Elliott interrupted excitedly. "We could even come up with a cassette that automatically makes you satisfied with exactly who you are and what you've done."

"The possibilities are almost endless, aren't they? The looniness just keeps going. The trouble is, who would control all this? What if some real crazy person ends up in a position where he or she is the controller of all this? Then what have we done? We could make things worse."

"You're right. Let's forget all this and go for the hot dog."

"Wait a minute." Art stopped, hesitated, scratched his head. "Maybe we could come up with the 'perfect leader cassette.' By the time this becomes possible, if it ever does, we are going to have some super-duper computers; I'm certain those computers could figure out the characteristics of the perfect leader. Then we could have a steering committee, composed of a cross section of humans, examine that cassette program and agree on it or make some consensus adjustments. Then we'd find some men or women with existing leadership charisma, choose one by lot, and have the cassette installed. We'd have the perfect leader. Someone the whole world would trust. Someone who, with the help of those super-duper computers, could figure out the best way to apply this cassette program to the entire human population. We could end up with a happy, harmonious planet yet—that is, once we figure out the technology for all this."

"It could work."

"It just might."

"Maybe we ought to get drunk tonight after work and talk about this some more," Elliott said. "Somehow it all feels too far off the wall from a sober point of view, if you know what I mean."

"You're implying that all this might be a bit unreal."

"You think it's real?"

"I don't know, considering all we've talked about. Like we said before, the eerie thing about it is the fact that something like it might be possible. So talking about it now is not totally beyond reality."

"So you don't want to get drunk tonight?"

"A drink or two or three might not be out of the question," Art said.

"We do have a day off tomorrow."

"Yes, we do have a day off tomorrow."

"So now that we've agreed that we're going to have a couple of drinks after work, what about getting the hot dogs?"

"For God's sake, Elliott, we have to be at work in less than two hours. We can eat something there."

"But I keep thinking about a hot dog covered with relish and onions, stuffed with a pickle, and dripping with mustard. Somebody must have put some crazy cassette in my head back there on the path while I wasn't looking. Some fast and clever perverted hot dog manufacturer who is also a mad scientist and marvelous illusionist."

"Yes, I'm sure you're right," Art said giving Elliott a look that implied he was crazy.

"I'll even pay for the damned things," Elliott replied.

"You're right. It must have been somebody fiendish back there who slipped the cassette in. You offering to buy convinced me."

They laughed.

"The timing will be just right," Elliott said. We'll turn back and take the short cut through the park. There's a concession stand on the way. I know the owner intimately. We'll get the best area of the counter to rest our elbows on. You can count on it."

"You know, I almost believe you."

"Then let's go for it."

They turned around and ambled back in the general direction of the concession stand and their hotel. On the way they talked about the pros and cons of several hot dog brands. They could never agree.

THE POINT

The brain is basically a chemical machine. While we don't know very much about how we think and remember, there are scientists all over the world who are trying to figure it out. Once they do, there could be an explosion of new technology that might be adapted to the brain, just as we've experienced it in the computer industry.

By the year 2500, or much sooner, the musings of Elliott Simmons and Art Meyer could become reality. Our entire education system could be replaced with implanted brain chips or the like that carry the knowledge and experience we desire.

No scientist worth his or her salt could stand up today and tell us it can't be done. None of us, Nobel Prize winners included, has the vaguest idea how human life will be led five hundred years from now. Practically any technological innovation we can dream up may eventually be possible.

If the brain is a chemical machine susceptible to technological enhancement, then how smug and arrogant can we be if we occupy positions of power? Power emanates from knowledge, experience, motivation, and innate energy that one day could be absorbed with a computer chip.

We live in a society whose businesses, professions, and organizations require layers of authority. If we are in a position of authority, that is fine, as Art Meyer noted, as long as we don't get carried away with it. On the other hand, if we have no authority, we needn't be unhappy about it.

We are being guided through our lives by a computer, a brain machine whose design we had absolutely nothing to do with. We need to absorb this fact. It's humbling; it can be good for us.

9

The Basic Economics of Wealth

It was a Monday night and the two famous economists were having coffee in a small restaurant just behind Pittsburgh's Golden Triangle. Roger Steele was a university professor with a flourishing consulting practice on the side. Sid Festenstein headed an economic forecasting company specializing in international affairs. Both had received their doctorates in the same class twenty-five years earlier.

"This is a funny thing to bring up, but I have to admit, Sid, that at this point in my life I feel a little guilty," Steele said. "I've made a lot of money not with my faculty salary, but with my outside consulting practice—enough to retire, but something tells me it's wrong. Why should I be able to retire when I'm only 48, while other people on the faculty who are older and certainly as capable as I am will have to work into the foreseeable future?"

"Hey look," Sid said, "it should happen to more people. Get off your guilt trip. Whoever said life was fair?"

The two men were studies in contrasts. Roger Steele was tall and lean, an attractive man, who was a popular member of his university's faculty. Sid Festenstein, 42, was short and somewhat plump. However, like Roger Steele, he was worth a considerable amount of money. He had recently sold his economic forecasting firm, with its staff of more than two hundred, to a publishing company. He continued to manage the company under contract, but could retire comfortably at any time.

"I guess that's the point," Roger replied. "Can life ever be fair? Can we ever devise an economic system that is satisfactory or fair to all human beings?"

"I don't think it's possible," Sid said. "Look at the human condition. We are basically acquisitive. We want material things, social status, power. The world is full of people who want all they can get. They were conditioned this way and they'll condition their kids the same way. The result is a dog-eat-dog world, and only a relatively small handful of people are able to rise above it. What kind of economic system can you wrap around these characteristics that can work and be fair?"

"I really don't know, Sid, nothing I've seen so far."

"And that's not even the worst of it. Have you ever observed who is successful in business—the people who make money? They all seem to have certain characteristics, some combination of intelligence, shrewdness, motivation, toughness, manipulative ability, and the like that gives them the capability of acquiring more wealth than others no matter what training those others have been given. There are a lot of poor Ph.D.s out there who have the intelligence but not enough of the other characteristics to be successful entrepreneurs. The simple fact is that the minds or the brains of the world are unequal in performance capability."

"I agree, Sid. There are probably combinations of specific characteristics like those you mentioned that make it possible for certain persons to accumulate wealth. It's probably been that way since well before civilization."

"You're damned right," Sid replied. "You can go back to the caveman days. Even in today's underdeveloped countries there have always been those who barter better and end up with a few more cows and maybe some special status to boot. Take a look at your history books: those who acquired power were usually the ones who were capable of accumulating and controlling wealth, or who were able to manipulate the wealth of others."

"And power controlled the governments that mandated the economic systems."

"Right on. So the thing perpetuated itself. Even when exploited segments of society managed to rise up and create a revolution, nothing really changed. Some of those poor people, those with the characteristics we spoke of, became wealthy and the dog-eat-dog world continued with systems containing inequities."

"You know," Roger said, "I always thought the free enterprise system was the best thing going in the world because you could make your own destiny. One's family and background, the caste systems of earlier times, were no longer roadblocks. But I'm not sure that free enterprise is really the economic system of the future."

"I don't think it is either," Sid answered. "It gives the person with high brain performance *business capability* the opportunity to thrive. His or her father doesn't have to be a nobleman. But it's very frustrating for those persons who don't have that capability. They are constantly told they are living in a land of opportunity. But without the right combination of mental characteristics, they can't take real advantage of it. They are unable, through hard work alone, to end up with a mansion in a plush suburb. Yet the proponents of free enterprise keep implying that they can: Work hard. Be competitive. Learn a trade or profession. Keep your nose clean. Stay tenacious and you'll go far. They say these things but it isn't really fair. It doesn't work for everyone. You need some combination of those specific characteristics to make it big regardless of what else you attempt to do unless you luck out with a lottery or something."

"But many people without those characteristics do seem to take for granted what their situation is. As a matter of fact, they *are* the primary marketing demographic for lotteries and other games of chance."

"And damn it, Roger, luck is another part of the system that isn't fair. There are children born into a free enterprise system who may never have to work seriously a day of their lives, nor feel the anxieties of economic uncertainty. They come from wealthy families, who pass the wealth from one generation to another. Only the circumstances of birth decide their economic future.

"The upshot of it all is that unless you're born with the right mental characteristics, or grow up in an environment that brings those characteristics to their full potential, or unless you are treated kindly at birth by luck—emerging in the home of a wealthy family, or having the potential physique and coordination of a professional athlete, or the looks of a movie star, for example—you are not going to enjoy full economic equality under free enterprise. If you're on the bottom end of the scale in mental performance, you can be in real deep trouble. During any mild recession, you'll be on unemployment and maybe even food stamps. Socialism was supposed to have made things more equal, but it really hasn't happened."

"I agree with that, Sid, but only to a certain extent. Socialism did end the miserable working conditions heaped on ordinary working men, women, and kids that existed around the turn of the century and before. It also created welfarism, which improved the lot of the working man, the disabled, the retiree, and so on. But I guess there's a pretty big gap between that and economic equality."

"You're damned right there is," Festenstein said. "The extreme form of socialism, communism, has come closer to that goal, but it's far from being really workable. The same kind of people who end up with more cows in Africa thrive very well in most orthodox communist countries, where they end up in the power blocs or in control of the black markets. The black markets comprise a significant percentage of the economies in those countries.

"What Marx, Engels, Lenin, and Mao failed to take into consideration were the basic inequalities in brain capacity and environmental conditioning. The murder of millions of land owners and other property holders didn't solve the problem. It only gave communism as a concept the space to exist. But what happened? The theory was that once the ownership of all land, institutions, and businesses was turned over to the government, all citizens would become comrades, brothers and sisters in destiny, who would be so sharing and loving that the government itself would ultimately disappear. We would have what Marx called utopia. But this didn't happen. What happened in fact was that communist governments had to become stronger, not weaker, to keep their systems in place. This might sound silly to say, with all the millions of people killed or affected adversely by the installation of communist states, but I think it was at least a good try. It was a noble effort aimed at doing something about the inequities of the world. But it just didn't work.

"Our very basic human brain drives continued to emerge, thwarting any possibility of a classless society and total economic equality, thus spoiling Marx's dream. Marx understood something about society and economics. But he and his followers were short on recognizing basic, hard-to-change brain drives."

"Didn't Mao finally recognize this fact? Wasn't this the impetus behind his Cultural Revolution?"

"I think he saw that things weren't working, that the basic human drives were beginning to corrode the system, but I'm not sure he understood that it was the structure of the brain that was his real enemy," Sid answered.

"He saw the pure communist theory breaking down. He saw people with high intelligence emerging as experts, an elite, and while the country needed them to thrive, they were forming a new core of class consciousness. This Mao saw as a threat to the pure equality he was seeking in society and so he initiated the Cultural Revolution. Among other things, schools were closed and those persons with high intelligence, the 'experts' within the government and society, were forced to move to the country and into manual labor where, supposedly, they would lose whatever drives were making them unequal. The process was repeated by the Khmer Rouge when they took over Cambodia. It didn't work in China or Cambodia. Unless some real mental damage has been done, those characteristics will usually reemerge."

"An interesting thought," Roger said.

"Thank you. And one other point that's important about the imperfection of working everyday communism is that the governments themselves force structural inequality."

"What do you mean?"

"The government of an orthodox communist country needs to control the vocational destinies of each individual. They attempt to do this on a very objective basis. There is almost no avenue of escape from the results of government tests given to eighth-grade children that determine whether they are to work on an assembly line, sweep streets, or be allowed to get additional education to train them for top-level jobs that pay more. I think this was an important underlying cause behind the revolutions that took place in Eastern Europe and Eurasia. Under free enterprise, a lower intelligence level is not a sentence to mundane labor. If a person has other mental characteristics like shrewdness, motivation, and ambition, he can still end up owning a chain of laundromats."

"So what's the answer?"

"Damned if I know," Festenstein said shrugging his shoulders. "I don't think anyone knows. Maintaining the concept of communism certainly isn't worth murdering millions of people. The fact is, we haven't as yet invented an economic system that is worth creating the ravages of any revolution. If we had a broader viewpoint, we might be better able to tackle the issue. Even then, I don't know. How do you design an economic system around the need for persons with higher intelligence to run our complex institutions in some degree of personal comfort? How do you really determine who is to do the dirty work? And how do you proportionately spread wealth and living comfort without eliminating the motivations to which our brains react?"

"Those questions have been the traditional toughies," Roger answered.

"Maybe what this world needs is a worldwide committee made up of unsung, humble, yet extremely capable economists—if they exist—who would be asked to work for years with a staff of dedicated researchers and computers to figure out some new global economic approaches. We probably couldn't get any radical new system in place even if we figured one out that could work equitably, given the power blocs of the world, but at least we would be making the effort. In so doing, the message could get out that there is some wrong to be righted. So far all we've been able to do is substitute and accept one inequity for another."

"Nothing is fair yet. Anything is worth a try," Sid said.

"Who knows," Roger said.

"Yeah, who knows."

"Let's order a brandy."

"Make mine a double."

They both ordered doubles.

THE POINT

When it comes to the basic economics of wealth, unless you're lucky with the makeup of your brain, your physique, or your family, the cards are stacked against you. Your only hope, if you are not blessed with these genetic-based virtues, is that the fortunes of life will be good to you, that you'll get the right breaks at the critical moments. This is the long and the short of it.

10

Sex as Robotics

It was late Sunday afternoon and Elsa Dixon still hadn't gotten out of bed. She worked six days a week as a psychologist at a local hospital with mentally disordered patients. The hospital was under-staffed and her days were long and hard. She cherished her Sundays. Often she would awaken late in the morning and read the newspapers in bed late into the afternoon.

Her husband, Alexander Dixon, the fashion designer, sat on his favorite contoured sofa, which was crammed into the bedroom exactly where he wanted it. Their apartment on the east side of Man-hattan was unpretentious yet comfortable.

"Well, that's enough for the current events of the day," Alex-ander said, looking up from the newspaper. "I can't handle any more news."

"I've had it, too," Elsa said, putting down her newspaper. "I sometimes feel compelled; I've got to know what's going on in the world so I won't think I'm ignorant. Or so other people won't think me ignorant. Maybe both. The truth is, I'm beginning to find current events a little boring."

"Me, too. Maybe we ought to start reading the supermarket tabloids—do something to add a new dimension to our lives."

Elsa smiled.

"We don't have enough dimension? You look very pretty, today, by the way."

"Is that an invitation for a little sex?"

"I was thinking about something more than a little. But first I'd like to order in a pizza, if you don't mind."

"You're really romantic, Elsa. You look at me and I remind you of a pizza."

"Hey, I could have thought of a bagel and cream cheese. Don't complain."

"You're right. A pizza is better."

Alexander walked to the phone in the kitchen and ordered a vegetarian pizza with extra mushrooms. He poured himself a glass of milk and came back to the bedroom.

"Okay, Elsa, get your thinking cap on and tell me what you think about sex in general, you know, the whole process: physical attraction, love, doing it, not doing it . . ."

"What did you put in your milk?"

"No, come on, let's talk about it. We'll have one of our great, deep and incredibly dull conversations until the pizza gets here."

"Isn't there anything on TV?"

"Nothing good."

"You feel like deep, dull talk, huh?"

"Yep, let's talk sex and its trappings. You know, all the things connected with it."

"Maybe I'll get you a personal computer for your next birthday, something to keep you occupied."

"Computers scare me."

"Me, too."

"Then talk."

"Me, Jane."

"No, be serious," Alexander pushed on. "Start with what you think is behind the sex drive in general. Then we can go from there."

"All right." Elsa thought for a couple of minutes. "Okay, let's start with the fact that the sex drive probably involves some very hard brain wiring. Nature wants us to fuck and so we have the program for it."

"An interesting start, Elsa. I can always count on sex to get your thought processes juiced up. Go on."

"Well, our sexual potential is obviously there when we are born, but it's one of our latent physical drives. It doesn't emerge until later in life. A time clock of some sort comes with our brain at birth. One day you reach the beginning of puberty, some hormones are released, some hairs sprout, voices change, and among other things you are ready to have sex. Now that's the hard wired part. Overlaid on that, I think, are some learned sexual programs."

"Like what?"

"Like the fact that all societies don't find the same things sexually attractive."

"Hey, Elsa, a behind is a behind."

"A behind is a behind to you and to a lot of other men in this society . . . and let me add, to many women as well, to mute your sexist comment. But there are some cultures where fannies mean nothing. In Japan, many men are attracted to the neck. In Africa there are tribes where the women mutilate themselves to be attractive. In some cultures the men like fat women; in others, thin. Our brain becomes programmed by what we see as we grow up, I guess, to find those of the opposite sex who are attractive to us. You with your rather weakly hidden lascivious sex patterns would be totally turned off by a slightly chubby, sweating aborigine woman, who might be a real turn-on for someone else."

"Hey, I'd be turned off by anybody who sweats a lot. I thought I had kept my lascivious thoughts hidden."

"Oh sure, really well hidden. That's why we have a library full of porno movies."

"I didn't think you noticed those."

Elsa broke out laughing. "Honest to God, sometimes I think you're totally nuts."

"That's why I married a trained psychologist. What an ideal thing for a needy nut. You can not only love me, but treat me, all at no charge."

They both laughed and paused for a few seconds, looking at each other. Then Elsa continued.

"In any event, the most important part of sex, the thing that makes babies, is definitely hard-wired, mechanical, and rather robotlike."

"Oh, that's a marvelous comment, Elsa. Being told that sex, which I assume includes ours, is robotlike."

"Let me ask you, Alexander, do you not feel a sudden lust for sex when you quite suddenly see a woman who is really attractive to you? You know, someone *you* think is a real sexual turn-on?"

"Yes, I guess I ordinarily do."

"And when you are thinking about sex, is the lust there before that woman suddenly comes into view, let's say wearing a tight bathing suit over a tanned body on a gorgeous beach on a beautiful day?"

"No, not before."

"She has to come into view."

"Yes, either in reality or in my mind, in a fantasy."

"So, isn't that a little mechanical? There you are sitting on the beach reading a book, you are not thinking about sex, and your penis is as limp as a wet rag."

"I just love your lurid narratives," Alexander interrupted.

"Then you look up and whammo. There is this woman who to you appears voluptuous. She's there unexpectedly at that second in your sight. That sight triggers some neuron cells in your brain to start sending out signals. Automatically you feel sexually interested, perhaps lustful, maybe you even get a hard-on. That's the beginning of the mechanical side of sex, in my opinion. You have no control over it. You and all other humans, male and female, who find their sexual interests suddenly aroused by a lurid sight or thought, are just victims of their brain drives."

"Yes, but your sick description of sexual arousal is not quite accurate. I for one don't always feel affected by similar sexual emotions every time I see a woman I find sexually attractive, and if there are strong feelings, they will often vary. I'll only rarely get an erection, to be euphemistic, just looking at someone walking down a beach. So it isn't as mechanical as a transmission changing gears, doing it the same way thousands of times."

"Then let's just say that sexual attraction, including the lust for sex, is a robotic brain drive that varies somewhat depending on your mood. There may be variations on how you do it, there are emotions and passions involved, all part of the ridiculous sexual trappings, to use your word, we have to contend with, but there is only one way to have natural sex, the natural object of which is to create a baby. A hard penis penetrates the vagina and after some thrusts it spurts sperm all over the place. That is one fixed natural process. We can't change how that works outside of artificial insemination or other laboratory methods. It is part of being human. We become horny, we get lucky, we fuck, sperm shoots. It is robotic. End of story."

"Well, I didn't think you would get quite so graphic."

"But do you get the point? Despite all the romance and the soap opera dramatics, sex ends up being a mechanical act that we are driven to by our nature, which wants us to make babies in the worst possible way. It is one brain drive or a combination of thousands, nobody really knows, that we are simply stuck with. It is a mechanism that is a given. We cannot change it like we might a hat. It is there, that is it. Nature wants us to have babies to keep our species going. So we are driven to fuck, no questions asked."

"The way you put it, sex is already beginning to sound a bit mechanical to me. I'm not even sure I'm going to like it anymore."

"I wouldn't worry about that, Alexander. But let's go on. Nature didn't make it easy for us to combine the drive for sex with a family relationship, even though a human baby has to be nurtured. In other words, it didn't give us an automatic predisposition to spot a potential mate to whom we can give all our love and on whom we can focus our entire sex drive. Sometimes it happens, but it's a chancy thing. What too often happens is that one mate or the other or both are still attracted sexually to other persons after marriage or whatever form of union.

"And this outside sexual attraction can disrupt not only families, but whole societies. It can create frustration, fear, violence, and all kinds of emotional pain, depending on the situation. It is, in my opinion, one of Nature's cruelest tricks. It's really one of the major reasons why there have been so many customs and laws about sex, just to try to keep this unmerciful madness under control."

"Now that's an interesting thought, although a little strong."

"Maybe it is strong, but if you look clearly at the whole thing, it underlines the fact that Nature is just tinkering with us. It doesn't play by what we consider are sportsmanlike rules. I will grant the need for a sex process, given the fact that Nature insists that as we die we have to be replaced. The process of species replacement is where sex as we know it starts. Maybe penises and vaginas are as good a way to do it as any, but I doubt it. I can also understand the need for a family environment, given the way we are constructed. But to repeat myself, why don't the two always meld? Why is it that after marriage, or a committed relationship, one partner or the other or both frequently become attracted sexually to others? Why didn't Nature give us a brain mechanism that would allow this sexual energy to be focused or the drive tempered?"

"Maybe you are overstating the problem, Elsa. There are a great many couples in the world who are so chemically linked to each other and in love that while one or the other might feel sexual interest in someone else, it becomes only a passing fancy. It's like getting a small hankering for some greasy food you know is going to give you a lot of heartburn. You avoid it and the feeling passes."

"But I'm not only talking about the concept of marital fidelity, Alexander. I'm talking about the animalistic *hankering* for outside sex, the attraction of it, whether one party or the other weakens and does it or not. The feeling of wanting to screw someone, just to screw, can be as confusing to some individuals as actually doing it, particularly for those with puritanical beliefs. It's a bad program, a lousy idea."

"I'm not sure I get that."

"Look," Elsa continued with greater intensity, "sex as it was designed for us included a very strong drive to do it. A lot stronger, for example, for most people, than our drive to eat chocolate bars. And that was probably a good thought when we were crawling around on all fours and couldn't think much. But as I said before, Nature with all its brilliant achievements should have anticipated the fact that one day we humans would learn to think very well and so adjust the sex drive and maybe the whole damned process itself."

"What you're suggesting is that Nature might have changed the entire reproductive process as part of the evolution of the human being from a grunting cave dweller to a thinking person?"

"Well put," Elsa said. "The whole thing could have been changed to a more rational method as humans became more civilized."

"Hey, hold it. I have one truly creative idea we could suggest to Nature if we ever can get in direct touch with it."

"What's that?"

"Very simply, a man sticks an old fingernail into his right ear. And that's it. An egg in there, or whatever, germinates. One sex, no bother, no dinners, no fights." Alexander stared off in space for a few seconds, then looked back at Elsa and said, "Or maybe that isn't such a good idea. Maybe I should keep thinking."

"Please, don't bother," Elsa said with a grin.

Alexander feigned a hurt look and then laughed. "Yeah, you're right. I never was too good at designing reproductive processes. I'm good at designing trench coats, though."

"Now let's get into the trappings of the sex process, as you called it. That's where we really get taken to the cleaners."

"Oh, brother, explain that."

"Okay, sexual jealousy is a really good example. The higher animals have it and we humans *still* have it, even with space shuttles circling the Earth. Once two people settle down in a serious relationship, a sort of sexual jealousy syndrome kicks in. The couple becomes possessive of each other. They don't want anyone else sharing the other's love or sex life. Look at us. I recall when you and I first began to date, I didn't have the slightest interest in who else you were seeing. Then as our relationship became more involved, the jealousy syndrome kicked in. For both of us.

"I really began to care about who you were seeing. And from the questions you were asking me, I felt you had the same attitude. We both became victims of the jealousy syndrome, which made us possessive of each other. I frequently believed that we often spent time together just to make sure that neither of us was spending time with anyone else. Sexual jealousy appears to be one of Nature's tricks for keeping two people together, once a serious relationship has started, whether there is love or compatibility or not. Nature wants a couple to stay together as a unit, to fuck and to nurture young, come what may."

"That's an interesting point, and I'm happy to observe that as the day wears on, your capability for graphic description doesn't wear down."

Elsa just looked blankly at Alexander and continued, wrapped in thought. "I do think that the jealousy program, this trick of Nature, this element of the sexual process, is not significantly harmful when true love exists. But it's terrible when a loving or compatible situation doesn't exist, because it can force togetherness when the parties should really be apart. It's another irrational aspect of this whole process."

"Interesting, indeed interesting. And in your professional opinion, is it possible for us to control sexual jealousy, this trick of the brain?"

"I think so. Of course there are various levels of jealousy. Some feel it much more intensely than others. In many tribal and in some modern cultures, husbands feel no jealousy when *they* offer their wives to visitors. When the wives sneak around on their own, however, it's another story. But in general, there are some mind games we can play that can subdue jealousy; in some cases, we can get rid of it altogether. But sexual jealousy for most of us is a stubborn emotion. It has a tendency to come back when you least expect it and overpower rationality."

"You talk about sexual jealousy as being irrational, Elsa, but what about the sexual mating dance? Do you realize that each day and night hundreds of millions of persons who are looking for sexual partners eye each other to see if there is any chemical response, the first step in the human mating dance?"

"I never thought about it in those numbers," Elsa replied, looking surprised.

"It's another irrational thing about sex. Another trick. The whole process of the mating dance, when we are forced to go through it, is damned uncomfortable. In the first place, no one is attractive to every other member of the opposite sex. Did you ever think about that?"

"No, I never thought about that, either, Alexander."

"Well, it's true. I know a single guy who is really a handsome man. Really beautiful."

"Why haven't you introduced him to me? What's his name?"

"Do you think I'm nuts? Nature endowed me with a terrific sexual jealousy program. That's why I don't introduce you. Anyway, this fellow told me that even with all his looks and charm . . ."

"He has charm too?" Elsa interrupted kiddingly.

"Would you shut up? Even with his looks and charm, he can only attract 24 percent of the women he finds interesting and pursues. The guy actually keeps count."

"You can't call that a major study, but it is true that no one person can be sexually attractive to every other member of the opposite sex. But once the attraction comes into being and the circumstances allow, a form of mating dance does take place; it can be very irrational and often painful, I agree."

"Damned irrational," Alexander continued. "I remember seeing a public television program about animal mating dances and the various forms they take. All it did was remind me of a hot singles bar."

"And so presto, we as humans fall for it all," Elsa responded enthusiastically. "An excellent point. We become *victims* of Nature's mating dance program just as we do its jealousy program and even its romantic love program. Look at us, look at how we dress to be sexually seductive to each other. It's as if the mating dance never stops, even if you've been married fifty years. We go for it. We watch two fish sniffing around each other, we can look at public television's minute examination of other animal mating habits and we never realize that nature has given us humans the same ridiculous program. Of course, we carry it to high levels of sophistication with colognes, low cut dresses, open shirts, tight jeans, gold chains, fancy hairdos, and so on. We get right into it, become a part of it, without understanding that our own brains trick us into doing it. People can get really hurt in the process. They can get unmercifully snubbed, and their esteem lowered. It all stinks. Boy, you got me going on that one."

"I like it. What else?"

"As long as we're down on Nature, let me repeat what I said earlier that Nature is out for its own good. In terms of the real-life world, it is simply intent on having us humans fuck and propagate the world. Why I love to be so profanely graphic with you I'll never know," she interrupted herself. "At the office I'm the original Miss Mild Manners. Anyway, Nature is not necessarily concerned for our own individual happiness, particularly when it comes to relationships."

"I don't get that," Alexander interjected.

"I mean that Nature throws all these emotions at us, including love, to get us together, form a relationship, and have kids. That is its ultimate goal. But that isn't necessarily good for us unless we luck out and find a relationship where the emotional variables work to support the relationship and not fight against it."

"So you're saying that having a good relationship with someone is primarily a matter of luck."

"I think so. We touched on this before during that last weird conversation we had up on the sun deck. First, it's a very chancy matter to meet someone where the potential for a good relationship exists. There are probably millions of other people on this planet that you and I might have become attached to individually, had we not met each other."

"When we happened to get on the same bus, together, one day ten years ago, standing on the same corner in a city of eight million people."

"Exactly, Alexander. Look at the odds on that one. If that isn't a chancy thing, what is?"

"Oh, my God," he said suddenly. "Are we going to get into a big discussion on chance again? Are you going to talk about my mother and father in bed again?"

Elsa grinned.

"I'll spare you. But chance is a strong factor and that's only the start of it. The next thing is, do all the emotional variables involved in the relationship create a positive support ambience? Is, in fact, the relationship solidly positive or does it have a high potential for turning negative? We have to use our reasoning power to examine it ourselves, if we can, because Nature doesn't seem to give a shit. Even romantic love, which is one of the few nice bones Nature throws us in the whole sexual process, can begin to wither under an umbrella of hostility. Once the relationship does turn negative, either before or after marriage and kids, it becomes unbelievably difficult for the two persons involved to see through all the emotional drives, tricks, and other programs to neutralize the negatives."

"If they can't," Alexander said, "it's divorce or separation time."

"Theoretically, or the couple stays together for one reason or another and they live with the negative feelings. It's been done for centuries. Let me add as an aside: in my opinion, the success or failure of any relationship depends to a great extent on whether each partner is able to handle the emotional brain quirks of the other. Before marriage, instead of blood tests, we probably should have quirk handling tests. We all have quirks, you know."

"I agree, Elsa, your quirks are unbelievable."

"Let's not get personal, Alexander."

"All right, so I have a few weird quirks as well. At last count they were under five."

"Oh yeah, sure," Elsa responded sarcastically and then went on. "But the point is you have quirks and I handle them. I accept them. I don't want to change them. And you are very patient with my quirks; so the deep love we feel for each other hasn't been affected. The love is primarily unconditional. We are not in a power struggle."

"So we're lucky. We've been able to perpetuate the most positive aspect of our relationship, love. It's a fantastic feeling for both of us and we've managed to work around the negatives, so we're comfortable as well."

"You're right, we're lucky with all of that. Except for this very hour, Alexander, when I'm starving for that pizza and the driver is probably twenty miles from here, being kidnapped by a gang of frustrated terrorists who can't find an unguarded diplomat."

"In this city, anything is possible. Wait a second, I'll call."

Alexander walked to the kitchen where he called the pizza parlor. He returned shortly.

"It's on the way. The guy is close. Should be here soon. 'Trust me,' the guy said, believe it or not."

"I believe it. Any time a guy in a pizza parlor says 'trust me,' I believe it totally. It's one of my quirks. But getting back to my earlier point, when the quirks between a couple get out of control—and that usually happens when *neither* person can handle the quirks of the other, since often it only takes one good quirk handler in a relationship—then love and respect usually disappear. That's when it's time to split."

"And that can be painful."

"Painful as hell. It's Nature's last throw of the dice, another sexual trapping. What it does is throw every negative emotion at you to keep you together, even when rationally you know the relationship is over. Even if you get through all of that and actually do make the break, the pain Nature then throws your way can last months or years.

"But for the most part, we don't recognize Nature's merciless aims and the tricky, bullshit emotional programs it throws in to achieve them. We simply accept the pain and the emotional punishment as our due. We don't look at it objectively and say, 'Nature sucks, we don't deserve all this bullshit; the thing didn't work between us; it's no one's fault, let's stop this pain program.' But no, we have to start playing games with our brains to trick them into getting back on track."

"What kind of games?"

"Well, seeing people like me, for one thing, or reading some of the hundreds of books out on the subject of recovering from a bad relationship or marriage. What it all amounts to, once you recognize those hurtful drives as programs, is playing tricks back on your brain to alter it so you'll be happy again. The stupid thing about the design of our minds is that we have to play the tricks. Our rationality isn't enough. You can't believe the people who come to see me who are just out of the most sordid relationships imaginable. There is absolutely no question in their minds nor mine that the relationships were bad. Yet they are going through the worst pain. It's unbelievable. And for what? The brain is definitely not our friend when it comes to the emotions it throws at us. In fact, it can be our worst enemy. It's a remarkable instrument, but in so many ways it can really screw us up."

"So what have we really said in all of this, Elsa?"

"I'm not sure. But if I had to put it all in a nutshell, I'd say as I said to start with, sex is a mechanical, almost robotic process that Nature endowed us with without telling us why, and that as a total program it is not necessarily good for everyone in today's world. We get hung up in the strength of its drives, the sensuality Nature drapes it in and the related emotional by-products. We just get sucked in by it all.

"The sex process also dictates too many things in our lives, including how we act and how we dress. Why do men and women have to dress so differently? It's part of the game. And another important point: love does *not* have to be included in the sexual process. What a lunatic thought that was in this whole design of things, considering the fact that babies need guardians. So what happens? We too often get sex and its infatuations confused with love. Nature doesn't always help us out there. So we get a lot of one-night stands. And for what? What the hell is really happening? What is supposed to be happening?"

"I like what you're saying, Elsa, I think."

"Thank you, Alexander, I think."

"So please continue until the pizza man rings."

"Okay. Another thing that is screwed up in this process is that sex can become so overwhelming for many of us that we can be bewildered by it. I touched on this before. If we are unattractive or for some other reason are not dating or relating much, or not doing well in the mating dance, our self-esteem suffers.

"Why? Because we are not answering Nature's call to have sex with someone, which has translated itself into a social expectation. I say fuck Nature's call to have sex. What *are* we reproducing for? Let's get right down to it. Nobody has left us a message saying that all you folks on Earth should reproduce because you are part of some grand, universal experiment on the uses of sodium. And in the process, we have to have more and more new people out there because we can't figure out yet how to make permanent humans. So get out there and fuck because fucking to make new humans was the best idea we could think of. Well, at least that would be something.

"Then we'd all know what we're fucking for. But no, we're in the dark and so sex becomes too big a part of so many lives. It leaves a lot of us wrecked. Nervous, fucking wrecks. I wish I could tell everyone: *Get off it. It's not that important. It's a brain trick. Your brain is trying to bring you together with someone. Don't always fall for it. Be rational. See what's happening. Watch your drives, your programs, whatever you want to call them. Let them be while you do what you think is rationally best for* you."

Elsa was shouting, sitting straight up on the sofa, shaking one of Alexander's magazines over her head.

"Good God, Elsa, I think you're really mad about all of this."

Elsa looked about for a moment and began to cool down.

"I was a bit loud there, wasn't I?"

"Well, I thought you were. And probably about two dozen neighbors thought you were, too."

"Ah, it's aggravating to be human. If Nature does this again on some other planet, I wish it would consult me, particularly when it comes to brain drives. I think I could help."

"Wait. I'll send a wire. Collect. What's the address?"

They both laughed. Then the doorbell rang.

"Right on cue," Alexander said.

"I can't believe it," Elsa replied.

"It's as if your trust in pizza delivery men has been rewarded, Elsa. You get the paper plates and I'll pay the bill."

"I like the way you give almost autocratic direction when a pizza arrives. What a quirk that is and how well I handle it. How well we mesh together. What a relationship. What a stroke of luck. Maybe Nature isn't so bad after all."

"For some of us. I love you, Elsa."

"I love you, Alexander. Now get the pizza."

Alexander walked over to the dresser in the bedroom, picked up his wallet and walked to the front door.

THE POINT

We are totally victimized by the sexual process. It permeates our entire lives because it involves not only the need for two sexes to live together and mate, but it includes the nurturing of the young as well, the products of sex.

Most of us respond to the total process without giving it a second thought.

At an upscale cocktail party composed of married couples, the women and men are all decked out, using every designer trick to appear sexually attractive. Is this to attract their mates for a night of sex? Of course not. It is simply the manifestation of Nature's genetic call to reproduce, to be socially accepted, and to wield power. It is an unthinking response.

In the fundamentalist Muslim countries, when women are outdoors they are required to cover themselves from head to toe so as not to be sexually attractive to the men who look at them. This is an interesting answer to the brain drive and would be fine, considering our sexual design, if it weren't so uncomfortable and restricting for the women. However, it has been interesting to see what women do in those fundamentalist countries when, because of a change in government, the women are freed from these restrictions. For the most part, out come the short skirts, the jewelry, and the makeup.

It is there, the drive is genetic. Like everything else genetic or conditioned, some are able to control it better than others.

There are some very intelligent people on this earth who will question practically everything. But they will be standing there arm in arm with a mate when they get the awards for their work. They aren't questioning the fact that they even need a mate and yet it's one of the biggest imponderables of all.

These same people will worry night and day when their father or mother dies and the survivor is left alone. Nature's design is for two people to live together, and we are convinced that the design is right because we can feel it. So we worry for others who are alone, when they might be doing just fine, particularly if they fight the brain drive that wants them to couple.

Homosexuals are part of the sexual process. They grow up thinking that they'll be like everyone else, but some brain flaw, some imperfections in the trillions of miles of connections have caused two persons of the same sex to be attracted to one another. But that's one of the few differences. There is still the same urge to have children and nurture them, even though they live in a society that does not allow them to adopt.

I am not homosexual, but I can feel their outrage at a society who thinks that the only normal way to have intercourse is for a penis to penetrate a vagina. Think about it, what is so creative about this process? What is so clean and heavenly? As Elsa Dixon observed, it is a robotic process that is part of our genetic program. If it weren't, we might be sexually attracted to deer. Our brains control this within a wide parameter, but the genetics are obviously there to anyone who uses a little common sense.

We are victimized by this sexual process and all its trappings: the mating dance, the sexual jealousies, the pairing and the union, how we make ourselves up to look, the love, and the potential pain of separation.

This isn't to say we can't enjoy the entire experience immensely. Of course we can. But we need to know that it wasn't our doing, it wasn't our choice. We are blindly following a much more skillful and seductive lover, the dictates of Nature.

11

The Enigma of Death

It was another bright, sunny day on Mackinac Island on northern Lake Michigan. Alfred Hoffman and Andrew Hill sat on the porch of their rented cottage, facing the beach. The two retired philosophy professors had been talking all week about various concepts of purpose, but today, the conversation took a new twist.

"Let's get off of purpose, today, Andrew, and focus, if we can, on death."

"Are you always this cheerful, Alfred?"

"It is a gloomy subject, isn't it? Even the business of death is gloomy: morticians dressed in subdued clothing with artificially long faces, people weeping at cemeteries, caskets, vaults, crematoria, and whatnot. The whole thing can make your skin chill."

"Death is not only gloomy," Andrew responded, "the entire issue is ambiguous. We know that it's imminent for anything living and yet we hold it in an odd, contradictory context. We are attracted by death, for example. Someone is killed in a car accident and we'll slow down to see if we can quickly spot the body, even though we are simultaneously repelled by it. We don't like to look at corpses, and we scrupulously avoid the entire subject of death if we can."

"Just as we avoid the subject of purpose."

"Yes. In that sense, the two subjects, purpose and death are intertwined in that they both remain unsolved mysteries for us."

"Unless we have belief systems that spell it all out for us," Alfred interjected.

"Of course. Those poor boys who are sent to their deaths in war by leaders who have literally brainwashed them into believing that a *heroic* death is a sure entrance into some glorious afterlife, aren't inwardly debating the various theories about death on their way into battle. They actually *know* something good is going to happen to them when they die. To them it is not a belief, it is actual fact, transmitted to them by their leaders—governmental, religious, or both—who give the perception of having a direct line to a God."

"And who are also excellent communicators."

"Communicators? Good grief, Alfred, these people could head the top public relations firms in the world. They know how to do it. Think of how skilled they must be if they can perpetuate and transmit an idea that will send you gladly to your death. And they've been doing it all through history. Tell me, can you think of anything you'd gladly go to your death for?"

"Well, there are possibly a handful of happenings I'd accept death to prevent, but there are none for which I would do so gladly."

"But why not? You've told me before that you believe in a hereafter that is more spiritually harmonious than life on Earth."

"I believe in it, yes, but the whole process of death quite frankly scares the bejesus out of me and I'm not getting any braver as I get older."

"I understand your fear, Alfred. I have it myself. But don't you recognize the contradiction? Here you are, like possibly billions of other people on this planet, thinking there is some kind of better hereafter, but scared as the dickens of going to it. How do you explain it?"

"Because, Andrew, we are, in fact, active here in a real world. It is a world we can sense. The spiritual world of the hereafter is not within our capacity to perceive, nor can we anticipate its experience. The prospect of it is a little frightening. Humans as a general rule are normally frightened by the prospect of a dramatic change. And dying is a really dramatic change."

"Quite dramatic."

"Exactly."

"And yet, Alfred, there are a good many people, including those poor patriots we talked of, who go to their death gladly on the basis of their beliefs. So I imagine that one's willingness to die or to accept death depends to a significant degree on how *deeply* one has been ingrained with a belief system that encompasses the nature of our spiritual being, both in life and in an afterlife."

"I would say that is substantially correct, Andrew."

"The fact that you are a little frightened of death probably indicates that your own belief system designed to deal with the process isn't rock hard."

"I would say that is also substantially correct. I have beliefs about a hereafter, but the leap of faith to achieve them didn't set any record. I, unfortunately, retain a healthy skepticism, which I would gladly give up if a more convincing communicator came along. But now tell me your views of death, Andrew, from the perspective you've been able to achieve in India."

Andrew rose from his chair and began to pace the porch.

"Wouldn't you agree, Alfred, that during the course of our careers, we have minutely examined most of the organized religions and cults of the world and the beliefs that each espoused?"

"We've looked at a lot of them."

"How many would you guess?"

"I really couldn't say."

"Give it your roughest guess."

"Oh, I would say about 1,500, if you include all the tangential sects."

"And didn't each one have something to say about death in terms of some form of afterlife?"

"Yes, they all touched on it in some way, although there was a wide variance as to how specific they were about it."

"Some just espoused an afterlife in an obscure form, while others stated with some precision what it would be like."

"Yes, and that includes the more primitive religions."

"If you were to categorize into just three or four broad theories what these religions and other belief systems tell us is going to happen to us after death, how would you do it?"

Alfred thought for a moment.

"Okay, but this is really narrowing it down. The first theory is that we all go to a heaven, or whatever label that religion or group places on a 'heaven' to indicate the spot where your spiritual life continues in some way under a more direct presence of God. And it's much more pleasant than living within impure bodies on this material planet. Evil is left behind. We may reside in this way permanently or according to some beliefs, we come back as the soul of a new human being."

"Yes, good," Andrew remarked, looking intently at Alfred.

"A second theory is that we get to that 'heaven' or to a 'hell,' depending on how we lived our lives here. We are judged in this by a God or his delegates. Living in a hell, of course, is extremely unpleasant. Heaven is as I've previously stated. A third theory is that we pass to a new spiritual existence in that our soul simply floats free and a 'heaven' per se isn't absolutely specified."

"Yes."

"And one more. When life is through here, we are through. In other words, that's all she wrote."

"Well done."

"I wouldn't say that, but those theories do cover the subject in a nutshell."

"Thank you, Alfred. All I wanted you to do was bring out the contradictions between these beliefs. They are obvious even in capsulized form. The more you would fill in these beliefs with detail the more obvious the contradictions would become. What we come back to once again is the problem that nobody left a note with the first humans advising them on the nature and purposes of life and then what happens, if anything, after we die. As with purpose, we appear to have a brain predisposition that creates a belief about what happens after death. So all the belief systems about life and death evolved to fill this programmed need.

"The problem is that these beliefs are all man-made. They all came from extraordinary human beings who have brains like yours and mine. What most of them did, in essence, was to point up the division between bodily needs and the pure rational mind. Then they gave the mind a spirituality or soul-force that in some way was continuous. In other words, they created the concept of a soul as a transcendent force that enters the body at birth or some time prior to it and leaves the body at death. It's this lingering soul or spirituality which goes to heaven, or wherever."

"And I imagine your point is, Andrew, that the existence of this soul-force is only speculative."

"Exactly. That's all it can be. If a soul-force does exist, it must reside in the brain. Why? Because we are transplanting or creating artificial devices for even our most vital organs, such as the heart, without dying or affecting our thought processes. And within the brain, neuroresearchers, according to the reports I read in the journals sent to me, have yet to detect any semblance of a soul-force. Nor have they been even able to find any specific area that is the absolute center for thought."

"Do you personally believe in a life after death, Andrew?"

"I just don't know. Who is really to say? I would say that everything we know so far rationally points to the fact that there is none. Yet I work very closely with some quite reputable gurus in India who tell me they already transcend their bodies, see previous lives, and can communicate spiritually with the dead. Their arguments are fascinating. The problem with this sort of thing is you have to be able to do it yourself, experience it, before you can believe in it. I just sit there as they tell me these things, nodding my head somewhat disconcertingly.

"The peculiar thing about all of these afterlife theories is that many of those who espouse them, including the authoritative religionists, usually never tell you point blank what actually happens. Their communication is always obtuse, never fully articulated. Or if it is, they can't account for the process itself in a reasonable way. They all seem to imply that you have to undergo what they've undergone, whatever that is, to understand."

"Perhaps they're right."

"Perhaps so. But it also makes it difficult to separate the charlatans from the true students of life. What I see is that life is focused on the brain. It is the home of our consciousness. And we don't really die until our brain stops functioning. What, if anything, leaves the brain to continue its spiritual quest is, of course, speculative."

"But there have been people, Andrew, who have come back from what they thought were deathlike states, who have reported quite similar experiences. A feeling of peace and calm, a bright white light and so forth, supposedly a pleasant thing, all in all."

"Yes, but they lived to report it. So there never was a complete brain death. Now if somebody crawled out of the grave, after being down there three months, embalmed or not, and told me what death was like, I'd believe him. But nobody has done that. It's quite possible that when the brain senses an oncoming death, it finally lets the person relax and enjoy his or her last few moments or seconds in peace, with appropriate thoughts and images. That's the least the brain could do, in view of the suffering it puts us through during our lifetimes. I need my brain to live, but there is wiring up there

I'd dearly love to exorcise. Wasteful impulses, cravings, and desires, in particular."

"What about those, Andrew, who are hypnotized or in other ways spiritually activated and report on prior life experiences that appear so real? How do you feel about that?"

"It's possible. We both know that anything's possible. But don't forget that the brain is inventive. It can create great fictional novels and superbly innovative dreams, complete with emotion, narrative, detailed imagery, perspectives, and smells. What this tells me is that it also has the capacity to create a fictional prior life."

"An interesting point," Alfred said after pausing to think about Andrew's statement. "What about a heaven," he continued, "an after-life meeting place. What are your views on that?"

"It's an interesting speculation, Andrew. But every time I think about it, I wonder about dogs and mosquitos."

"Dogs and mosquitos?"

"Well, yes. Most of the theories about a heaven describe it as a place for humans only. Dogs, mosquitos, and other living things are left out. There is this concept that because humans are spiritual beings they are different from animals. I quite frankly believe this is a prejudicial attitude. I've had some dogs, for example, whose company I would much prefer to some humans I've known. And if it was off to some heavenly place I was sent after death, I would truly be disappointed if my old dog friends weren't already there.

"I think my point is that a life force exists in animals as well as humans. If part of that force consists of a soul, then animals and insects should have it as well: caterpillars, mosquitos, perhaps even trees, any organism that emanates from the basic coding of DNA. And if there is a heaven, how do we all communicate with one another? What language? What age level do we settle at? Who is old, who is young? Are there sexual differences? Do we have memory, imagination, and creativeness? Who keeps track of all the individual spirits? There would have to be billions upon billions of them. And where the dickens is the place?"

"The questions could be endless, Andrew."

"Then what about life on other planets? There are billions upon billions of other stars. Perhaps an infinite number. Surely some have planets that hold life. Where, then, do all those other planetary souls go? And if all of us do go somewhere, do we all mix together?

Some spiritualists claim that in our afterlives we are usually mixed up with the same nuclear family units out of the untold trillions floating about.

"Yet despite these questions my guru friends do claim to have definitely experienced some form of spiritual transcendentalism that they say exists after death. And who am I to argue with them? For all I know, they can be absolutely correct. For all I know, anyone can be correct. Come up with the most harebrained scheme about life after death and there is nothing one can do to dispute it, because we aren't able to prove it one way or the other."

"Having said all this, Andrew, what is your own gut feel about the whole subject of life after death?"

"As I mentioned before, my rational self is inclined to believe that death is final. It's the very end to one's existence. But there is some emotion that nags at me that tells me I'm wrong; that at death something indeed takes place that explains what all of this has been about, and the concept of life in its essence is revealed. If that doesn't happen, then we are all just pawns of Nature, keeping alive, assuring survivors for reasons that we'll never know. And that thought simply repels me."

"I think it's time for a little, quiet walk."

"I think you're right, Alfred. And now that we're through talking about death, do you know any good jokes?"

"Give me a moment. I had an uncle who was a comedian. He passed away, but maybe I can get in touch with him."

The two men laughed, stood up, looked at the sky for a moment with the sun beginning its late afternoon descent, and walked toward the hard-packed sand near the water.

THE POINT

We are so imbued with a sense of purpose that the thought of departing our earthly lives without some form of continuation repels us. We see the evidence of finality before us, but our brains trick us into believing otherwise. Because life is such a great mystery to begin with, any idea about death is feasible, no matter whose idea it is. We can't prove anyone wrong.

The thought of death as an eternal end to our lives should be one of our major preoccupations; it should be discomforting from the moment we are old enough to know that it will happen. However, the brain appears to trick us into leading our lives for most of our years as if death can't happen to us, even though we know, logically, that it will, or that if death does happen, we will continue in some way or have a peaceful end.

The process of death is such a brutal thing. It would have been so much more sensitive for all of us to live a specific number of years, after which we might board a conveyance that would take us to some unknown destination. At least we'd know for sure we are going somewhere with the prospect of rejoining loved ones, even if at some point along the way we might be peacefully extinguished.

It would seem that the best idea about death is simply to let our brains trick us into any comforting perspective about it. In other words, whatever belief feels comforting to us, believe in it with all we have. Any of the available theories could be right. When it comes to death, the tricks our brains play on us appear to be a good thing.

12

The Human Land Grab

Ed Grogan sat bundled up in his overcoat, scarf and wool sweater on the screened-in front porch of the Sunnyday Home for the Aged.

Christ, it must be thirty degrees out here, he thought, as he stared out at the vacant front lawn and street. The day was sunny and relatively dry. It was refreshing just to be outside for a quick breather. He stood and looked up and down the street. No one in sight. He didn't like that. He would have rather been living where there were people on the street. He liked watching people. But all things considered, he had decided some time ago the Sunnyday Home had been the best choice for him. It was clean; the food was borderline edible; he didn't have to give up everything he owned; and, best of all, he rarely had to talk to anyone.

Grogan had been labeled an eccentric the day he arrived. His language was salted heavily with profanity and he would walk quickly away from any conversation that bored him, which was most of them.

Grogan heard the front door to the home open. He turned his head and saw Essie Beecroft walking toward him. Essie was the only other person in the home who Grogan liked to be with, although he never admitted it. She pulled up the one remaining chair left on the porch during the winter and sat down.

"I saw you sitting out here so I thought I'd join you," she said.

"I noticed."

"What exactly are you doing out here?"

"Good God, Essie, what the hell do you think I'm doing out here, brushing up on my volleyball slam? For Christ's sake, look around you. There is nothing on this porch except these two rotten chairs, now occupied by you and me. And nothing is happening out there on the street. During the past twenty minutes, the most exciting thing that occurred was an odd noise that I believe emanated from the sewer. It sounded to me like a fart."

"Please, Mr. Grogan."

"You see, you shouldn't have asked me what I was doing out here."

"I knew what you were doing. You were getting some fresh air."

"So why ask me?"

"I was just trying to make some decent conversation with you for a change. It didn't work."

"Obviously."

They sat in silence for a few minutes, staring at the bleak city landscape outside the home.

"You know it's strange," Essie said tentatively, "but even at my age, I sometimes dream about owning just a little bit of land up north, in the country, where I could just sit on a screened-in porch like this and look over some beautiful rolling farm land."

Ed Grogan whirled quickly around, slammed his arm on the chair and practically shouted, "Goddamn it, that's the trouble with this whole, rotten, lousy world."

"What on earth . . . ," Essie looked startled.

"For God's sake, woman, do you know what this obsession for land has done to us as human beings? Do you realize what a ridiculous thing it all is?"

"Well, I never really thought about it very much, and I don't appreciate your outburst."

"Then goddamn it, why did you come out here in the first place? You know damned well that something you say is going to cause me to go nuts. It always happens."

"It doesn't have to happen," she said sounding upset, "and I can't see what's wrong with wanting to own a piece of land."

"But don't you realize that that's nothing but some useless addiction, as bad for us as some drug that renders us senseless?"

"What are you talking about?"

Grogan sat back in his chair attempting to calm himself. He tapped his fingers on the arm rest and took a few deep breaths.

"All right, all right. Look, Essie, there is nothing wrong with you personally wanting to own a few acres of land. What are a few acres in the whole scheme of things? Nothing. It's all the rubbish, the problems that develop out of this addiction we have for land, that infuriates me"

"I'm afraid I still don't understand."

"The fighting, the arguments, the wars, that's what I mean. All about some goddamned land. For Christ's sake, we just seem to have this very basic, very weird need to have our own land, our own space. And all the evidence points to the fact that it's some inherited trait, some goddamned thing we had no choice in."

"Like what kind of evidence, Mr. Grogan?" Essie asked, giving him a skeptical look.

"What we see in animals, for one thing. With only rare exceptions, animals are very land oriented, very territorial. And I don't see how one ant can teach that to another. It's got to be an innate thing."

"But you can't prove it."

"Goddamn it," Grogan yelled, "I know it can't be proved yet. But with all the genetic research they're doing, the genes they're finding that cause this bad thing and that one, they're bound to find that territorial gene, the fucking thing that . . ."

"*Please,* Mr. Grogan, your language . . ."

"My language has nothing to do with what I am trying to say." Grogan stopped talking. He thought an instant about what he said and then broke into a chuckle.

"I don't suppose that little comment made much sense."

"It didn't make any sense at all and I still don't like your language. Besides, what do you really know about this land thing?"

"Quite frankly, I don't know that much, but neither does anyone else for sure. I spent the first three years of my time in this holding cage for the elderly reading every book about anthropology that I could get my hands on and understand, as well as devouring books written by people who sat out there in the wilderness for years and studied the habits of animals."

"Three years is a long time to spend on any single subject, Mr. Grogan."

"It is, but I found it all very compelling. That's how I know at least a little bit about the subject. For example, there is a theory that this attitude we have toward land comes directly from a natural genetic design to give us space for self-defense. That may sound a little crazy but if you think about it and we go back in time only 35,000 years, things had to be pretty rough on this planet. It had to be a *totally* dog-eat-dog world, instead of just the *partially* dog-eat-dog world we know today. Practically all living things were potentially something else's dinner. As a result, humans and animals had to possess some pretty fierce characteristics, either for killing or defending or both. So what we ended up with was sort of a dichotomy. On the one hand, humans and animals had to come equipped with characteristics that were fierce enough to allow them to kill. On the other hand, the nuclear families, tribes, and herds had to live together peaceably. This one theory contends that animals and humans were given this instinctive territorial drive to stake out a land area so that like species wouldn't destroy one another."

"I'm not exactly sure of what you've said."

"It took me a little time to figure out what they were saying myself. Let's use a family of wolves to illustrate. When that nuclear unit of wolves stakes out a piece of land, they simply pee around the edges so that the family next door knows not to trespass. This is Nature's way of giving the families within the species some breathing space. Now a wolf's piss is not going to keep hungry lions and tigers out. But it helps to keep strange wolves out and lessens the chance of social and territorial fights among each other. Nature obviously wanted us to have space for ourselves, so it gave us a way to make it happen. Call it a built-in land addiction or a territorial program or whatever you want to call it."

"A fascinating view, Mr. Grogan."

"You think so?"

"Yes."

"That's interesting, because when I start reciting facts like these, most people think I'm a crackpot."

"I didn't say you weren't a crackpot. You probably are, but continue anyway."

Grogan smiled.

"Well, I think until the research people get this all nailed down, you have to look at animals to figure out which of our brain drives are learned and which are instinctive or genetic. Now maybe a wolf learns to pee on his borders from watching his parents or maybe it is a built-in wired brain drive. It doesn't make a whole lot of difference. The fact is that behind the act itself is a drive or brain predisposition that allows for it. We don't, for example, have a general predisposition that allows us to feel comfortable in cutting off a hand, if you don't mind the brutal example." Essie winced, but Grogan continued, hardly noticing.

"Canaries are another case in point. According to some students of the subject, they sing in their natural environments primarily to make sure that others in the area know that the space is being occupied. Now the anthropologists can't know these things for sure, who can get inside a canary's head, but it sounds like a pretty solid observation. So really what we are looking at here is a natural balancing act. Nature gives us fierce characteristics but also instills in us a need for our own land or space to prevent us from getting in each other's hair, and triggering those characteristics that can cause us to turn on our own kind. However, in my opinion, Nature really fucked this thing up."

Essie Beecroft winced visibly. She was about to object again to Grogan's language but concluded it was useless. Instead she said: "And how do you believe Nature *went wrong,* Mr. Grogan?"

Grogan missed her innuendo.

"Because we shouldn't have been saddled with these fierce characteristics in the first place. What on earth did Nature or the Creator or God or whoever perpetrated this life process on us—this joke—have in mind when it gave us fierce characteristics? If Nature wanted this planet to live in peace, it could have been a little more clever about it. I mean, look how clever the design of the human body is, or even a simple house plant. Nature came so close to creating a harmonious setting for this planet. But what did it have in mind when it determined that a lot of living things should have to kill each other for food? It certainly could have devised a better system for allowing living things to feed themselves. But no. Why make it easy? And so mice eat bugs, which eat other bugs. Cats eat mice. Foxes eat rabbits. Tigers eat deer. Man eats cows, chickens, ducks, sheep, fish, and there are some people with gourmet tastes who would eat just about any goddamned thing that could wiggle. Now what kind of mercy or justice is there in a feeding process like that?"

"Put that way, none that I can really think of."

"So you agree that Nature came out a little wanting in this area?"

"From that viewpoint, yes and I do like the gentle way you put that."

"Thank you. The point is, if Nature would have provided some *inorganic* substance in ample quantity that *all* living things would just love to eat as its bodily fuel, the need to kill would be practically nonexistent. Even animals like cows and horses that are not carnivores wouldn't need violent instincts because they wouldn't have to defend themselves from a decidedly homicidal attack. Nobody would want to eat them. They'd only have to defend against primarily social attacks, which don't have to be fatal. I'm talking about a few fine adjustments that could have added a lot more harmony to life."

"You sound angry about it."

"I *am* angry about it, for Christ's sake, at least when I start to think on it. What the hell did whoever did this have in mind?"

"About life in general or how we eat?"

"Well, both, I guess."

"I'm not sure we'll ever know, Mr. Grogan."

"I'm not sure either. But you would think that we as humans, with thought processes and powers of observation, should be able to see what Nature more or less had in mind, at least with regard to this drive for land."

"I don't quite understand."

"I mean we should be able to see quite clearly that Nature gave us this brain drive for land to assure protection or some kind of reason along that line. But now that we are wise enough to recognize that fact, we shouldn't have to be shoved around by it."

"I still don't understand."

"Having land itself is not that important in today's literate world. We don't have to *own* land. We can't own land anyway. Somebody makes up a piece of paper that says *legally* we own some land. But we don't own that goddamned land. How can you own land on a planet that is floating about for no reason we can comprehend?" Grogan paused and Essie was about to respond, but Grogan quickly continued. "How? I'll tell you how. Because a bunch of governing bodies back there in history created customs and passed laws that told you so. *Told* you you could own land. *Legislated* the damned concept. What the hell did they know then? What do we know now? What I'm saying is that the concept of land ownership is absolutely crazy. Anybody who thinks he or she actually *owns* land ought to be committed to some mental institution. All you really have is some land that you've borrowed until you die or someone else *borrows* it from you. This idea of actually *owning* it only satisfies some stupid brain drive that has caused us more grief than it's worth. All through history, people have been fighting and killing for *their* land. What bullshit. They've been tricked by this ridiculous drive."

"Are you saying that people don't have the right to defend what they think is theirs, including land, Mr. Grogan?"

"Oh, sure they do. At least until we find some way to rise above this fantasy of land ownership. If you, Essie, actually owned that piece of land up north, or were inhabiting it because you had a piece of paper saying it belonged to you, there would be no sense giving it up to someone who came up to you and said, 'Oh, Essie, I believe the concept of land ownership stinks and therefore I am going to inhabit your land. You can go somewhere else, thank you.' You'd tell the guy he was off his rocker and he should go visit the first shrink he runs across. And if he didn't leave, you'd call the cops.

"What I'm saying is that we have to live within the systems that have been set up here on Earth and more specifically, within the countries we live in. They may be wrong, but it's better than sitting around in some jail. We just shouldn't be so serious about these goddamned systems even though we have to live within them."

"I'm afraid you've lost me again."

"What I'm saying is that we have some lousy brain drives that trick us into setting up concepts for living that are ridiculous, and the least we can do is make some attempt to begin recognizing them, just like we recognize our arms and legs. If we acknowledge them, maybe someday someone will get some ideas on how to cope with those drives and set up some better ways to live. We should assume, for example, that we do have a natural drive to have our own space. Our own place to be. For cave dwellers, it might have been some nice corner of the cave. Today it might be a home in the suburbs.

"We should also assume, for humanity's sake, that this drive goes *farther* than our own little family's space. It also extends to the borders of the community we live in and beyond that to our state or nation. We should assume further that we are brain driven to have this sense of belonging. To have roots identifiable in the soil of some established entity that has definable borders, be it our own home or our entire country.

"And then we should look at the foolishness of it. We should see that if we are born in Switzerland we then are compelled by our upbringing to call ourselves Swiss. If we are born in France we are then compelled to call ourselves French. If we are born in Mexico we are compelled to be Mexican. All just slick labels, with which too many of us become obsessed. What the hell difference does it make who the fuck we are? Can't we see that where we are born is accidental? And once we get stuck with a label describing our accidental origin, we are then simply brainwashed into identifying with it so strongly that we'd even die for it. Now that is one sick brain drive. A ridiculous trick of Nature. When will we begin to see all of it?"

"But what's wrong with belonging somewhere, Mr. Grogan, being a part of something, identifying with it? I think you are making too big of an issue out of all this."

Grogan stood up and paced the length of the porch, his hands in his overcoat pockets, eyes down, lost in thought. Then he walked back to where Essie Beecroft was sitting and stood in front of her.

"I *am* making too big an issue out of this. But what the hell, I would rather be making too big an issue out of the human obsession with land than going inside and dying of asphyxiation. You've got to know that the rotten lima bean and ham casserole they served for lunch is probably at this moment causing a record level of farting among the inmates of our beloved Sunnyday Home."

Essie Beecroft looked away, wondering why she spent so much time with this crude individual. It had to be Grogan's assertion that she would rather spend time with him because his mind was so much brighter than most of the people who lived in the home. She was friendly with many of them. She liked quite a few and spent time with them. But she had to admit that Grogan was a genuine diversion for her.

To be sure, she couldn't stand his language. Indeed, she had never really heard language like that actually spoken by anyone close to her. Words like Mr. Grogan's were never used during her upbringing in Muncie, Indiana, nor were they permitted in her household while she was raising her own family. She had only seen vulgar words and phrases in books. So being with Grogan was both an enlightening and degrading experience. She was trying hard to accept this contradiction and to live with Grogan's vulgarity. But it was difficult.

She looked at Grogan and broke the brief silence. "As long

as we agree this is not the big issue you are making it out to be, why don't you go on?"

Grogan looked at her with surprise.

"Now wait a second. I agreed with you that *I* might be making too big an issue of the subject. But I didn't say it wasn't a big issue. You and I just sitting here and talking about it can't accomplish much. So in that sense, I could very well be making too big an issue out of the subject. But in terms of our existence on Earth— all human beings, that is—it is one *hell* of an issue."

Essie Beecroft gave him a blank stare.

"Okay, let's attack this subject from another angle. Say you and I are up in the sky on a space shuttle. And . . ."

"My, that would be exciting, wouldn't it?" Essie glanced at Grogan with a faraway look.

"Yes, it would be."

Grogan paused to think about it. "But for the moment it's a fantasy. Anyway, we look out a window and we see the Earth in all its natural beauty. There are no borders, no lines of national sovereignty. Only telescopic instruments can detect fences and customs gates. But these are human contraptions. What we could see quite plainly from that shuttle is that all national borders are human inventions. We can more easily imagine from our viewpoint in space that at a specific time in history some big wheeler-dealer might have started it all by standing tall and saying, 'I declare this country India and these are my borders.' Maybe he even went around and peed on them. I don't know.

"Other fellows through the centuries declared this place China, that place Peru, and so forth. The borders shifted back and forth as wars started to rage over who owned what. Then, to make things worse all through recorded history, there were assholes who would stand up and say, 'Oh men, do you know that that little country over there used to be a part of our Motherland? Let's get our army together and go over there and get the darned thing back.'

"So they invaded, killed thousands of people in the process, took the land back, and the borders shifted again. But nothing really shifted except a man-made border. Some satisfaction for such a lunatic land drive. As human beings we have gone through centuries of that bullshit. Now you'd think that at some point we'd have caught on to how silly it all is. You'd think that humans would have one day said to all governing bodies, 'Enough of this. You guys ought to catch on to what's driving you. It's nuts. Nature fucked up. Let's all live in peace.'

"No way. It hasn't happened because governments and opinion leaders just continue to feed these drives, making no attempt to observe them and then control them. So they allow this limbic bullshit to perpetuate the separateness of their states."

"So you think there should be no countries or states."

"No, I didn't say that. I said we perpetuate their *separateness*. Humans still need to be governed and for that we need districting. What I'm saying is that we can't go off our rocker over the concept of a Motherland or a Fatherland. So, we are born in France. That's nice. It's a pleasant place to be. Let's hope we can organize ourselves well and live lives that are relatively ordered in the district or department as they were once called. That's enough. Let's not become obsessed with patriotism for our districts and let's hope there are no similar obsessions in other districts. Let's all just try to get along while we're living."

They both sat for a moment staring out on the street as a large moving van rumbled by. Then Essie turned to Grogan and said thoughtfully, "But how does all this high-level talk about land drives relate to my little place up north in the country?"

One nice thing about Essie Beecroft, Grogan thought, is that she rarely loses sight of the central issues in their interesting little discussions.

"Well, do you agree that this need for space, for land, is a natural drive?" he asked.

"I don't know if it is or not. Whether it's natural, instinctive, learned, I don't know. I will agree that by the time we are adults most of us have a desire for some space of our own. Yes, something we own, be it a piece of land, a home. . . ."

"Even an apartment you own," Grogan interrupted, "like a condominium. A marketing gimmick that makes us feel better because we *own* rather than *borrow or rent*. Right?"

"Yes, even an apartment we own," Essie replied.

"And for some it's just not a simple little desire. It is an obsession, a lust, an addiction. Agreed?"

"Yes, some people have this terrible need for land."

Essie Beecroft became startled as Grogan practically leaped out of his chair, clapped his hands, and said, "But there you are."

"But there I am what?"

"We have this need, this drive for land. We agree. It emanates from the brain, nowhere else. It is there regardless of how it got there. It could be harmless under other circumstances. But in today's world it's not. The bare fact is that under the systems we now have on Earth, all of us can't own a piece of land. With our twentieth-century economic systems we all don't have the money or capability to own or in other ways lay claim to our own space. As a result, we have a very basic inequality among the Earth's people, and that inequality translates into a conflict between what exists and what we are driven to want. That conflict then translates into frustration or hostility or both.

"For many that means discomfort, uneasiness. For others it generates aggression, sometimes dishonesty, sometimes injustice, sometimes crime, either as a nation or as individuals. We are all so hung up in this land ownership concept, the result of the damned drive, that we can't see that it is keeping us from trying to bring decent lives to more people."

"And so what would you suggest?"

"Hell, I don't know what to suggest. I'm no genius and I'm not so sure there is anyone on Earth capable of coming up with a few decent concepts that are acceptable to everyone. In all parts of the world we all think so differently. We have so many varying beliefs that have become deep, deep attitudes. Even if a few power brokers of the world could sit down and agree on something, I'm not sure anything could be accepted totally. We are too structured for it."

"Tell me, Mr. Grogan, what do you think one decent concept might be?"

"Damn it, Essie, I said I don't know of anything."

"Well, you must have had some thoughts on the subject."

"I don't know," he repeated lamely. "Maybe I'm talking about a concept that would involve things like computing the Earth's resources. How many people can we really support on this planet at one time with the resources available: planning for specific family development while not allowing for overpopulation? How can we make sure that the families who do live here can do so in some reasonable degree of physical comfort? How can we find enough land or space allowance to satisfy a computed average of world-wide brain drives? These are the questions we'll face if we don't find the goddamned gene that causes the drive and then learn how to adjust it. We'll have to find enough to eat for everyone, as well as outlets for aggressive, ambitious people. Maybe it's not wealth that these motivated nuts get in return for their efforts; that would continue the inequality. Maybe plaques, awards, recognition on television for being really aggressive and ambitious without killing or hurting anyone."

"That sounds a bit unreal."

"Sure it is. What do I know? Maybe there are other answers. But I can tell you, Essie, that either this planet is going to eventually achieve some equitable way to live or we are going to kill each other off; not that that would make much of a difference to whoever started this life farce. The way we are going, it looks like that was the general idea anyway. Some warped form of an evolutionary life process that will end in a nothingness."

"My goodness, why don't you just snap out of all this and cheer up?"

Grogan looked startled. "Cheer up? What the hell for? For seeing things in a real life way? For realizing that what I see as an ordinary human being is a microscopically narrow picture?" He paused, looked at Essie, and then stared at the street. "Hell, maybe I should cheer up. The fact is I'm not really convinced about anything. I see so much confusion surrounding almost everything that I find it impossible to have strong, consistent convictions about any future or any direction. I only have feelings, ideas that I like to talk about, particularly on miserable days like this one. Maybe I should cheer up. But then, on the other hand, why should I?"

It was getting a little darker outside. A little colder.

"So I suppose," Essie interjected, "I really should work on *not* wanting that lovely screened-in porch looking over some beautiful land."

"Good God, Essie, what are you trying to do? Go ahead, want your land. If you get lucky in next week's lottery, for Christ's sake, go ahead and buy it and take me with you. But let's sit up there together understanding that we don't own a goddamned thing. We have only borrowed a little piece of land, a little bit of nature to satisfy brain drives that for you and me aren't bothersome enough to worry about. We'll sit up there and enjoy it all. If we can't be up there, we'll enjoy what we have here, which includes complaining about it."

"That is probably the most sensitive thing I think I've ever heard you say, Mr. Grogan."

"Well, don't get carried away with it."

"I won't."

"You want to hold your breath and go inside? It's getting cold," Grogan said.

"The smells don't bother me very much."

"Then what I'll pray for most of all is someday to get a transplant of your type of olfactory nerve system design, your sense of smell. At this time of my life, in this place, I could use that more than a dream about a piece of land. I just can't stand all those people in there eating and . . ."

"Please, Mr. Grogan," Essie quickly interrupted. "You have already been explicit enough about all of that."

Grogan looked at her and chuckled.

"You've got my number, all right. Okay, let's go inside and suffer."

Now it was Essie's turn to chuckle.

They got up, walked to the door, turned around, gazed at the darkening city landscape one more time, opened the door, and stepped inside. Grogan gagged as he always did when he came in from the outside.

THE POINT

Of all the programs that cause brain tricks, our territorial program is the one that wreaks the most havoc. The prime culprit behind wars for as long as recorded history has been written, our territorial program is still at it. In 1992, it continued to create misery as small wars abounded in dozens of breakaway republics, wars being fought over boundaries and land in eastern Europe and the former Soviet Union.

But this territorial urge goes beyond war, reaching deep down into the very fabric of our social lives. The battle cry becomes: "My land versus your land." Or "I have more land than you." Or "A bigger house or apartment." We read about wealthy people buying ranches covering 100,000 acres or more because they crave more space. Then we read about others obsessively collecting new homes and apartments in various locales throughout the world.

We read about these things and don't give them a second thought because we recognize the addiction in ourselves. This is natural, or so we think.

But until we begin working on controlling and disciplining these drives, we will continue to create chaos.

On a social level, our territorial program will allow those with the mental characteristics to do so, to continue acquiring more land, more space that they can "own." This will result in higher levels of visible inequality and separateness that will increase the disharmony and crime among us.

On a worldwide scale, the problem is worse. We continue to bomb cities and commit murder as this drive impels us to stake out lands we think belong inherently to us. As Ed Grogan pointed out, the land belongs to no one. Our diplomats and politicians need to understand this and begin from the beginning while recognizing and overriding their territorial compulsions.

Most brain tricks, the irrational attitudes that affect us, are not necessarily lethal. Not so for the territorial brain trick.

13

The Game of Choice

Ed Sanders, the insurance broker, called his brother, Roy, the neuro-researcher to have dinner at a quiet, small French restaurant only a few minutes from where each of them worked in Madison, Wisconsin.

They met about 6:00 P.M. and were seated near the rear of the restaurant. It was a Thursday night and the restaurant wasn't crowded. They went through their usual small talk until the drinks arrived. After a few sips, Ed said somewhat abruptly: "I have to tell you, Roy, that our conversation on the way to mother's three weeks ago has been on my mind. You know, about the brain and human programming."

"You're kidding."

"No, it's not only been on my mind, I think it's affected my life. Because while I was puzzling over it, this out-from-nowhere thought hits me that I was nuts to give up tennis three years ago for a reason I hardly remember now. So yesterday I played a set with my old partner. Whether or not this experience was related to the talk we had about the brain, I am interested in talking about this programming thing some more."

Roy gave Ed a studied look.

"That's a bit remarkable. I didn't think what we were talking about was all that profound."

"Well, Mr. Blasé Scientist, it certainly affected me, but I'm still a bit confused."

"About what?"

"On the one hand, I think I can see a little more clearly that

146

our brain controls us, that it's a chemical computer of sorts, but I'm still nagged by the thought that there is something more beyond that."

"Like what, Ed?"

"Hell, I don't know. Like a spiritual world or something. The concept of the soul, or whatever it is that enters our lives and makes us conscious, reasoning beings. Something beyond cold chemistry."

"We talked about that," Roy said, with a touch of impatience. "It may be present, but scientifically, nothing of that kind has ever been found. There is not the slightest evidence that anything spiritual enters or leaves the body in humans or in animals."

"But it may be possible."

"Hell, anything is possible."

"Do you mind if we talk about this some more, Roy? I realize you work with this subject all day long and talking about it now might be boring."

"No, not at all," Roy said in a calmer tone. "I like to talk about it every chance I get, although that last comment may not have sounded like it. It helps focus my own thinking."

"Okay, let's talk about the concept of choice and how it relates to brain programming."

"You're right, that's boring."

They laughed.

"No, I'm kidding," Roy said. "Go ahead, what aspects of choice do you want to discuss?"

"Okay, let's assume that your concept of the brain program is correct. Our brain does direct our individual lives totally and is programmed to do that, through some combination of genetic structure and conditioning. But how does it make a choice? It's something I've been thinking about. Our range of choices seem infinite."

"You mean, how can we be programmed to make the choices we do?"

"Yes."

"Look, Ed, this is not part of my field, but I can give you some thoughts I've had about it."

"That's fine."

"Okay, let's start with the premise that a choice we make at any instant in time is how we are programmed to choose at that instant. Tomorrow we might be programmed differently enough to make another choice."

"I think you lost me."

"Let me give you an example. You're in a supermarket and you see a package of your favorite double chocolate ice cream bars in the freezer. You want to buy them, but you're on a diet. There is conflict. One instant you decide to buy those chocolate bars, and you put your hand in the freezer. The next instant you decide not to get them and you stop. Back and forth it goes in your head. Finally, the urge is so overpowering, you make the *choice* to buy the chocolate bars and you take them home."

"This conversation is making me hungry."

"It's making me thirsty. Let's have another drink, Ed."

They ordered a second round and then gave the waiter their order for dinner.

"Getting back to the original example, let's stage that supermarket scene a week later. Everything is the same. Our man is attracted by the thought of the chocolate bars, and he's still on a diet. The difference is that on this day his total brain programming, which is always changing in some way, has given him a more disciplined mood. He *feels* more in control of himself. He sees the chocolate bars and once again begins changing his mind as he did in the first example. But because his brain is programmed somewhat differently at this instant in time as against the week before, his final *choice* is different. He decides *not* to buy the ice cream bars. Now I'm getting hungry. But do you see what I mean?"

"I think so."

"We are indeed changeable. But the thought processes, the emotions that make change possible are all programmed in. On any given day at any given instant, the choices we make are affected by how all the trillions or possibly quadrillions of brain wiring connections containing that programming are interacting. And given the complexity of it all, it's a wonder that we can be as consistent as we are. Our very basic attitudes, broad outlooks, values, and habits, once established, ordinarily remain very consistent and strong. Major changes in the human brain program appear to take place only gradually. Sudden changes usually require some traumatic experience."

"I don't understand, Roy. First you say we are changeable like the guy with the ice cream bars, and then you say we're consistent."

"We are both. We are changeable, but within specific parameters. And those parameters are generally consistent. Having chocolate bars and breaking a diet is pretty superficial. Deciding to change some deep-seated mental attitude like one's belief in a political system, or in a religion or breaking a deep, robotic emotional response like envy, that's different. Those are the kinds of strong programs that are very difficult to change and they are the ones that keep humans generally consistent."

"So we're programmed with that."

"Yes, attitudes, habits, emotions, other feelings. They all emanate from brain programs that feed into our rationality and influence it."

Roy thought for a moment, then continued.

"I have an idea. Why don't you fill in some answers on a questionnaire I passed out during one of my seminars. I have one with me."

"Sounds good."

The waiter brought the salads.

"Where's the paper?"

Roy leaned over and reached into his briefcase. He fished around a bit and found a copy of the questionnaire. He handed it to Ed. It had on it the following:

Given the absolute freedom to do so: Yes   No

a. I would become a nudist.   ___ ___

b. I would refuse to shave.   ___ ___

c. I would outlaw abortion.   ___ ___

d. I would command women to wear asexual clothing.   ___ ___

e. I would steal whatever I wanted.   ___ ___

f. I would have adulterous sex.   ___ ___

g. I would live in a commune where total equality exists. ___ ___

h. I would ban all exploitive pornography.   ___ ___

i. I would build a monument commemorating Musso-   ___ ___
   lini's attack on Ethiopia.

j. I would ban ethnic jokes.   ___ ___

"Here, Ed. Use my pen and just check your answers off."

Roy handed Ed his pen. After barely a minute, Ed handed the pen back and began eating his salad.

"These are my answers and maybe this is telling me something."

Roy didn't look at the answers. He handed the paper back.

"What it should be telling you is that we are indeed programmed with different attitudes and outlooks, most of which come through social conditioning including *self-conditioning,* which I'll explain later, but I would suspect with a good deal of genetic influence as well. I gave this paper to twenty-four people in the seminar I conducted and the answers varied all over the place."

"I can imagine."

"One fellow was even serious about erecting a monument to Mussolini about Ethiopia. During our discussion period, he made a great pitch for it. He actually said it was a dream of his. That shows you how programmed we can get."

"I suppose that's a program, all right."

"Hell, Ed, we are just programmed individuals. We're programmed with nationalism, religion, custom, language, knowledge, emotion, job obsessions, skills, motivation, lust—everything we think, believe, and feel. It all comes out of the storage in our brains, billions of circuits firing every microsecond, creating all of it."

"All right, all right, but how does all of that relate to our ability to choose—you know, the concept of choice—to get back to the original point."

"What we choose at the moment we do, Ed, is what we were going to do anyway. All of our programming leading up to the instant of choice makes the choice for us."

"Let's order another drink, Roy. You're repeating yourself."

"Good idea."

Ed signaled for the waiter who took their order.

"All right, I know it kills you to do it," Roy continued, "but look at my head. Encased in it is a brain that is creating every thought I have and every physical action I take. It can only do that because it is programmed to do so. Up here is this extremely adroit electro-chemical computer capable of unimaginable ranges of perception and power. And it is programmed for it. The fact that I'm eating with this knife and fork is a habit that is programmed in. If I grew up in an underdeveloped tribal unit, I'd be programmed to eat with my hands. Or if in China, with chop sticks. I am also programmed to be able to converse with you tonight. Tomorrow I'm all programmed to deliver a lecture on the genetic habits of ants."

"Fascinating."

"Yeah, really. As I said before, Ed, people don't like to hear somebody say they are programmed. Instead of being annoyed about being programmed, admitting it to ourselves can be somewhat of a relief."

"Why?"

"Because it can alleviate a lot of guilt and anxiety in our lives."

"How so?"

"Let's take another example, the case of the accountant who seizes an opportunity to embezzle money. He is soon caught and thrown in jail, where he is wracked with guilt about what he did—his career blown, his family in dire straits, the whole nine yards. End of example. But looking at what happened, the fact is that it is ridiculous for him to be wracked with guilt."

"Why?"

"Because when he made the choice to embezzle, he was programmed at that instant to do so. He might have weighed the pros and cons for weeks or months, just the way our man worried briefly about the chocolate bars, but ultimately the final input created the program that brought about the *choice* to steal. While rationally he knew that the act would be wrong and risky, his security and power drives were strong enough to push him over the edge. So instead of feeling guilty about the choice, what he ought to be is just plain pissed off because Nature and chance stuck him with a combination of genetics and conditioning that created a program of emotional drives that moved him at that exact point in his life to choose to steal."

"So what's the difference?"

"Hell, Ed, there's a big difference. Guilt is a rotten emotion. It is an uncomfortable feeling that doesn't very quickly go away. Anger and disappointment are easier to handle, particularly if you can accept the inequities of the world and of Nature. Why be angry for very long over something that you were *programmed* to do and did."

"In other words, I shouldn't feel guilty that I swatted my dog this morning because he crapped all over my shoe?"

"Not really. At that instant, your dog was programmed to crap on your shoe. And when you saw it happen, your program directed you to swat your dog. Nothing to feel good about. You should be cursing your *program* for not giving you the ability to restrain yourself from a violent reaction."

"And that's it?"

"That's it. If you didn't like your reaction and knowing you, you didn't like it, then it's time to see if you can change that specific program so you won't swat your dog when you rationally don't want to."

"And how do you do that?"

"Hell, man, that's a big question. Some people see shrinks, some consult their priests or commit to Jesus, others go through higher consciousness movements, others try meditation. Another way is to strategize, to trick your brain back. Some of us succeed simply by recognizing that a specific program is bad, others of us don't succeed at all. There are a good many programs I'd like to change about myself, some of which I think would be almost impossible, others of which I think I could handle if I gave them a try.

"In the meantime, at this instant in time, sitting with you in this very nice restaurant, I am what I am because that is how I am programmed to be. If I make a choice at this instant, this very second my programs all combine to *preordain* it for me. All the input of whatever kind or origin combined to make it. So, while I think I have the ability to choose, that I am a free spirit, in reality I am only the victim of my programs. They make the choice."

"So you really don't have a totally free choice about anything."

"Not in the context in which the phrase has so often been used. We choose what we are programmed at the instant to choose. If you want to call that free choice, go ahead and do it but just understand the process that takes place."

"Well, I'll try to think about all this the next time I'm about to swat my dog."

"It probably won't help."

"I don't think it will either. You mentioned something before about self-conditioning and that you would explain it later," Ed said. "How about explaining it now?"

"Well, it's probably the one thing—self-conditioning, that is— that makes humans far different from both computers and animals," Roy said, "because through it we can be our own programmers. We are able to program ourselves."

"I don't get that."

"What I mean is that some of our social conditioning is self-induced. Because of the brain's capacity for random, rational thought, we can develop independent outlooks of our own that can either complement or conflict with how we've been conditioned by others . . . how we have been taught, for example. Some of those independent ideas or outlooks might not last very long. Or, they begin to build, become stronger, and before you know it develop into a genuine brain program, something that affects our rational or emotional responses when triggered."

"That's a little clearer," Ed said, "but give me an example of something that might be self-programmed."

"All right. To go to an extreme, let's go back to that guy I told you about who was in my seminar and was actually serious about building a monument commemorating Mussolini's invasion of Ethiopia."

Ed grinned. "Please, I was trying to forget that."

"Too late," Roy grinned back. "Now in terms of that one idea as an independent entity—not related in any way to similar programmed feelings such as a deep love for fascism—this guy could only have become programmed with this idea about the statue in one of two ways. First, he might have heard about it from someone else or read about it. Depending on the circumstances and level of that exterior input, he either formed a program about it right away or it slowly built up. In any event, the program ultimately developed as a result of *exterior* conditioning. Something that was inputted by others, just as our original language, education, and religious beliefs are inputted.

"Second, the program might have been self-conditioned because the guy might have come up with the idea himself. One day the thought just struck him. Who knows how or where in the brain it happened. But like an exterior input, it immediately became or eventually grew into a genuine program. It was a self-induced thing; he programmed himself."

"So when you said before, Roy, that we are the victims of our programs, it doesn't necessarily mean that we are victimized by the thoughts and ideas put into our heads by others."

"That's essentially correct. I don't know how you could determine which of our conditioned adult programs are totally created or influenced by others and which are created or influenced by self-inducement, just as we don't know which are created or influenced by genetics. The brain, as I've emphasized before, is for the most part a mystery. We are still at the tip of a giant iceberg and for all we know everything I've said is nuts and some person we consider a lunatic could be right.

"But the evidence all points to the programmed nature of the brain and to the conclusion that we as human beings are the victims or the beneficiaries of those programs, whatever their origin. And the programs, as they exist at any instant—to get back to the original point—create our choices for us. So all we can hope for is that our programming at critical instances in our lives will work positively to allow us to make what eventually turns out to be good choices for us and those around us. In other words, we need to understand the futility of feeling bad about a poor choice in the past, whether it was two minutes ago or twenty years ago. Curse the programs that created the choice instead of yourself and you'll feel a lot better. Analyze those programs and maybe you'll have a better shot at not going through a repeat."

"What about dessert?"

Roy smiled.

"The ice cream?"

"I always said, Roy, I just love your program."

"I've always liked your program, too, Ed."

They both had double scoops of double chocolate chip.

THE POINT

I recall reading an article quoting a designer of a highly sophisticated chess computer program, that it needed an enormous capacity to operate. The designer pointed out that like every other computer program, his had to be inputted with the information that was eventually to be outputted.

But there seemed to be a difference with this chess program, he said. The computer, in some cases, had to access so much information that it was actually making a choice on its own. In other words, the designer didn't always input the precise answer to the situation the computer was pondering. But inputs had to take place and computer circuits were working nonetheless.

This reflects, in a way, the process of choice in the human brain as described by our Dr. Roy Sanders. The mind is not the free-floating, free-spirited entity that we like to think it is. It is a computer-like instrument that delivers to our mind screens the same types of images that are digitized by computers. It processes input and thought with identical digital techniques.

A major choice that we've made in the past is exactly what our brain programming combined to preordain for us at that given instant in time, just as a high performance computer flashes a preordained chess move on its screen.

The big problem with this is that our brains don't like us to think that the choices we make at any instant in time are what our programming preordained for us. They are busy tricking us into a different reality, one where we perceive ourselves as totally free-spirited.

Like many other things that deal with the brain, there's a good likelihood that you will forget all about this tomorrow. If you are driving a car and make a wrong turn, bet on a losing football team, choose the wrong golf club, misbid while playing bridge, or send your kids off without raincoats and it storms, chances are you will curse yourself for your stupidity.

At those times, it might be a relief to think about what Dr. Sanders said and blame the villainous programs that combined to make the choice, rather than yourself.

More about this later.

14

Brainwashing

James Atwood was 58. He had been a political science professor at Ames University for more than twenty-five years. Today he was standing in the same lecture hall and at the same podium where he had begun his career at Ames. His course on world governments was considered a snap. The lecture hall was always crowded.

He recalled his first few years at the university. It was a period of excitement. He had spent a significant portion of his time researching and writing. One of his earlier textbooks, now several times revised, was required reading for this class. He served on various university committees, and even went to Washington during the war in South Vietnam to serve as an advisor with the State Department.

It was immediately after the fall of South Vietnam that he began to feel some deep, inner uneasiness about the world's system of governments. He initially attempted to blot out these feelings, but they persisted and in a few years turned into a dour cynicism. He became more withdrawn.

Today was to be his last lecture of the semester and the last of his career. He had decided two months ago to retire. He had never married, so with his pension and other income could live modestly. His plan was to spend six months doing very little with himself, hoping that some opportunity would develop that would allow him to become active in another field. He wanted to do something new, but didn't exactly know what. First he had to rid himself of the malaise that had infected him and that he attributed to a subject matter he now found offensive, but was obligated to immerse himself in every day.

He looked out over a sea of faces. He could recognize none of them. The thousands of students who attended his lectures through the years had become a huge blur. They deserved someone new, someone fresh, he thought. He already had a replacement to recommend, one of his associates.

He had been shuffling his notes at the podium while taking in the surroundings for one last time. It was odd, he thought. There was nothing on earth he could think of that would make him change his mind about retiring, but he still would miss coming to this place. The experience of being a professor wasn't what created the cynicism he felt, it was the subject matter. He would miss being a professor, an authority figure. He wouldn't miss world government.

He cleared his throat, called for attention and the following dialogue took place:

PROFESSOR: "May I have your attention please? I would like to begin this lecture period by telling you that I am retiring. This will be my last lecture. I am retiring primarily because I no longer place much credence in *any* current worldwide political system. Beyond that, I no longer believe in the concept of national sovereignty and all the headaches it has caused the world. I would like to tell you that I am not a quitter. Having seen the errors of the world, I now intend to devote the rest of my life to finding a better system. I won't do that. Something far deeper than academic research and preachment has to take place before the majority of the people of this world begin to understand the predicament we have been placed in by the concept of sovereignty and all the side issues related to it.

"Rather than bore you with a long diatribe of my current beliefs, I will accept questions. I might add one more thing. I have queried the quiz instructors and they have told me that none of you has sloughed off enough to deserve a failing grade. So please, in this relaxed atmosphere in which the fear of failure has been totally erased for all of you, fire away with your questions."

There was a brief period of silence. Then a ripple of applause began to grow and spread quickly through the lecture hall. Soon the students were on their feet giving Professor Atwood a standing ovation. The first of his life. He stood there soaking it in for a full two minutes and then raised his hands signalling for silence. The students sat down. Then one stood up just behind the front row.

STUDENT: "I would like to tell you, Professor Atwood, on behalf of this class, and I know I speak for the hundreds of classes preceding ours, that it has been a privilege for us to be given the opportunity of learning this subject matter under your direction."

More applause.

The student continued.

"We hope you enjoy your retirement. You will be missed by the university."

PROFESSOR: "Thank you for your generous remarks. I have enjoyed my time here at Ames, but I also look forward to a future that will divert my thought processes in new directions. And now let's have some questions dealing with world governments."

The class period then began in earnest with a number of students vying for recognition by the professor. One by one they rose.

STUDENT: "You appear to have been disillusioned by the concept of varying world governments, the division of the world into sovereign nations. What fault do you find with the concept?"

PROFESSOR: "The concept itself is antiquated and no longer useful. It dates from hundreds of centuries ago when the world consisted of isolated tribal units. No one really knows for certain where on this planet humans evolved. Was it in one place or many places? Whatever happened, the result was that we did become scattered and the tribal unit resulted. We were separated from each other, each unit developing its own customs and cultures. If at first we could have all been in one place, gradually occupying more land as the population increased but within reach of one another, we might have one world government today. But that didn't happen. The tribes, instead, became our first sovereign units because of their isolation. They did relatively well at keeping peace *within* their societies through a system of justice, superstition, simple brutality, or whatever. But distrust and unfamiliarity between these tribal units as well as simple avarice frequently led to conflicts and full-scale wars. That problem still exists, today."

STUDENT: "But how can you compare the tribes of antiquity with the great nations that emerged out of them?"

PROFESSOR: "What really changed? The concept of the tribal unit simply grew into cities, city-states, and sovereign nations. It was a change of form rather than substance. Nations continued to tangle with each other and still do. The world was out of control then; it is still out of control today."

STUDENT: "But hasn't all the fighting, in modern times, meant something? Surely we have learned from it."

PROFESSOR: "What can you learn from something as senseless as war? Do you realize how inane it all is? Here we are floating about on this planet amongst trillions of stars like our sun, without the vaguest idea of what our lives are ultimately all about. The only things we feel we know for sure have been programmed into us by others. Our brains have absorbed this stuff like sponges and so we go about our way and do things like fight wars. What we need to be doing instead is to look outward and try to figure it all out. When is the last time any of you watched some documentary or film about war on TV and wondered how crazy we must all be to be killing each other? The thought probably never entered your minds because we feel that war is natural. But for civilized societies, it shouldn't be natural. We need to stop it. We should start by keeping the nuts out of power, people who have crazy ideas about the destinies of their countries. We have to begin understanding that no human being knows ultimately what our purpose is. If we knew that, we would stay away from the nuts. Instead, we would look to reasonable people whose only objective would be to do the right thing for their populations and the world at large."

STUDENT: "But what about the hundreds of millions of people who have died in wars fighting for causes they believed in. Are you saying they died in vain?"

PROFESSOR: "They died fighting for causes created by their leaders. They were programmed to die. It has been relatively easy for government and military leaders to prepare their populations for war, to program them as you might an unthinking computer. They could create magnificently conceived causes or lies about the imminent enemy, if the real causes didn't sit well. Any given war might have been avoided if other leaders were in place at the time. Like everything else in human experience, wars were a matter of bad luck."

STUDENT: "But what about those who died to defend their home and families, who were victims of aggressors?"

PROFESSOR: "There is little difference between dying to defend one's family or possessions from a single criminal and from an entire nation led by someone with criminal traits. We have lived, and continue to live, in a tumultuous world. If there is no chance of accommodating an aggressor, there is really nothing noble about defending ourselves. It is simply part of the human condition. We don't want our loved ones harmed. We don't want our property taken. We defend them."

STUDENT: "Isn't it more difficult to create the circumstances that could lead to war, today?"

PROFESSOR: "One would think so. There are certainly more literate people in the world today, who have gone through colleges and universities like ours. We are a much smaller world in that any population center can be reached by jet within twenty-four hours. We have technology in the weapons of war that make it more fearful to start a confrontation. But despite all this the wars go on because of the reasons I cited previously. The people the world over are programmed with attitudes that conflict with one another, and we allow idiots to come to power who, through compelling arguments, can still program us to go to war. End of story."

STUDENT: "When you say that government leaders can program us for war, do you mean we can be brainwashed?"

PROFESSOR: "If you are asking if we can be mentally bullied into following a specific course of action, the answer is absolutely yes, given the right circumstances and knowledgeable technique. How else have we gotten soldiers to scale walls or to attack out of trenches and foxholes, putting their lives at risk? How else do we get people to set themselves on fire for a cause or die from a hunger strike? They are programmed to think they are doing it on behalf of a great concept: liberty, individual freedom, religious belief, their home-land, and so forth. Now war has been a necessity when it's the only alternative to get rid of a despot or an authoritarian government. But even when it is a necessity, the population still needs to be pro-grammed for it. Nobody wants to volunteer for possible death un-less they are convinced of the reasons. This is the job of the propa-gandists, the public relations people who are employed by govern-ments."

STUDENT: "If the statesmen of the world are still ineffectual in providing long-term, enduring solutions for world conflict, why are they so concerned about how history treats them?"

PROFESSOR: "An excellent question. I have never ceased to be amazed at the obsession of statesmen with their place in history. What history? We have 4.5 billion years left to live on this planet, if we survive. What difference does 5, 10, or even 50 years in the public eye mean? What will happen to the history books 10,000, 100,000, or a billion years from now? Will they even be around? Will anyone care at those points in time, if there *is* anyone left to care? A few written words in a history book are meaningless. We have no capacity to judge anything because we have no context to judge anything against. As inhabitants of this planet, we are both isolated and insulated. We can only make judgments within our own narrow context and so we'd be better off not making any at all.

"Diplomats deal with high-level power; they believe they perceive a broad sweep of history, including the history that the future will create. This broad sweep, however, is barely discernible against the total life of this planet. Diplomats are as narrow and brainwashed as the rest of us."

STUDENT: "Your use of *brainwashing* offends me. We like to think that nothing can brainwash us, and I believe that."

PROFESSOR: "Were you at our football game last Saturday?"

STUDENT: "Yes."

PROFESSOR: "Which team did you cheer for?"

STUDENT: "Ours."

PROFESSOR: "Why?"

STUDENT: "Because I go to school at Ames."

PROFESSOR: "Well, that's the core of it, don't you see? You go to school here and so you become rapidly *programmed* with the concept of Ames being *your* school and so you cheer for its football team. The result of programming, brainwashing, attitude adjustment, conditioning, indoctrination—they all mean the same thing—is that a strong attitude you *didn't* have before is now a new attitude for you.

"For example, if you had chosen another university, you would be cheering for *its* football team. The point is, we become easily indoctrinated—or to use the more brutally perceived term, brain-washed—with loyalties and concepts. The entire spectrum of our living environments, including relationships with other humans, at the moment or in prior time periods shapes those loyalties and the traditional thinking that surrounds them. This applies not only to football teams, but to friends, family, companies, neighborhoods, cities, states, nations, religions, clubs, bowling leagues, and so on.

"The phrase 'brainwashing' has a negative connotation. But forget the label for a minute and look at the brain as an organism and how it reacts within your skull. The brain and how it's programmed is what impels us to fight or cheer for causes. That program has to be inputted. We are not born programmed to cheer for Ireland, Israel, or the Chicago Bears. We are brainwashed into doing so."

STUDENT: "So you are insinuating that we are brainwashed or programmed, as you like to call it, into being loyal to the United States, for example."

PROFESSOR: "Exactly."

The student remained standing.

STUDENT: "But how can you say that when this is our country?"

PROFESSOR: "I thought I have already pointed out that this is your country because you were born here or are living here. If through the accident of your birth you were raised in Japan, you would undoubtedly be loyal to Japan and you'd be cheering for its causes including the baseball team playing in the city in which you live."

STUDENT (the same one): "Please, professor, let me get this straight. You are contending that loyalty to a state is nothing more than a brainwashed virtue."

PROFESSOR: "Yes I am."

STUDENT (the same one): "But then why is it that so many people from underdeveloped countries, and from countries such as Russia are so anxious to emigrate? Obviously they have not been brainwashed."

PROFESSOR: "That is also correct. I use the term 'brainwashed' in a broad context. There are many students on this campus who couldn't care less if our football team wins or even if this school remains open or closed. In any population among the countries of the world you will find those who are ambivalent about their nation, their communities, their athletic teams, even their families. In this country, we have people whose views on the United States range from total noninterest to fanaticism.

"On the average, however, I would say that most are happy with this country and would defend it. The average loyalty level here is undoubtedly higher than in those other countries you mentioned because we do have more freedoms, more wealth and opportunity, and more of our population can indulge in greater creature comforts. Were those same conditions existent in the disadvantaged countries, there would probably be no groundswell to leave. Most persons would be content to stay where they are, all things being equal."

The student sat down, another stood up.

STUDENT: "When you say we are 'programmed,' you put it in the same context as brainwashing. Are they the same?"

PROFESSOR: "As I said before, I believe so, even though the term 'brainwashing' has a bad connotation."

The student interrupted.

STUDENT: "So does the term 'program' in my view."

PROFESSOR: "If the brain, according to scientists, uses the binary system and is wired much like a computer, the term 'program' should not be objectionable. It is, in any event, only a label to describe a process. I like the label, program. It is not my invention. I saw the term used in this context some time ago and thought it fit as a label. You can pick your own.

"I believe, therefore, that we are *programmed* to direct our lives. And we are programmed with such nationalistic patterns as language, customs, mode of dress, and values. We are also programmed with loyalty to our country, our families, our religions, our fellow workers, and so forth. We have flags, patriotic songs, national holidays commemorating some stirring event, all hallmarks of government propagandists throughout the world. Let me add that most of us in this room, including yours truly, would cheer for the United States during the Olympic games. Most of us would not shout and cheer for the Peruvians. It would be primarily the Peruvians who would."

STUDENT: "And you think that this separateness is harmful?"

PROFESSOR: "I don't think that when our football team plays the Ripon Warriors the division of loyalties between schools is harmful. It is simply part of our human existence today and so it can be great fun. As an aside, I have found it interesting to watch a student change schools. When one doesn't realize one has been part of a brainwashed program, it can be mentally enervating to switch loyalties.

"In actuality, it should be very easy if you can see that program. There is nothing wrong with being brainwashed. Our brains are programmed to soak it in. So what? However, to get back to your point, separateness is indeed harmful when you have sovereign nations, each with its own armed forces, who disagree. There is no higher authority to force a settlement. History and the present have shown us how harmful that can be."

STUDENT: "Do you think eventually there will be one world government with this authority?"

PROFESSOR: "I don't know. I hope so. The United States is an excellent example of the potential. Before we declared war and fought for our independence from England, the states among the eastern colonies were in effect individual sovereign governments. The Continental Congress was initially considered a temporary necessity. The results of the war showed that the states could work together and that a confederation under a strong central government had some real advantages.

"The states gave up total sovereign authority to a central government while maintaining their own identity and local governing authority. With the communication we have today, the same could happen worldwide, certainly more easily than fifty years ago. However, it can't happen, as I stated previously, until we all recognize the programmed nature of our brains and sit down together with a perspective of nonbelief, looking to doing the right thing for the world as a whole."

STUDENT: "Do you have any suggestions on how things can be improved right now?"

PROFESSOR: "None. Our time has run out, I can take just one more question."

A student in the last row stood up.

STUDENT: "If in your retirement, Professor Atwood, you think of any quick solution, would you send a telegram to each of us? I think you have succeeded in scaring the hell out of us."

The professor laughed and so did the class.

PROFESSOR: "I will certainly consider that. Until then, good luck in all you do, and thank you."

The professor got the second standing ovation of his life.

THE POINT

We don't like to hear that we are capable of being brainwashed. Rather, as Dr. Roy Sanders pointed out previously, we prefer to think of ourselves as free-floating spirits in complete charge of our own destinies.

But we are programmed. Look at the clothes we wear, our

mannerisms, our eating habits. These are programs of our cultures. True, many of our attitudes are self-induced, the result of ideas we developed on our own. But they are all based on knowledge we were programmed with elsewhere. We don't come out of the womb a born-again Hindu. As the professor emphasized, there is nothing wrong with accepting the reality that we are capable of being programmed or brainwashed, and that in fact, we are. Our minds are based on computer-like technology, and programming is a part of it.

This is a big concept to grasp. If you can get through it, it will be much easier to figure out ways to trick your brain back when the time comes.

15

The Frightening Scales of Reality

"Hello, this is Carl Ullman, again, with another edition of 'Unlimited Reality.' A very unusual thing happened two weeks ago after our interview about evolution with Henry Heiman. We received a good many phone calls and letters asking us to have him back again, which, frankly, we had planned to do anyway. For those of you who missed that interview, Henry has no academic credentials whatsoever. I sat next to him on a bus . . . I guess it's about a month ago now, got caught up in conversation with him and thought his views unusual enough to invite him to be on the program. The reaction of listeners to that program, as I said, was overwhelming. And so sitting next to me right now is Henry Heiman. Henry, welcome back to 'Unlimited Reality.' "

"Thank you, Mr. Ullman."

"You know, this program has been on the air for seven years and I do believe you have set the record for listener reaction. The calls and letters have been phenomenal."

"Your other guests must not have been very good."

"Oh no, not at all," Ullman responded enthusiastically. "We've had some very famous people on this show: psychologists, psychotherapists, transcendentalists, psychics, neuroresearchers, just to mention a few. Many enjoy worldwide reputations as scholars. But few created the interest you did among our audience."

"That sounds flattering, Mr. Ullman, but it really isn't. Just because a person has credentials doesn't mean he or she knows very much. A person might be an expert in some field of specialization, but in terms of knowing what things are really all about, none of us is ahead of the others. We are all equally in the dark, even though we don't all know it. The crazy thing is that people are so impressed with credentials. So somebody has a doctorate. Big deal. Or has written a book. Or has been a mayor, or a governor or a congressman or a president. None of it is any big deal. Can any one of them tell you how the brain was designed and then encoded in our genes to be passed on from generation to generation?"

"Some credentialed people sound like they might know," Ullman said.

"But what do they know? Beyond what they see and know logically there is only speculation. When you put speculative beliefs in the hands of a credentialed person, it takes on the aura of fact. Credentialed people will tell you to believe in this god or that one. They'll tell you when it's important to fight or give in. They'll tell you to go out and win no matter what the cost. They'll tell you to jog three time a week. It's incredible how people with degrees or other credentials tell us what to do. Strip them of those credentials, have them give advice while being employed as a factory mechanic, and who would listen to it? They take advantage of the public's insatiable quest to learn how to live with greater emotional and physical comfort. They use credentials to do it, usually benefiting from it in some way: monetarily, or with a feeling of recognition, esteem, power, importance, and so on."

"I see you're in good form, again today, Henry. So let's get into the subject we had planned to talk about, which has to do with the scale of time, space, and size. Where do you want to begin?"

"Two weeks ago we talked about how the universe is some 15 billion years old. Can you get a grip on that figure?"

"What do you mean?"

"I mean can you conceptualize 15 billion years? Credentialed scientists drop that figure as blithely as some sports announcer reading off a football score. But think about it, who can get a grip on 15 billion years? I was once married for 10 years. It was a torment. It was a lifetime. People go crazy with enthusiasm when somebody finds a relic 2,000 years old or 6,000 years old. But in terms of time in general, it's nothing, a passing fury. Even 15 billion years is nothing under the concept of eternity.

"There is simply no number that can describe the history of what exists, since the space in which our universe exists has probably never *not* been here. Something has always probably had to exist. But who can visualize that concept? Who can get a grip on it? You can't, I can't, and neither can credentialed scientists or mathematicians with their obscure equations, or religionists for that matter."

"Believe me, Henry, neither can I," Ullman said whimsically.

"What indeed is time after all?" Heiman continued. "We have no idea of what it is. Its very substance. If one were to get fussy, one could say there was no time at all."

"How so, Henry?"

"Look at it this way. We cannot say that time has ever begun . . . that there was an actual beginning of time, can we?"

"I don't know."

"But *can* we? Can you and I, sitting here, point to any proof that there was ever a beginning point in time?"

"No physical proof I can recall anyone referring to, Henry."

"All right. I recall an article written by a mathematician who contended that time began about 2 times 10 to the 10th power years ago, as he framed the formula. Now if we can look beyond this useless puttering about and view eternity as a concept of time without end, then there is no reason not to view eternity as stretching endlessly in any direction. That would cover what we earthlings perceive as a future and a past. In other words there is eternity both ways, ahead of us *and* behind us. We can't discount that idea, can we?"

"No, if you want to ignore what you say some mathematicians contend, then I think the idea is probably as valid as anything else, Henry."

"So then we can say that since eternity also goes backward there may have never been a beginning of time. Something always had to be taking place in some context."

"Yes, you're right, I think we can say that."

"So if time has no beginning and no end, then it simply may not exist at all, since we can't realistically measure it."

"Yes," Ullman shot back, "but we experience time. We feel the passing hours and passing days. We see ourselves growing older through time."

"That may be only an animal phenomena, something we experience as a living, observing being, an inhabitant of a rotating planet in a moving universe. But what is *outside* of what we perceive as this or other universes? That's the question. Maybe *that* is not moving. Maybe that's what really counts, that what is outside is not moving. Hence there may be no real passage of time. It is still. We simply live out our lives in a time context that is a phenomenon of our Earth or our universe or a series of universes."

"What is your point in all this?" Ullman asked.

"The point is, Mr. Ullman, that we as average humans should begin rethinking our ideas about time."

"How so?"

"Time is important to each of us, primarily because it is a measurement of our aging and how long we live as humans. Basically we are all wrapped up in our own lives and the lives of those close to us. Time measures how long we and they will be around. It also measures the flow of events and activities around us. Now this may all sound simple, but the end result is that time becomes one of the most critical things in our lives. Clocks, watches, calendars are necessities, at least in civilized life."

"But how should that change?" Ullman asked.

"That can't change, I don't think. Unless, however, as Einstein said, once we can travel at the speed of light, clocks will stop. In the meantime, time is an element that is strongly programmed into our lives. It allows us to live comfortably in our own little spheres of reality and activity. What should change, however, is our perspective of time. If it's possible that eternity stretches without end and in that sense is timeless, then that should tell us something. It should tell us that in a real look at the world, we are relatively meaningless. And that means not only you and me, but others around us and our great historical figures as well."

"And what do you mean by meaningless?" Ullman sounded a little uncomfortable.

"Meaningless with regard to anything in the long run. The fact that you and I are sitting in this studio talking about this whole subject is meaningful to you and me. We are both in our own spheres of reality. But in a real view of life, as measured against the concept of eternity, what you and I are doing here is meaningless. Nothing that we can think of in a longer term can result from it."

"Yes, but people can get something out of this. As a result of our conversation here or discussions taking place elsewhere, things can change." Ullman sounded hurt.

"That's true," Heiman replied. "But I count that as part of what we perceive as our own realities. Yours, mine, your listeners—everyone else on Earth. What I meant by a longer term is something like 20 billion years. In what we sense as time, that is a very long time. But under the concept of an endless eternity, it is still nothing. It is just a frame of reference for us as earthlings. What you and I are doing here today will probably influence nothing that will happen 20 billion or a trillion years from now, and in that sense what we do is meaningless. Do you see the difference? Things are only meaningful in terms of the false realities our brains trick us into creating. In terms of the real world of endless eternities, it doesn't mean much at all. The problem is, of course, that most of us don't even want to *think* about this concept of the real world. We tune it out. In that process we become narrowed. And when we become narrowed we become indoctrinated with beliefs that can make life rather unpleasant."

"I think I see what you mean." Ullman sounded placated. "You are suggesting that we actually look at two realities: that of our own world, the world that we sense, and that of what we don't know, which includes the concept of eternity."

"Yes, that sums it up very nicely. Of course, the problem is carrying out this dual belief system in everyday life. During moments of ecstatic happiness or sadness or while we are experiencing other strong emotions, it is very difficult to step back and view the reality of what we are experiencing against real-life—the reality of undefined time. Those persons who can do so find it somewhat of a comfort because they can balance what is happening today against long-term meaninglessness. It actually becomes possible to enjoy life more."

"Interesting, Henry."

"I think so."

Ullman began staring at the ceiling, lost in thought. The studio became silent. This caught the engineer's attention. He began waving frantically through the glass at Ullman, who spotted him, sat up with a start, and said: "Sorry, Henry, that last thought carried me away for a moment. Ahmmm . . . there was something you said before that I wanted to question you about. I made a note of it. Oh, yes, you mentioned when you talked about present-life humans as being meaningless, that all historical figures were as well. Did you mean that?"

"Oh, quite definitely. In the first place we can only trace the historical figures we know about to the first Sumerian writings, which took place just some 8,000 years ago. Now what is 8,000 years, Mr. Ullman, against the scales of time we've been discussing?"

"Nothing, really."

"Exactly. And what did all our great historical figures accomplish when viewed against the perspective of where this planet, this universe, our spirits, or whatever will be 100 billion years from now, as measured in human time?"

"I'm really not sure."

"Quite so. Who can be? What great historical figures did, literally, was to change in some depth how our lives have been lived or what we've believed in. Hammurabi, Aristotle, Alexander the Great, Julius Caesar, Jesus, Charlemagne, Genghis Khan, George Washington, the Duke of Wellington, Napoleon, Abraham Lincoln, Karl Marx, Adolf Hitler, Franklin Roosevelt, Richard Nixon, just to name a very few. What did they do? They altered life around them when they lived. The earlier figures undoubtedly affected the fact that you and I and all others are living today, since among our ancestors some met and married because of events caused by these people. Now that may sound important, and to most people it is. But is it?

"These great historical figures were all humans like you and me, but with brain patterns that allowed them to gain power under the fortunes of life that came their way. So they used that power to sway living customs and thought. But in the broad sweep of the time scale, what they did is as meaningless as what you and I do. There is probably nothing that we as earthlings can do to change whatever is going to take place in the scale of time. For all we know, nobody is even noticing us. We might be some forgotten experiment, or those the creating forces have given up on in disgust. So here we are treasuring the thoughts and actions of these historical figures when in the long run nothing will be affected by them."

"But they did make an impact on this planet."

"Yes, I said that. They did, for better or worse, affect the living conditions of many in their era and beyond. The influence of their lives has also affected you and me. I admit that in our everyday reality this is important. In the real-life world, it is probably totally meaningless."

Ullman felt it was time to get on to another subject. "Let's switch to something else, Henry, something that relates very closely to the term eternity, namely, the term infinity. How do you feel about that?"

"Eternity and infinity. Interesting words. For all we know they both mean the same thing. Infinity means that there is no end to anything we can see, feel, or in other ways sense. Once we leave the solidness of Earth, we have nothing but empty space in front of us: space that is littered only with small solid and gaseous objects called stars, planets, and the like. What this means is that, aside from these floating objects, there is nothing totally solid we can ever touch, no matter how far we go.

"In other words, space pilots could never reach a perceptible end to space, because there may be no perceptible end, although some credentialed scientists contend that the reason has to do with the universe being circular. But who knows . . . and what does it matter? If it is a circle, what's beyond the circle?"

"But what does all this mean, Henry?"

"It means that this is just one more way we are deceiving ourselves. Let me repeat that almost all of us go through our lives thinking, 'Well, here things are and this is my reality.' What would you say, Mr. Ullman, if someone came up to you and said: 'By the way, there is a definite possibility that what you see out there and what we call the cosmos goes on absolutely endlessly. There is no ending to reach and we haven't the vaguest idea about what our universe's part is in this scheme, let alone our own solar system and the planet Earth. We are just floating around out here like some discarded mothball!' If somebody would say that to you today, Mr. Ullman, what would you say?"

"I don't think anyone has ever told me that before, Henry."

"But that doesn't make any difference. Let me guess what you would probably say."

"Go ahead."

"You'd say, oh, that's interesting. A good bit of knowledge to pass on to my kids and my associates here at work. Yes, thank you for letting me know."

"Wait, Henry," Ullman sounded a little annoyed, "I'm sure I wouldn't quite put it that way."

"But you agree you are not going to get overly excited if someone came up to you and said those things."

"No, I would not get excited," Ullman said, struggling to hide his annoyance.

"But that's the point," Henry responded. "You should get excited.

You should at the instant that information becomes absorbed say something like . . ." and Heiman stood up and began to shout: "*Are you crazy? Are you nuts? Are you absolutely out of your mind? Telling me that there is no end to space? That I am just floating out here as part of this planet and our hi-tech engineers haven't figured out precisely what our role is? My God, what if the current forces of Nature get out of kilter and this planet starts to drop like a rock? No universal forces. No gravity. We just drop. No bottom. No top. No nothing. Who is going to prevent this? Where are our scientists? Until they give me some real answers instead of something smug like 'Don't worry, we know about time, it is 2 times 10 to the 10th power years old,' . . . I am going to get drunk and move out of reality. This bit of news has been a lot more than I can take.*"

Ullman simply stared at Henry. He was now on his chair pointing to the ceiling. The engineer in the control room appeared mesmerized. Then Henry blinked hard and looked around him. He nimbly stepped down off the chair, straightened his tie, and said in a very calm voice: "I'm sorry, Mr. Ullman. I didn't mean to get carried away like that. I was only trying to make the point that the term infinity has much broader implications for us as humans than we currently perceive. Infinity and eternity should be the most interesting and absorbing of all concepts for us. What is out there? How big is this thing? Is there even a concept of bigness? What is time? What is space? Who am I really? Who made me really? Just think of it. We look back a blink of an eyelid in time to the periods before Jesus and we laugh and scoff at the idols and superstitions that were worshipped by those early tribes. But really, do we know anymore?

"I mean think about it: do we know one darned thing more . . . *one goddamned thing?*" He began to shout and rise, caught himself, and then sat down: "Excuse me, Mr. Ullman, but in my opinion, we . . . do . . . not . . . know . . . one . . . thing . . . more . . . *not one thing more.* We *think* we do, with our society and our technology and our telescopes and our space probes and our microscopes and our great universities and libraries. But in terms of really knowing what is—what this all is—we don't know one thing more. If our ancestors were frightened of the elements and prayed to their idols, then we perhaps should also be frightened sick about the concepts of eternity and infinity. Where do we fit in? Who are we, for heaven's sake?"

Ullman began to feel drained. At one point in Henry's descriptions he actually felt a twinge of fright.

"Isn't it also interesting," Henry continued, "that we actually measure space in terms of time? Light years we call them. It is easier for us to measure space distances in terms of the time it takes light to travel. Oh that thing, we'll say. It's only one light year away! We'll say it without realizing that *one little light year* is 5,865,696,000,000 miles away. In our reality, that means that if we could rig some spaceship to travel at 100,000 miles an hour, it would still take us just about *75,000 years to go that one lousy light year. You see what the scientists are doing?* They are trying to trick us into believing they have a handle on things when the only thing they can do is attach some terms to what they have observed.

"They will say, 'Well, that is only 400 light years away. Now isn't that marvelous.' We don't stop to think that if an object is 400 light years away, it would take our spaceship, traveling at 100,000 miles per hour, 28,000,000 years or so to get there! If we could get beyond our limited brain programs to fully comprehend that piece of information we would probably say something like: *What? Twenty-eight million years? Who do we know who lives 28,000,000 years? How big is this universe? What is this all about? I cannot visualize spending 28,000,000 years trying to get anywhere. Let's not try to get there. What would we find anyway? Niggers?*"

"Please, Henry, this is going on the air!"

"Are you going to edit out 'niggers'?"

"Yes, probably."

"Please do me a favor and let this program go unedited. I am the least bigoted man you'll ever meet. I threw the term 'niggers' into that remark purposely. To remind people how silly it is to discriminate against anything when we are so lost in time and space. The least we can do is try to get along. Who knows, maybe somebody among all of us will get some idea as to how we can get down from this planet. Crawl or fly somewhere where we don't have to live life in the inconsistent way we do now. A place where we might be permanent beings with minds that are programmed to be content and happy."

"I see, well then, I'll leave this segment all intact."

"Thank you."

Ullman sensed it was time to shift directions again. He felt calmer now.

"Henry, I'm sure our listeners will agree that your ideas about time and space are interesting. But let's turn to another subject. Instead of thinking in large concepts such as space and time, let's think about smaller ones. What are your views on small?"

"The concept of small, Mr. Ullman, is just as confusing and unsettling as the concepts of eternity and infinity."

"Why?"

"Well, let's start with one simple fact to better illustrate the point. There are mites no larger than two one-hundredths of an inch, so small they aren't even visible. If you look at microscopic photos of these mites, you'll see that they look like everyday insects. Now, the point is, there are possibly millions of other organisms in the world the size of these mites and they all have inner workings that are hard enough for us to imagine in something the size of a grasshopper. Who is capable of designing something so small, we can't even see it. Its reproductive system is smaller yet. Moving closer to home, how do you visualize the sixty trillion cells that make up your body? The fact that each of those cells is made up of thousands of smaller moving, living parts, including a DNA molecule that carries billions of bits of information—enough to reproduce the entire human body—is considerable food for thought."

"It is incredible when you think about it," Ullman said.

"And that's not all: then we get down to atoms and their electrons and protons. Small, very small. Scientists have found what they call quarks, which are even smaller. We probably haven't found the most minuscule of particles and we may never, despite all the giant accelerators and other clever devices scientists are building. Whatever we think is the smallest thing might not be. And that, like eternity and infinity, can be a totally absorbing concept when you think about it."

"I imagine it could be. And now, Henry, what do you think all of this discussion about scale means? How can you summarize it?"

"As I said before, the brain is somehow programmed so that we block out these scales. It is as if we are purposely being tricked by our brains to focus on the challenges and problems of living on Earth. I suppose we should be thankful for this on the one hand because it keeps our minds focused on our own little worlds, our own little realities. But on the other hand, let me repeat, it blocks out a viewpoint that would allow us to work better together as humans, and that is unfortunate. I am fairly sure that this blocking program is one that, with some work, can be adjusted. Many have claimed to do so. Perhaps they have.

"In any event, I think if all of us could cooperate in overcoming the blocking program, find a center spot where we aren't exactly consumed by it, but remain in wonderment of the real life world, we could sit down together and find a way to disarm totally and lead a life with some degree of harmonious coexistence. Nature might seem to be doing us a favor by blocking out of our minds the actual state of the real world, tampering with the scales and all that, but it went too far, in my opinion."

"And how do the scientists figure in all this?"

"The scientists aren't helping at all. They accumulate a few academic degrees, get interviewed on TV, and then assume this relatively smug air of 'we really know what's going on.' What in fact they have done is make limited observations. They have used highly advanced mathematics, for example, to move closer to what the concept of time is. But they are far from understanding it, in particular its relation to anything outside what we perceive as a universe. And they are no closer to understanding the concepts of infinity and scale in general. What they've done is put lofty terms and equations on what relatively few things they have discovered. They have created a language all their own, and behind the shield of their credentials they say to us, 'look, we have a handle on things.'

"But they really have a handle on very little. They, of all people, should be more puzzled than the average person. If we could see some total puzzlement on some famous scientists' faces, that would help us neutralize our own program of complacency; it would help us look our nature squarely in the face. That would help us gain the viewpoint I spoke of previously. I wish they would stop creating lofty words for things: it's only camouflage to keep us nonscientists within our own realities."

"Henry, I think you did it again. You made an interesting broadcast for 'Unlimited Reality' and I want to thank you for being present with us, today."

"Thank you very much, Mr. Ullman."

"Maybe you ought to write a book, Henry, about your views."

"I could, but it would make no difference. The world would still be the same."

"Well, good luck to you and perhaps you'll come back to visit us again."

"Call me any time, it's a nice bus ride."

"Goodbye, Henry."

"Goodbye, Mr. Ullman."

Ullman cued the music, shook hands with Henry, watched him leave the studio, lit a cigarette, and sank back in his chair.

THE POINT

Henry Heiman's contention that our brains have a mask that shields us from the realities of the boundless scales we are discovering is a poignant example of how our brains were designed first to trick us into focusing on our own realities and then to absorb beliefs that make us comfortable. Without these beliefs, we would probably be frightened to death. Without this masking effect, we would certainly be terrified to read a book like Stephen Hawking's *A Brief History of Time,* in which he describes the brutal and barren nature of the universe, with its black holes—stars that have collapsed inward with such force of gravity that time stands still.

Instead, we casually react to books like these, rather than being jolted by them. What this illustrates is that the brain is deceitful. It appears to be designed to deceive us into carrying on our lives as part of some bizarre experiment, and it doesn't want us distracted by asking too many key questions, such as where might the Earth be located.

For example, if a stranger walked up to you and asked you where the Earth was located, within the universe or multiple universes, what would you say? If the question were asked of me, I would reply: "Well, I'm not quite sure, but I do know we're close to Mars. Does that help?"

Do you see what I mean?

This is about as far as our brains let us go. If they are capable of deceiving us, what can be so wrong about deceiving them back with our own trickery?

16

Accepting Ourselves and Others

The narrow path seemed almost familiar to Ludmilla Denisov as she climbed her way upward. The TASS correspondent had left on a late-evening train out of Moscow and after a long and uneventful trip was again in the foothills of the Ural Mountains. She had come to revisit Ilyich Barkeloff, the 110-year-old man who had retired some 35 years earlier from the foreign service.

She had visited him three months ago on his birthday and had written a feature article on Ilyich's concept of the aging process and subjects related to it. The article had been picked up by a number of foreign newspapers and had caused quite a sensation, not only in Russia, but in other countries as well. Now her editors asked her to revisit Barkeloff. They wanted another story.

The trail wound torturously upward. The cottages were widely spread out. Ludmilla thought about how the region was well known for the number of persons who lived long lives. She wondered how the inhabitants could walk these mountains. Just at that instant Ludmilla heard the thud of hoof beats behind her. She quickly stepped off the path as a man who had to be at least 80 was moving fast up the hill on a young quarter horse. He waved happily at Ludmilla as he rushed by, dust and dirt flying. She wondered first how the horse could take it. Only later did it strike her how strange it was to see such an old man ride so hard. But then, it all seemed to be quite natural in this area.

She reached the top of the hill and continued on the path which now swerved to the left. Ludmilla could see Barkeloff's home through the trees. She walked another hundred feet and saw him almost as she had left him three months ago, sitting on a bench under a tree lost in thought.

"Greetings Comrade Barkeloff," she called out.

He opened his eyes with a start.

"Ah, Ludmilla. How good to see you again. Please, how many times must I remind you, call me Ilyich."

Ludmilla broke out laughing, ran up to Barkeloff, and they hugged and kissed. He asked her into his home where he poured hot tea as they talked about her trip. Later, they walked outside and sat on Barkeloff's favorite bench, which had a remarkable eastward view of the Urals.

"I must tell you, Ludmilla, that I was very happy when they brought me the wire from the village that you were returning. I very much enjoyed the day we spent together."

"It was enjoyable for me as well, Ilyich."

"So, what brings you back? Certainly it is not lust for a 110-year-old body."

Ludmilla chuckled.

"Don't sell yourself short, Comrade. Who knows what will emerge from these meetings? But no, lust was not uppermost in my mind in returning. I am here to do another interview."

Ludmilla described the enormous response generated by the article on aging and how Barkeloff had become a relatively well-known figure in Russia and elsewhere in the world because of it. Her editors wanted a follow-up story.

"I did see the article," Barkeloff said. "A fourth or fifth cousin of mine, I can't remember those details, brought the newspaper up from the village to show me. I was impressed with your style. I am happy for you that the story was widely recognized."

"And what about you? Aren't you pleased that you have become a celebrity?"

"There is one thing that living to my age does for you when you spend a good deal of time thinking about the life process: it allows you to put life in a more real context. The fact that I am known or any person is known to a great many others is not important. In 100,000 years—barely a speck in terms of universal time— I daresay that *nobody* known today will be remembered. What would it matter anyway? Fame is not only fleeting, it is irrelevant. Unfortunately for this world, most human beings do not believe that.

People want to be recognized. In far too many hearts it flames an ambition that can be cruel and bitter to others. The world would be better off without powerful and famous figures. It would make reason and compromise easier to achieve. We could live in greater harmony. But enough of this, what do you want to talk about?"

Ludmilla simply stared at Barkeloff. His mind was so crisp. It was as if he had special fluids surrounding and preserving his brain. As if catching herself in a trance, Ludmilla blurted out: "My editors are interested in your views on the acceptance of others."

Now it was Barkeloff's turn to stare at Ludmilla. After a few seconds he broke into a hearty laugh, slapped his knee, grasped Ludmilla's arm and shook it, then hit the bench.

"Amazing," he said.

"Perhaps I've missed the humor."

"Oh, don't mind me. I see too many ironies in life and when I sense a good one, it hits me better than a good joke."

"But why do you see such an irony in this?"

"Because, my dear Ludmilla, TASS has had a long history of being judgmental and nonaccepting, although that is admittedly now changing. If an ape in the Moscow Zoo would piss in the wrong direction, TASS would probably scold it. It believes there is only one right way to see and do things and attacks whatever conflicts with its views at the time. But let me also say this in TASS's defense. It only reflects the narrow beliefs held by the majority of the people in this entire world. It is a rotten aspect of life. Now that I've gotten over this little joke to myself, I must commend TASS for opening the subject. Where do you want to start?"

"Where should we start?"

"Ludmilla, you have the makings of a great politician. However, as a favor to me, don't pursue it. Remain a journalist; you're good at it. Politics is only a good career if you see life as a game. A deadly serious politician who gets into power can often be the scourge of his country and the world. Oh, there I go, always getting off the subject. Okay, where to start? I think the starting point is relatively easy. It is the acceptance of one's self. This has been said many times, but it is an important element in accepting anyone or anything else."

"How so?"

"Unless one can see one's self from a higher perspective and accept all that is going on with that self, it is much harder to break through all the obstacles our nature throws in the way in accepting others with whom we feel alienated."

"Describe that perspective."

"In essence, it means being able to look in a mirror and see a chemical, human organism run by a brain that will react and do exactly what it is going to do anyway at that time. It means accepting what is happening at that time as well as what has happened in the past."

"An interesting way to put it, Ilyich."

"A simple and short statement, is it not?"

"Yes."

"And yet for most human beings that simple statement is impossible to practice."

"Why?"

"In the first place, most of us still do not believe that we think with our brains or that the brain is chemical. Second, most of us do not realize that the brain controls our thought processes and that it is simply reacting to its own experience when a response is called for. You ask me for a statement from my perspective on acceptance of others and the response is based on the experience of my brain. How I and others have conditioned it to believe, feel, and respond. I have accepted the response my brain offers on the general subject of acceptance today. That is simple. The trouble with acceptance doesn't come from this kind of normal give and take, nor usually with anything to do with peace, harmony, or success. The trouble begins with trouble. We have our greatest difficulty with acceptance when it involves failure, trauma, and things that are negative. Do you see what I mean?"

"I think so."

"Not long ago a nice boy from the village came to see me. He had flunked his examinations for medical school. His parents were afraid he was going to take his life. His biggest problem was that his parents and teachers had taught him since childhood how to live in their own custom, how to read, add, think; how to understand history and geography; how to study great thinkers and writers; and so on. What nobody ever taught him was how to accept himself, even in his failures. If they did, that boy, instead of trying to kill himself, would have said something like: 'Well that is too bad. I flunked the exams for medical school. Either my brain is not facile enough for those studies, or I don't have the motivation to push my own learning abilities to the maximum. Perhaps I will try once more if my advisers think I have a chance, although I'm not sure I can try any harder than I did. Or I will do something else. The world is full of mystery, and being a doctor is not the only vocation that will give me pleasure and contentment.

" 'In the meantime, I am surprised that I don't feel anything except some mild frustration that my brain is not up to what I hoped it could do. I still feel happy and will continue on my way through life.' Now," Barkeloff continued, "what a marvelous thing if that boy could have been taught at an early age to think that way."

"It would have been indeed."

Ilyich paused for a moment as if to collect his thoughts. "But of course, there is one missing ingredient in that hope."

"Which is?"

"Everyone surrounding him would have to think the same way."

"Why?"

"Why does that boy, instead of being only terribly disappointed, also want to blow his brains out? Because he will not be a doctor? Not at all. It is because he is being perceived as a failure by his parents, his relatives, his friends, even his teachers. This has dramatically heightened his own feelings of failure. Not one of those persons would come to him and say: 'Ah, it is too bad what happened, but it makes no difference. We love you no less than we ever did. It is absolutely no fault of yours that your brain and its conditioning did not qualify you for medical school. If you are obsessed with medicine and want to be around it, you can train to be a technician or a nurse. There is no station in life that is more important than any other. We all do what we have the capacity to do. Having a greater or lesser capacity is of no real significance in a life process that itself is shrouded in mystery.'

"Now if those close to the boy would all say something in that vein, if they all truly accepted what happened to him and wished him nothing but well in the days ahead as he looked for alternate courses, do you think he would be disappointed to such a profound degree that he would want to die?"

"I believe I see your point."

"It is easier to accept one's self if each of us lives in an accepting environment. The problem is that we live in an ugly world full of competition, social snobbery, nonacceptance, bigotry, and discrimination that all of our education and religion have been unable to eradicate. To be truly accepting of one's self takes a stronger personality in this environment. By that I mean not so much strength of character but a strength to be able to look through all the beliefs one has been taught and then to see the world and one's self in proper perspective."

"The perspective of looking in the mirror and seeing that one is controlled by a chemically actuated and imperfect brain?"

"Yes. It sounds rather simple, doesn't it? But achieving that perspective is very difficult. Not only must one recognize that the perspective is possible, it must be worked at constantly. The brain attempts to eradicate this kind of perspective. It is busy making us do whatever it is that our nature intended. It doesn't like the artificial interference of strong reason."

"But tell me, Ilyich, doesn't religion attempt to provide a similar perspective in terms of accepting one's lot? The will of God or the will of Allah are well-worn phrases."

"Quite true. Religion uses spirituality rather than pure reason in an attempt to lead believers to that perspective. My observation of it, however, is that it hasn't worked well enough. Some of the most orthodox religionists of the world are often the most nonaccepting and bigoted. They become so obsessed with their doctrine that they are unable to see either the true goals or thrust of their religions. Religion really hasn't helped us enough, Ludmilla. Neither has the atheism espoused for years by the old Soviet government. Extremes of any belief are usually not helpful."

He looked back toward the mountains. The two remained silent for awhile as Ludmilla looked over her notes.

"You said before," she continued, "that we must be accepting of the past as well as the present instant in time. Please get into that a little more, if you would."

"That is the easiest part of all. How many times I have had heard in my life 'If I only didn't do this, or if I just would have been smart enough to do that, this or that would have turned out differently and I would have been better for it today.' What rubbish! We did what we did. Who among us is perfect? Who has ever lived who was perfect? We make mistakes. We make poor decisions sometimes. The process of life continues through an illusion of time we have created to measure movement. We must move with it. Memories do not always teach us. They are primarily valuable for storing experiences we've been through and the results that ensued from them.

"When we make the same mistake a second or a third time, which we so often do, our memories simply serve to give us a better notion of the consequences. When I was in the foreign service I made a simple clerical mistake that ended up costing the lives of twenty-two people. At the time it was terrible. I was guilt-ridden for many years. However, when I achieved what I will simply call a Higher Perspective, the guilt vanished. My emotional temperament became stable. I saw clearly that I did not want to cause the deaths of those people. I would have gladly given my own life as a substitute. It was the nonthinking mistake that caused those deaths, not a premeditated desire on my part. It was not murder but a tragic part of the process of life with which I was unfortunately involved. Some would want me to feel remorse for my entire life, but that is ignorance. That is nonacceptance of what has already taken place.

"It is like saying that one should refuse to accept history. History is what has already taken place. We might not like it, but we have to accept that the facts did happen and that they are buried in a past that is totally dead. If we do not accept this dead past totally, then a considerable amount of bitterness may remain."

"Explain that."

"Well, we see it so often. A family is wronged by another in the past and a grudge continues with injury and killings. Maybe it's one ethnic group or an entire nation remembering the past wrongs of another and looking to seek revenge. Ethnic fighting and wars have many times been waged in the cause of simple revenge. What a waste. Somebody makes a mistake and for years the progeny must pay for it. The only cause worth risking physical injury for is self-defense.

"If there are maniacal people coming after you and you are enjoying life, then it is appropriate to fight back. After the maniacs have been subdued, pick up your life where it was and enjoy it. Forget the maniacs even existed. There will be more around or there will be other trouble to contend with. That is the way of our lives. If you are killed in the process of defending yourself or your loved ones, so be it."

Barkeloff looked off to the mountains for a moment, then turned back to Ludmilla. "Most of us make some decisions that will affect others negatively. We may have done it intentionally at the time, or it may have been accidental. If it was intentional and a dreadful loss was caused, we should have been removed from society until there was some assurance we wouldn't do it again. If it were accidental or a matter of chance caused by a poor decision, we must put the incident behind us. As I told you during our last visit, memory can be mentally debilitating. I prefer to live only with a minimal amount of memory so that each day brings an experience that is fresh and new. If we have accepted the past because it is already the past and there is nothing we can do to change it, we are on the road to that Higher Perspective. If we can accept ourselves just the way we are at this instant, then we are well on our way to that Higher Perspective."

"Why haven't we reached it by this point?"

"Primarily because of two things: We have also to accept what we probably will become, and we have to accept other living things. That is a remarkable leap of perspective; unfortunately, too few have managed it."

"Explain what you mean about accepting what one might *probably* become. How can one accept something that is going to happen in the future and is as yet unknown?"

"You strike upon the heart of the matter. How can we accept what to expect if we don't know what's coming? The crux is that once we accept ourselves, our past, and the fact that it's what's in our brains at the instant that makes us who we are, then we can also understand ourselves.

"We can understand that we might like to dream of terrible rape scenes because it makes us feel good or gives us a wonderful sensation when we masturbate. We accept that. We realize it's like a tape machine in our heads that turns on and plays a rape dream when something we see or think about triggers it. It's like . . . what do the Americans call it . . . oh yes, a juke box. A button is pushed and a prerecorded tape plays in our heads. Instead of music the pushed button creates a thought or response that each time is relatively similar. If we went out and acted on a potentially harmful thought, actually tried to commit an act such as rape, our best course of action would be to volunteer for confinement so the world would be safe while we work to neutralize that particular brain tape.

"Or we understand in the same way why we might be addicted to scenes of violence or other unpleasant things. We see or hear something that triggers it, or we fall asleep and the unpleasant yet stimulating tape plays. As long as we are not abusing others, we should accept it. Too many nice people in this world, Ludmilla, overburden themselves with worry because of dreams, fantasies, and illusions that go directly against their own moral standards or codes of ethics.

"However, there is nothing wrong with these responses of our mind as long as they aren't acted upon. Literally, we must accept them, just let them be, without even worrying about where they came from. What difference does it make? They exist. They are there. That is a fact. If we do not resist they become harmless impulses and eventually may fade away. Then again, maybe not. With total acceptance of one's self and one's conditioning, it doesn't make much difference."

"That is very interesting," Ludmilla said. "There are some fantasies I have that disturb me very much. I would prefer not telling you what they are since I consider them private. But they have made me wonder what kind of person I *really* am. Am I the Ludmilla that most of my relatives and acquaintances know? Or am I the Ludmilla who has some very horrible and lurid thoughts and fantasies?"

"If you would ever act out one of these terrible fantasies, would they be abusive to others?"

"Quite possibly. Yes, I imagine so."

"Have you ever done so?"

"Never."

"Do you think you might attempt to do so?"

"I cannot say no categorically, but I truly cannot imagine myself in such a situation."

"Well then, that was precisely my point. You have these fantasies, illusions, or dreams that are not at all in character with the structure of your basic personality. Nobody understands the human brain, except superficially. No one can tell you exactly why you have these dreams or fantasies.

"For all we know, your great-grandmother had the same fantasies and so did her great-grandmother before her and it was all passed down through some part of a gene that may have been dormant in a generation or two. Or it might have been caused by something you read at a sensitive age or saw or heard. Some exterior conditioning. Who knows and, as I said before, who cares? It is something recorded in your brain and you must accept it now. Fighting it is meaningless. You cannot win. If it will go away, it will do so without any pressure from your rational self.

"The important thing is to continue exerting your rational will to prevent yourself from abusing others, either verbally or physically. This is what all thinking humans in the world must do if we are to survive. That is, if there is a reason to survive. But to get back to accepting what to expect . . ."

"Yes."

"You see, if we know ourselves very well and accept what we know, we can be more tolerant of our own expectations."

"I don't understand."

"Let's look at the example of a person who has studied piano for many years. He enjoys the piano. But he recognizes his technique will never be good enough to perform as a soloist in concert halls. He continues working hard but he is *not* frustrated at his lack of progress or his defeat at auditions, because he accepts himself and his abilities. So if he truly loves the piano, he will play in an orchestra or in a restaurant or with a band or at parties. He can alter his style, his music, to suit the piano-playing niche he selects.

"Or he might decide to do something else. This man will find much greater harmony in his life than the burgeoning pianist who does not quite have the necessary talent, who refuses to accept what is obvious to him as well as others, who goes on fighting for years in frustration. In the end, he winds up bitter and jealous of those who have passed him by. Perhaps he is encouraged in all of this by teachers, coaches, or relatives who espouse the 'winning is everything' attitude. They are as guilty of nonacceptance as the pianist is.

"Oh, certainly, we can all look at musicians, soccer players, gymnasts, mathematicians, scientists, and others who fight through every conceivable obstacle thrown in their paths, including physical or neurological impediments or whatever, and somehow successfully break through. But the odds of this are enormous. To me it is hardly worth the misery it causes among the masses who are not great successes. I find the concept of a 'winner' faulty.

"There is a religious concept that everyone is equal in God's eyes. It is a marvelous concept. It has just never worked consistently in the everyday world because we are driven through tricks of the brain to strive for social power and status, just like unthinking animals and insects. Do you get a feel for what I'm saying? Does it make sense?"

"I think so. What you are saying, it seems to me, is that I shouldn't feel bad if I'm not nominated as the 'Journalist of the Century' by a panel of professors in the year 2005. I should accept my ability; work hard at improving it, if I desire; but not feel frustrated because I see writing and other literary work I would like to emulate, but cannot."

"Yes, that is precisely it. Accepting an expectation does not mean that we have to quit. Working hard, trying to improve one's self can be great fun, a source of enjoyment. If we work hard, there will always be something coming out of the effort that will be rewarding. Feeling rewarded is an excellent sensation, like eating a delicious meal. While it isn't lasting, it is a pleasant emotion to experience.

"What a marvelous thing if we could all work toward our own betterment without the nagging fear of failure. Some of us do succeed in this. When it happens, it is a marvelous state of mind that brings us remarkably close to the Higher Perspective I have described."

"And that last step you describe as the acceptance of others."

"Yes, but before we get into that, how about another nice cup of hot tea? Perhaps some delicious fruit just picked yesterday."

Ludmilla put down her note pad, stood up, and stretched her arms while looking toward the mountains, now in some slight shadow.

"These mountains are beautiful, Ilyich. The trees are like a cozy blanket. Hot tea and fruit sound just fine."

Ilyich took Ludmilla by the arm and walked her inside the tightly constructed wood cottage. The stove was an old cast iron wood burner that looked practically as old as Ilyich. The fire had been stoked and Ilyich quickly had it ablaze. The tea kettle was new, she noticed. Water came from a hand pump on the sink. The drain, she could see, simply led through the wall outside. The cottage was small but comfortable. One entire wall was lined with books. There was a desk with a large oil lamp. A separate bedroom was the only other room.

"Your home feels warm," Ludmilla said.

"Yes, it has a nice feeling. I like it here. You notice, no electricity."

"I did. Why don't you have it? I saw electric wire and poles leading up the hill."

"I don't want it. I am not interested in modern conveniences or technology. Everything I want to study is in these books and in my thoughts about life in general. Don't get me wrong, I'm not an old eccentric. Television and radio are fine for those who want them. I make no judgments. They just do not fit my lifestyle. I keep up with current events through newspapers and periodicals. I would rather read leisurely than be bombarded with short, pithy broadcast messages. As for appliances and other conveniences, I like life without them. Up here in the mountains, they seem unnatural for me. I spent many years in cities and enjoyed their conveniences, including indoor plumbing and electricity. But no longer.

"Human nature is such that it adapts quickly to conveniences, wealth, power, and so forth. Over the long term, they do not really raise one's level of contentment. That only comes from love and the lack of fear. I love with all my heart. I ask nothing in return from people or animals. At my age, there is very little to fear. For awhile I feared death. Now it is only a curiosity. So my general level of contentment is high. In terms of lifestyle per se, I do not know what more to aim for. In terms of interests, mine range far and wide and I give my mind very little rest. This environment suits me well."

Ilyich laid out fresh tea cups from a cupboard near the sink. He then cut an apple and a pear into slices.

"Who brings your food up here?" Ludmilla asked.

"One of the villagers comes by every morning. The snow can be eight feet high in this area yet somehow they make it. On this side of the mountain we are somewhat protected."

"Could you direct me again, Ilyich, to your outdoor plumbing? In the months that have passed since I was last here I can't remember. Without memory I'll cherish this trip as a new experience."

Ilyich smiled. "Out the back door and down the trail."

"Thank you."

When Ludmilla returned, the tea had been poured and a dish was piled high with sliced fruit.

"Come, let's take this outside and enjoy the afternoon sun," he said to her.

Ludmilla carried the tea cups while Ilyich walked outside with the fruit. They resumed their places on the bench, with the tea and fruit between them.

"Now, Ilyich, what are your views on the acceptance of others? And how do they relate to what we've already covered?"

"An interesting subject, really quite complex. One would think that the mystery of our existence would be enough to allow all of us to accept one another. After all, from a purely rational point of view life is an absolute mystery, one in which every human being shares equally. When it comes to life's purpose, we are all equally ignorant. Unfortunately, soon after birth we are programmed, like an ordinary computer, by our parents or guardians to believe whatever it is they believe in with regard to our purpose here.

"As a result, we go around with our noses held high as if our group is the knowledgeable one. Those *others* are ignorant. Beliefs separate people, and the schism is particularly deep when these beliefs revolve around religion, nationalism, or cultural traits. What does this mean? It means that too many people are taught as children to look down upon others who believe or act differently. So we practically begin life by not accepting specific groups of others. We can't seem to transcend that original programming."

"Why do you think that is?" Ludmilla asked.

"To begin with, there is a strong theory that humans are much like animals in that we have a genetic predisposition against accepting aliens into our family or community units. It is an interesting theory and I tend to believe it, since the studies behind it consist of the close observation of the living habits of hundreds of species. There is, of course, no way to prove the theory scientifically. It probably doesn't make much difference: If we are sensitive to Nature, we can observe that most humans tend to reject what is alien to them. A perfectly marvelous black family can move into an all-white suburb of London and there is widespread prejudice and rejection for no reason."

"So you think that nonacceptance of others may be genetic."

"I think it is quite possible. At least a predisposition is there. So many things appear to point in that direction."

"Such as?"

"Like the concept of a social pecking order. The term, of course, comes from the social nature of chickens. The dominant chicken

'A' will peck chicken 'B,' who will peck chicken 'C,' and so on down the line. There appears to be a very definite genetic intuition at work here. After all, how else can it evolve? Among animals, there are no elections, no debates. A few stares, maybe a scuffle now and then, and the issue of social hierarchy is decided.

"In the more primitive and underdeveloped human societies, this same pecking order manifested itself quite clearly and still does. In modern, more civilized societies it still exists but is often a good deal more subtle."

"How so, Ilyich?"

"Just look around you. Even in the old Soviet Union, where we were supposed to be socially homogenous, there was a natural tendency to want to achieve social power and status. Some achieved a higher station through shrewdness, motivation, intelligence, charisma, and sometimes sheer strength. Observe today all the world's leaders. See the powerful 'A's in government, business, religion, society.

"They exist in every nation, every state, every city, every hamlet, every community. Beneath them are their immediate underlings, the 'B's, who still consider themselves among the leadership. The 'C's are just above the common people who we might call 'D's. It continues downward. So there is this naturally evolved inequality between us just as there is among animals."

Ilyich stood up and stretched. He walked over to the edge of the small clearing and gazed again at the mountains. He seemed to radiate energy, Ludmilla thought. What a marvel he was, such mental acuity for a man of his age. Then she remembered what Ilyich said in the earlier interview about aging, that it is only a concept. He and I, she thought, are sitting up here with our communication occurring between two brains. Bodies serve the brain. Yet she couldn't help noticing how trim and even muscular Ilyich looked. He couldn't weigh more than 135 pounds, but he wasn't at all stooped. His beard and hair weren't even all gray. Were she to meet him on the street somewhere, she would have guessed him to be in his seventies. The changes this man has seen. The world in the 1870s when he was born was only slightly different than it had been for centuries before. He had lived through a time of enormous technological revolution and incredible enlightenment. The amazing thing is that he absorbed it all. His very basic beliefs shifted as he learned. Very unusual in itself.

"Excuse me," Ilyich interrupted her thought. "I just had to stretch and look at those mountains again. I can't get enough of them. For me it is one of my few remaining sensual adventures."

Ludmilla laughed, then said, "Tell me more about the human pecking order."

"It is interesting, is it not? There is then one more side of it: the pecking order between entire groupings of people. Even among the early primitive tribes there were those who as a group looked down on others as some kind of scum. Historians who concentrated on American Indians saw this very clearly. As I recall, they noted that the Cheyenne looked down upon the Comanche, and the Comanche looked down upon the Shawnee. Or some such order.

"Similar prejudices were uncovered in studies of tribes in Africa. We have found them reflected in the art left by cavemen. However, most of us are never told about these studies and what they mean. If we were, we might get a better perspective on the very same prejudices that exist today between groupings of people, despite all the worldly advancements over the centuries. Here in the Urals, many of my neighbors look with disdain at the people who live down south in Turkistan. Dirty Bedouins they call them.

"Entire nations look down at one another. Religions do the same. Even sects within the same religion look down at one another. This I find most incredible since believers, of all people, are supposed to comprehend that we are all equal in the sight of God. The words are said, but not absorbed. They definitely aren't practiced. Then there is the obvious disdain between peoples of various colors, as if it makes any difference whether our skins are black, white, or blue. Skin is nothing. Features are nothing. Our brains are everything.

"If we could wear them outside our skulls we could then concentrate on making judgments based on what has been recorded in the brain rather than on the color or look of the body. An automobile can't go anywhere without a driver. A body can't go anywhere or say anything without a brain. In that sense a human body's frame is no more important than the exterior design of a car body. Yet we have fought many a war over whose physical characteristics are better."

Ilyich paused. He was getting a little worked up, Ludmilla could see. She was about to say something calming when he began again.

"I can see you want to calm me down. Please, let me enjoy

the excitement of what I'm saying. It is practically as sensuous as looking at the mountains."

"You are a wonderful man, Comrade Barkeloff." She just blurted it out.

Ilyich paused and stared at her.

"Ah, if I were only eighty-five years younger."

Ludmilla broke into a deep laugh.

"Now I will continue with my excitement. This skin color prejudice is the most ridiculous thing. It is a primitive trait, a brain trick, if you will, yet we cannot get beyond it. In this context, anyone who is prejudiced against any other group of persons taken as a whole has not gotten beyond the caveman stage in attitude and enlightenment even though that someone may be a genius at operating a computer. Do you realize, Ludmilla, that this type of prejudice even exists in our factories? One group over here is disdainful of a group over there, on the same factory floor. And this doesn't account for the prejudice that often exists between labor, clerical employees, and management.

"The same type of prejudice exists in schools and in other places where large numbers of people work. What else can it all be but a manifestation of a genetic pecking order programmed into our brains? We appear to be compelled by our own nature to stake out a station in society where there is somebody we can look down upon and be prejudiced against. If only we could discover the gene that contains this miscreant trait, we should attempt to exorcise it just as we would a gene containing a hereditary disease. If we could rid the world of prejudice, we could lift great weights from the minds of hundreds of millions if not billions of people who feel its oppressive weight. In the meantime, it is as if these genes are creating a brain that is flawed, defective for twentieth-century living."

Ludmilla began to talk.

"Wait, Ludmilla. I want to finish this thought. Another proof, in my own opinion, that a human genetic predisposition for prejudice exists is how easily nations have gone to war since recorded history began. One day we see a nation living in peace with a decent leader. The next day he dies and the new leader all of a sudden doesn't like the next country over. Or he wants its wealth, or he simply wants to enjoy the emotion that will come from overpowering them. What does he do? He propagandizes: he calls the people in the adjoining nation beasts, barbarians, and scum who must be wiped out. They are threatening us, he will say. He will have his propagandists develop posters that show the 'others' with dripping bayonets and fangs.

"Did you ever see the posters that were developed by the United States during World War II? They depicted the Germans and the Japanese as barbarian groups bayoneting babies. Most of the American people fell for it. They began to hate Germans and Japanese as groups, even though hundreds of thousands of Germans and Japanese had lived peacefully in the United States for years. Today, of course, government propagandists are faced with a real challenge—satellite television. How can you call a people barbarian when television takes you into their living rooms where they are petting their dogs? Fortunately for the propagandists in countries with leaders who are preparing for conflict, the media cooperates and so between antagonists we see mostly scenes of riots and people with clubs, in a state of excitement. There is not much drama in televising a nice family having dinner and talking about the weather. Ah, maybe I am getting too excited. I can feel my own blood, and for a man my age I'm not sure that is a positive thing."

"A marvelous discourse, Ilyich. I have been writing notes so fast my hand hurts. It's interesting what you say about satellite television. Right away I thought of the new tack government leaders intent on propagandizing their people take today. They no longer talk much about the enemy people needing to be wiped out. They talk more about the leaders."

"Yes, and you see we are still vulnerable to the argument. Forget the genetics for a moment and accept the fact that this is all a result of early upbringing or later conditioning. This would get the environmentalists off our backs. It really makes no difference where the brain program comes from. Someday I'm certain that neuroresearchers will be able to tell us. This nonacceptance is a result of how our brains in one way or another have been programmed to think.

"So prejudice against other groups, whether a religion, a nation, a skin color, a working class, a social level, or a group in a school yard only indicates to me that we have far more work to do as a global community than to improve the quality of our hockey teams."

"Then you are saying that all human beings should be able to accept everyone."

"Yes."

"Even if we truly don't like them?"

"If you are describing entire groups of people, yes."

"But what if we really don't like them?"

"An entire group whose homes you have visited and whose children you have met?"

"Well, say we just don't like some of them."

"Aha. That is the point. It is absolutely fine not to like somebody. More specifically, it is absolutely fine not to like somebody's personality. That is far different than disliking an entire group of people, not all of whom you've met. Here your dislike is based on a blind prejudice. But to dislike an *individual* of whatever group? What can be wrong with that? We are all different, chemical creatures. Not one of us is alike. We operate through the thought processes and demands of our minds. We are designed so that we cannot be compatible with everyone. Perhaps there are some rare fortunate persons who can be compatible with every other person, but I have yet to meet one.

"In a nutshell, I am saying that disliking somebody specifically because of how they think, what they say, how they act, even how they look, is okay. However, while you dislike a person you still must accept him or her."

"Look, Ilyich, there is a man I work with who I dislike very much. If he comes within ten feet of me, my skin crawls. You are telling me I should accept him?"

"Yes, accept him for what he is. You can't change his program, to use the word loosely. He is what he is. But you don't have to live with him. You don't even have to say hello to him, if the feeling goes that deep. But accept him. Let him be. What does it hurt? Who does it hurt?"

"But I can't even stand the sight of him."

"Then get another job. Leave the premises where he is. It's your problem, not his. If he bothers you or molests you in any way, I'm sure the management would step in. What I'm saying is, accept his presence here on Earth because he is here in the same historical time period that you are. There is nothing you can do about that except have him killed, which is not a recommended way to handle a deep dislike for another person. If it was, most of us would end up dead.

"There is usually someone in our lives who has a deep dislike for us, or there was at some time in the past. If they were smart, they avoided us, just as you should avoid those you dislike. If you can't avoid them, then you will probably have a problem. But then if you can manage to accept the problem, your level of contentment should not be unduly affected."

"I must admit something to you, Ilyich."

"What is it?"

"It's hard for me to say after everything you've said."

"Go ahead. Tell me. I promise not to tell anyone." Ilyich smiled and put a finger to his lips.

"Okay." Ludmilla paused, looked down at her fingers twisting the pen with which she was taking notes. Then she looked up and stared into Ilyich's eyes. "I've never liked the Chinese."

Ilyich stared at Ludmilla for a few seconds. Then he slapped his knee and bent over with another deep laugh.

"Ludmilla, that is marvelous. After everything we've talked about." He slapped his knee again. Ludmilla smiled at him sheepishly.

"It's true," she said. "I really understand everything you said and I don't disagree. But I'm not certain I will ever get over my dislike of the Chinese as an ethnic group, as stupid as that sounds."

"Have you ever been to China?"

"No, but my parents went there many years ago when relations between our countries were better, as part of a cultural exchange group. They came back with the impression that the Chinese were little better than animals."

Again Ilyich burst out laughing, slapping his knee several times.

"Incredible," he said.

"It's true. Practically the only thing my parents talked about for many months was how terrible the Chinese were. I did not come in contact with Chinese people until last year when I was sent by TASS to a special United Nations conference in Geneva. I spent many hours with Chinese journalists and I found them very cold, aloof, and obsessed with self-interest. I didn't like a one of them. I know you find this funny and ridiculous."

"Let me apologize for that, Ludmilla." Barkeloff took out a handkerchief and wiped his eyes. "I don't really know what's happened to me, why I find these deep group prejudices so ironic and hilarious. I understand they are serious to many people. You'll have to excuse me."

"I would excuse you for anything, Comrade Barkeloff," Ludmilla said, again looking somewhat sheepish.

Ilyich looked at her, smiled again, blew his nose, and put his handkerchief in his side trouser pocket.

"The interesting thing about this specific prejudice of yours is that I spent four years in China, from 1932 to 1936, I believe. I was in the foreign service at the time. The country was in the midst of a depression, as was most of the world. I became very friendly with many Chinese. I ate in their homes; we took walks in the park together; and we talked a good deal because there wasn't much entertainment, not a whole lot available to divert the mind. After seeing the country I can agree with some of what your parents say.

"Some Chinese lived in animal-like conditions and so acted as animals. Others, as you have noticed, are cold, aloof, and obsessed with self-interest. In my career, however, I had a great advantage. I lived in many of the major countries of the world and visited most of the smaller ones. It was part of my business to get close to the people of these countries. In practically every nation I visited there were people who lived under animal-like conditions. For example, some of the slums of New York City make our Moscow Zoo look good by comparison. I always found a cross-section of people everywhere who were cold, aloof, and full of self-interest.

"I am no different than most who have traveled the world with an open mind. We all saw the negative things, but we also saw the positive ones. People appear to be basically the same everywhere, including those in China. There are those who are warm and loving, others who appear uncaring, those who are lazy and unmotivated, and those who are aggressive and businesslike. One can go through an entire spectrum of typical human behavior and find similar examples in all human communities regardless of skin color or cultural traits.

"Now there are definitely some noticeable differences when nations or communities as a whole are considered. There appear to be certain tendencies. The Spanish appear to be more relaxed, emotional, and fatalistic than the Germans. Nigerians are less motivated than the English. The Americans are a good deal more idealistic than the French. And so forth. But if you dig under the surface, you will find people you can match across the board. In other words, you will find citizens of Spain who are as hard and aggressive as the toughest German businessman. You will find Germans who are as laid back as one might think all Spaniards are. There are Frenchmen who are every bit as puritanical or idealist as we perceive Americans to be. There are Nigerian businessmen who will eat you alive if you are not careful.

"We are all inhabitants of the same planet. We were thrown together in various cultures and societies and became indoctrinated by them. But those thrusts only magnify certain basic tendencies that would occur to anyone born into those cultures, regardless of color or belief. Ah, how about a drink of water?"

"I could use a sip."

"Good, come inside."

They walked again into Barkeloff's cottage. He was beginning to look a little tired, Ludmilla thought. Perhaps the interview was draining him.

"On second thought, let's forget the water and have a little wine," he said.

"An excellent idea."

Barkeloff opened a cupboard and reached for a beautiful crystal decanter filled with what appeared to Ludmilla to be a full, rich red wine.

"They make this down in the village, God knows from what."

Barkeloff poured the wine in two small water glasses. He handed one to Ludmilla, took the other himself, and held it up for a toast, clinking Ludmilla's glass.

"To understanding and the greater application of common sense," he said.

"To understanding and common sense," she replied, taking a sip. The wine was rich and sweet.

"Here, let me show you something."

Barkeloff walked to a dresser and began rummaging through drawers.

"I know it is here somewhere. Yes, here it is."

He brought to Ludmilla a photograph that was worn, tattered, and fading. The photo was of a Chinese man and woman in front of what looked like a clothing store. They were both smiling widely.

"It's odd that your prejudice should be against the Chinese. These are the Lims. They were two of my closest friends. A wonderful couple. Deeply in love with one another and unable to have children. Full of life and hospitality. Their home was my home, as the Spanish say. They killed and ate dogs, which I found disgusting. But eating habits, like most of our other habits, are customs we are conditioned to accept in our environments. If you grow up eating dogs or raw fish or whatever, that is what you will learn to eat. It is amazing the judgments made about others because of their eating habits. They mean nothing. I loved the Lims. I disliked their next door neighbors whose trash kept overflowing onto the Lim's property. There were many people like the Lims in China. You must live among a group foreign to yourself to have this observation. Come let's walk outside again. Take your wine with you."

Outside, Ilyich put his glass on the bench and did some odd stretching exercises. He continued to do so for a few moments while Ludmilla just watched. He appeared in a trance. Then he stopped just as suddenly as he began.

"Interesting exercises are they not? A combination of oriental yin-yang and an exercise book written by an American movie star I once came across. The exercises stretch and tone the muscles as well as relax and refresh the mind. We have been talking quite a while."

"Should we stop, Ilyich? Perhaps you are tired."

"No, not now. What time is your train?"

"It leaves the village at 9:00 P.M."

"Good, we have time to talk more and then we'll have a bite to eat before you leave. You should get down the hill before it turns dark so you can see the path clearly. Now where were we?"

"You were talking about the Lims and China."

"Oh, yes. I used that as an example. Can you see rationally, Ludmilla, that this prejudice you have against the Chinese is simply a brain program?"

"Well, according to what you say, Ilyich, everything we think is part of a brain program or conditioning or trick of some sort. I am not entirely sure of that concept but it does appear possible."

"For the purpose of discussion then, can you assume that your singular Chinese prejudice is a brain trick, to use that term alone for now?"

"Yes, I think so."

"Now ridding yourself of emotions and looking at that program from a cold, logical point of view—and knowing what you do about the world, forgetting even what I said about the Chinese—can you see that this prejudice against one entire group of people is irrational? That there are millions of Chinese whom you would like if you met them? And there are other millions whom you would dislike?"

"It is possible."

"Can you therefore pinpoint this irrationality as a program that is worth exorcising from your brain if you could? In other words, if you could get rid of this prejudice, would you?"

"To be honest, Ilyich, I'm not sure. I think I enjoy disliking the Chinese."

She expected him to burst out laughing. He didn't. He just smiled with a nod of understanding.

"And there you really have it. You *enjoy* the prejudice. Most people who are prejudiced enjoy it as well. It appears to fulfill some basic need. My own feeling is that this is a genetic need as well. You have a genetic predisposition for prejudice and you were environmentally conditioned to focus it on the Chinese, because of what your parents initially told you. The later observations you made on your own, which might have neutralized the program, instead deepened it. You are stuck with a very human conflict.

"You have a prejudice against a group of people, yet you find it possible to like some of them. But these encounters with those you like, either personally or in media, are not enough to wipe away the group prejudice. It is a very natural occurrence, but totally irrational, is it not?"

"Well, yes, the way you put it. I recall my parents saying that they really liked their Chinese guide."

"Which helps make the point."

"So what does the world do about this, Ilyich? All of us cannot travel as you did. I'm not sure that travel in itself is enough."

"Quite right. When a prejudice is deep enough, one can travel with blinders on, looking for justification of the attitude."

"So what do we do?"

"Let's now go back to our earlier discussion when I said we must accept ourselves before we accept others. I was really talking about a mental exercise to rid one's self of a negative prejudicial program."

"What do you mean?"

"If each of us does not accept him- or herself, we appear to be more attracted to disliking others. Within that range of dislike is group prejudice. It is much more difficult to reach a perspective that can neutralize a brain program of prejudice unless we start to become more accepting of ourselves as individuals. We are what we are at this instant. This is how we were programmed to be both genetically and environmentally, and at this instant there is not much that can be done to change. All change comes slowly. It may happen overnight, but a good deal of effort had to precede it.

"If we can recognize that, then we can also recognize that others around us are what they are and we must accept them as well. On this Earth no one has living rights that supersede those of others. Anyone who thinks so has simply been brainwashed by their authority figures who don't know any more than anyone else. We can dislike other individuals as we discussed. If we do, we should avoid them.

"But we cannot let this lead us into looking at the groups to which they belong in a nonaccepting manner. We must study this attitude within ourselves and see the irrationality of it. We must concentrate on it without willing it to go away. It is practically impossible to force the mind: the brain is a stubborn instrument. I would like to meet someday the source of its development. We would have a few words. But to get back: if we don't resist the prejudicial attitudes but simply concentrate on them, one day, possibly overnight, they will melt away.

"It is a trick we play back on our own brains. This overnight success, however, might take months or even years to achieve, depending on how deep the program is. However, once we become accepting of ourselves and of others, both individually and collectively, we will raise our level of contentment.

"Irrational dislikes and attitudes, those we cannot logically think through, result in conflicts within us that tend to bring us down. Our general level of contentment, that line from which we go to our highs and lows as humans, is lower when we have these irrational attitudes. When we get low, we are really low, and when we are high, we can't get as high as we might be if our general contentment level was higher."

"I like what you say, Ilyich, and I intend to quote you, but if you take your viewpoint as a whole, particularly this genetic predisposition for group prejudice, isn't this some fault of Nature?"

"An excellent point. It is. I am sure that, as a protective device,

Nature gave us the genetics to be nonaccepting of those alien to us. In an animal-like state, one can't be too careful of others. But as humans, we should be beyond that. This trick of Nature is useless. We don't need it any more. Nature didn't give that gene a phase-out pattern, when it designed us to evolve into thinking creatures.

"Today we can think and should be able to observe the world rationally. For one thing, to protect us instinctively, Nature tricked us into disliking people who are alien to us. But that gene and that attitude is now as useless as having a tail. Now we are capable, through our evolved thought process, of seeing what is really dangerous to us. We no longer have to guard automatically against alien groups as a whole."

"So all is lost in that sense."

"Oh, no, not at all, Ludmilla. Fortunately we are able to neutralize many of our negative brain responses through logic. It is normally a slow process, as I've said, but it can be done. What Nature did not do for us we can do for ourselves, since it did provide us with a brain that can think. We can fault it for not phasing out our animal instincts as we evolved, or we can just observe that we still have the defective traits Nature gave us and take action against them or we simply ignore them.

"Any human who has the capacity to think clearly—and not all humans do, which is why prejudice will not be eradicated soon —should be able to spot this conflict of group nonacceptance and work on it. There is a choice in this matter, if our mental disposition allows for a choice."

Ilyich stopped and gazed off into the distance.

"It is pleasant to be with you, Ludmilla. Do you have any other questions?"

"No, Ilyich."

"Well, then, there is a little trail that takes us through the woods and winds its way back. Let us walk. It is a beautiful day. Then I will fix you something to eat and you can get down to the village. How does that sound?"

"It sounds wonderful, Comrade Barkeloff."

He smiled as he reached over and kissed her on the forehead. Then Barkeloff took her hand and led her toward the wooded trail.

THE POINT

Our DNA has obviously been programmed with genetics that force us to push ourselves upward to reach the highest social and power levels of which we're capable.

The primologists have observed this quite clearly in wilderness animals. As was pointed out, there is relatively little difference in the DNA between humans, the primates, and other higher animals that have been closely studied.

This genetic system makes good sense for wilderness animals because it provides herds with a hierarchy and disciplined order. It would pay us to remember that humans were wilderness animals only an anthropological eyeblink ago.

However, humans, as we've also pointed out, can think rationally. As a result, we are capable of observing these limbic programs running in our brains and we can work to keep them from causing chaos in our lives. For example, we can look rationally at the United States of America, the melting pot of almost all major ethnic tribal units, and understand the prejudice facing this country. The experience would be similar to forcing strangers from all points of the globe to live in one small apartment building. It would be chaos.

In the United States, as in other countries where ethnic groups are legally free to live together, the cultural diversity provided by the mixture can never be enjoyed fully until all can see that their genetic programs are the culprit. We have too many programs running in our brains that were useful when we were living in caves, but whose high-intensity level we don't need anymore.

The idea is to understand that we have these programs and that we can do something about them.

17

Our Sameness

Ed Grogan sat in a lawn chair in front of the Sunnyday Home for the Aged. It was Armed Forces Day and the suburb in which the home was located had put together its own little parade, consisting of some National Guard units, the high school band, a dance school, the police and fire departments, the American Legion, and other local clubs.

The parade route brought it in front of the Sunnyday Home and many of the residents were sitting on the front porch and lawn to observe. Grogan sat on the lawn off to one side by himself.

Essie Beecroft, his sometime companion, walked over to Grogan and set up her own lawn chair.

"Why are you sitting over here by yourself, Mr. Grogan?"

"I like my own company," he said.

"Do you mind if I sit next to you?"

"You usually do sit next to me; you already are."

"I don't know why you can't be a little more pleasant."

"If I was, I'd be somebody else and you wouldn't love me as much as you do."

A slight blush came to Essie Beecroft's face.

"Please, Mr. Grogan. I never said I loved you."

"Do you like me?"

"Well yes, I do like you."

"At our age, that's close enough."

Essie grinned to herself.

"What do you think of the parade, Mr. Grogan?"

"I think it's full of shit."

Now she winced.

"To tell you the truth, Mr. Grogan, I think you are a very decent person. I don't like your language. It offends me. You use it as some kind of act, perhaps to attract attention. I can live with it, but I don't like it."

"But you like me."

"I said that before."

"I know. I was just checking again. At 86, I'm still insecure in my relationships."

He began to turn away as she said, almost to his back, "Why don't you like the parade?"

"Because it reminds me of a very bad and basic human contradiction," he said, turning slowly to face Essie.

"What do you mean?"

"Look at those Army guys all dressed in the same uniform, all trying to keep in step with each other. They are trying to look as if they were one single unit. They count cadence together, they salute together."

"What's so contradictory about that?"

"All that sameness is part of the human pattern. We just don't *think* it is. That's the contradiction. As humans, we attempt to emphasize our differences, not our sameness. We don't like to be compared to others. We don't even like to be told we look like others. We want to stand out in some way. To rise above the pack. This drive to be different has caused a lot of the misery in the world."

"But we *are* all different."

"Yes, but our differences are proportionately small. If all the humans in the world of the same sex were lined up along some enormous beach, you'd be hard pressed to spot *radical* physical differences. Coloring would be different, heights, shapes, and so forth. But the sameness would be overwhelming. A behind is a behind. A leg is a leg. An eye is an eye. A tit is a tit . . ."

"Please, Mr. Grogan, don't go much further," she interrupted.

"Well, you know what I mean. Even our mental patterns are similar. We can all think to some extent. Our emotional responses are, all in all, very much the same, as is our ability to absorb language and communicate. Think about it, every time a functioning baby is born it looks like another human, time and time and time, again. We never really think about that."

"Think about what?"

"Why it happens that way. How a string of infinitesimally tiny chemicals can combine to create a human being that each time looks like other human beings. Why doesn't a woman ever give birth to a canary? Look how lucky the world would have been if Hitler's mother would have given birth to a canary. Nature has such discipline in these matters. It's just totally beyond me, beyond anyone, really."

"But this is God's way, Mr. Grogan."

"Somebody for sure created us. But there had to be a screw-up in making us basically look the same, as against a canary, for example, while giving us a brain drive that makes us want to be different."

"But what's wrong with that?"

"It creates too much separateness, too much "you versus me." We overdo it. We become preoccupied with our differences without understanding that we are just part of the parade. I suppose you're wondering what that does?"

"Frankly, yes, Mr. Grogan."

"Okay, let's rattle off just a few of the bad things it does. It creates prejudice, for example. We'll discriminate against others because we perceive them to be different or separate from us. We'll be mean. We'll maim and kill. We'll start wars, or we'll deprive others of a good education or an opportunity to enjoy life. Sometimes we'll let people starve or live in intolerable slums.

"We look down our nose at animals, but you don't see dogs, cats, and chimpanzees preoccupied with how different they are from their brothers, sisters, and friends. Oh sure, a horse can be made an outcast from a herd, but that appears to be instinctive, not a result of what is supposed to be reasonable thought. Humans can think, but our basic thinking is lousy."

"But aren't you missing an important point, Mr. Grogan? If we were all the same, we wouldn't have any identity. Life would be dull and uninteresting. I personally like being who I am. I like making a statement to the world with my personality, with how I dress. I wouldn't like being part of a crowd of sameness, as you put it. I daresay that most people would agree with me."

"You're missing my point. I never said that we had to be clones of each other. We are all very different within our species. But we are more similar than we are different."

"When you compare humans to canaries."

"Yes, or to trees or rocks or volleyballs. We would simply be a lot better off if we could perceive that the differences between humans are really minor from that angle of comparison. Just stare at those soldiers for a minute. They look basically the same, don't they?"

"Yes, but I can also see some distinct differences."

"But are those differences enough to say to one's self: 'My skin is more pinkish than his, so he can't come in my locker room. Or I am smarter than that one, so I should have more money. Or I am more civilized, so it's okay if someone less civilized starves. Or I dress better, so it's fine if I snub someone who looks like a slob. Or this person talks funny, so it's okay if I laugh behind his back.' It goes on and on, and it's all crazy. Minor differences between us are often blown way out of proportion as if we are absolutely driven as human inhabitants of this Earth to create inequity and hatred."

"You should have been a philosopher, Mr. Grogan."

"Are you kidding? In my opinion, most of the great philosophers of the world never got the point. Guys like Nietzsche spawned as much separateness and hatred as your average Ku Klux Klan cross burner. Others just thought in wide circles. I read most of the great philosophers and to me it was just so much bullshit. They never got it."

"And you have it."

"Hell, no, I don't have it. But I know enough and have seen enough of life to understand that we are beyond figuring it out. So we might as well try to get along, and we won't get along until we understand how very much we don't know and how very much alike we are."

"You're back to that, again."

"My God, Essie, that's what we've been talking about."

"That's the first time in five years you ever called me Essie. As a matter of fact, that's the first you ever called me anything. You've never called me by name."

"Forgive me, I got carried away. Let me put this thing another way. Our sameness is dictated by some very basic facts. First and foremost, we are all born through the same process. White, black, mauve, you name it, we all come out of somebody's womb. Second, after birth, we *all* have to be cared for in some way. Third, we *all* need food and water to keep our bodies alive. Fourth, we *all* need clothes or shelter or both to protect ourselves against the elements. And finally, when we are through living, we *all* die. No one transcends the life process. No one is bigger than life.

"When you find someone who got here without being born, or who won't die or who can survive without sustenance, then send me a telegram and I'll get off all of this. In the meantime, as far as I'm concerned, every human on this planet, or probably anywhere else for that matter, is in the same damned boat and deserves equal consideration."

"Are you ever going to call me Essie again, Mr. Grogan?"

"Do you like it?"

"I really do."

"All right, let's start with once a month."

"You're a very stubborn man, Mr. Grogan."

"Watch the parade, Essie."

"You're also a rascal."

"I know it."

THE POINT

As Ilyich Barkeloff pointed out, our brains appear programmed to achieve the highest possible level of power within our social groups. In this effort to climb higher, we need people to look down on. Our favorite targets are people whose skins are of another color or whose perceived group habits or living conditions we find intolerable when measured against the standards with which we've been programmed.

This prejudice is usually triggered only when the ethnic group is unsubjugated and striving for equal rights. Our power drive overcomes what we can rationally observe as the basic sameness between us. The hatred generated causes unhappiness for the victims and imbalance for the perpetrators. Neutralizing this brain trick is one of the most difficult things to do. It might be one of the first things to practice. If this can be undone, the sky is the limit.

18

The Essence of Religion

It was the last week that Alfred Hoffman and Andrew Hill would spend together at their cottage retreat in Mackinac Island on northern Lake Michigan. For the past three weeks they had been enjoying not only their many conversations, but the nearness of each other.

They had been friends and colleagues for more than forty years. They taught philosophy at the same university for almost thirty years before retiring, Alfred specializing in the nature of truth, and Andrew in the history of philosophy. The two were once again sitting on the porch of their rented cottage facing the beach, which, despite its length, appeared more deserted than usual.

"We've covered a number of wonderful concepts this trip," Alfred began.

"We have," Andrew replied, "and the time has passed so rapidly. I don't look forward to returning to India and leaving you for another year."

"Nor I."

"The interesting thing about our talks, Alfred, is that they have been very broad in scope. We have avoided digging into specific examples and researches in an attempt to prove one thing or another."

"We have avoided proofs, Andrew, because nothing we've talked about is really provable. So there isn't much sense in dredging up references and obscure footnotes."

"But you know what we haven't talked about?"

"What?"

"Religion . . . as a concept."

"But we've certainly touched on it enough," Andrew said.

"I know, but we really haven't gotten into its very basic essence. Why do we have it, what has it done for the world, what is it doing? Religion is a powerful force in the world. It ranks only behind national governments in its ability to exert will and power over great masses of people. And it has often proved stronger than government."

"That's very true, Alfred. The odd thing about it is that most people don't have the ability to see religion from a distant viewpoint and note what it actually is in our lives. We all seem to have some abiding opinion about it, ranging in subtle levels from a deep, fanatic belief to complete nonbelief. We don't seem to be able to take that step back and see a truer picture."

"Which is?"

"First that religion is man-made and extends back into mythology and other ritualism that has to be tens of thousands, if not hundreds of thousands of years old. God, or whatever created what exists, has not manifested itself in its essence. As a result, we have developed our religious beliefs over time through insights of humans like you and me, who said they were messengers or interpreters of God, and who were then supported toward this end by disciples. You either believed them or you didn't or you ended up somewhere in between. Nothing was ever rationally provable. One had to take that leap of faith to encompass the belief system being espoused, very often doing so without the slightest amount of skepticism."

"And up to the point of religious fanaticism."

"Correct. Too many people are unable to look objectively at all the religious beliefs in the world to get a better look at the whole matter. We spoke before about the number of religious sects and cults that you and I have studied. I think we roughly guessed about 1,500. But if you took into consideration every tribal belief in primitive areas as a body of religious thought, there must have been thousands of them at one time or another. Wouldn't you agree?"

"Probably, Andrew, when you include the subtle shadings of belief that have existed just among the different sects of the larger religions."

"And wouldn't you also agree that among these thousands of religious belief systems, including various forms of agnosticism, there have always been fanatics who have believed that their religious belief was or is the only true religious belief?"

"I would say that is probably true. They are the ones who have helped sustain the beliefs through time."

"Now doesn't that tell you something right there, Alfred?"

"That there has been and still is wide disagreement about religious beliefs, yes."

"And beyond that, that nobody has known or knows today a darned thing for sure, because there is so much strength in those conflicting beliefs. The Jews think they are a chosen people, but then really . . . so do those who belong to most of the other religions. They all believe that their concept of the divine, for whatever reason, favors them. Where is the sign in the sky that says this one is right and that one is wrong? How can we believe fanatically in any one system on faith alone when we see so many conflicting beliefs?"

"Millions manage, Andrew."

"Yes and that's the tragedy of it, Alfred, because instead of bringing us together, religion has been splitting us apart, too often creating deep factionalism, misery, and wars. And for what?"

"Are you against religion as a concept, Andrew?"

"Not at all. I think religion can play a great role in this world. As we've discussed previously, we are surrounded by mystery. We don't for a fact know why life exists. We don't know for sure how what exists got here. We don't know in which context the universe exists. We don't know enough about our bodies and the workings of all living things. We don't know for a fact what happens, if anything, after we die. And so on. Now these are some pretty basic questions, wouldn't you say?"

"You couldn't get much more basic."

"We could go on for days with the rational unknowns. We appear to be bit players in an enormous mystery and what religion can do is bring order into our lives amid what otherwise might be chaotic uncertainty."

"So what you're saying, Andrew, is that you believe in religion as something to believe in."

"That's a good way to put it. I mean, why put religion down? Any set of religious beliefs, no matter how farfetched, could ultimately turn out to be true. The problem is that the peoples of the world don't look at it quite that way.

"If you drop out of the womb in a home whose inhabitants believe in the teachings of some obscure Moslem sect, likely as not you'll believe in those teachings as an adult and you might even go marching blindly off to some war to defend those beliefs—and do it without the slightest thought that those beliefs have no substantiation in fact and are thus no better or worse than any other. Further, you rarely think that your beliefs derived from the simple accident of your birth into a household where those beliefs held sway."

"A strong religious training has very deep roots in our brains."

"Deep? Alfred, it's one of the deepest of all brain teachings. How many other teachings include a propensity to give up one's life of comfort in its defense? Take a look at your religious fanatic. Try to talk to him about his beliefs on any kind of rational, intellectual level. You get nowhere. I don't care what the religion is. 'This is the word of God.' Or, 'That's the word of Allah.' That's the response you usually get when the questioning gets heavy. The teaching becomes totally ingrained."

"Perhaps as you pointed out with purpose and death, there is a built-in wiring system in our brains," Alfred said. "It is pre-set in some way to receive a religious or spiritual belief of some kind. Maybe Nature saw we would need some kind of deep-rooted belief system to persevere in this crazy world and simply wired in the apparatus to accept it."

"There might be something to that, Alfred. There is some opinion that the capacity for ritualism is indeed brain wired in the limbic area. But of course, brains differ, people differ, and for many persons the beliefs they grew up with diminish in strength or they change altogether."

"But one is rarely without some spiritual or religion-oriented belief system."

"That's true. One could even consider atheism a belief system within the religious sphere. Talking to an atheist who is a fanatic is just as tiring as talking to a religious fanatic."

"Would you say, Andrew, looking back at all of recorded history and beyond, that religion as a concept has been good or bad for us?"

"A very neat question, Alfred. On the one hand, throughout history, religion and mythology have been sources of inspiration. During the traumatic periods that all human beings have faced, a deep religious belief offers hope and comfort. It makes life bearable.

"On the other hand, religion has been the cause of major wars and social conflicts. The Crusades alone killed millions. Religious wars have been devastating, even into the twentieth century. We need only look at what happened to the Jews, the gypsies, and other ethnic groups in World War II; or the Protestants and Catholics in Northern Ireland; and then in the Middle East, with Moslems pitted against Christians and Jews. On top of this, look at the prejudice and hatred that religion has generated. People killed, abused, attacked, tortured, and chased from their homelands because of their religious beliefs.

"Reading the history of religious conflict and prejudice, it's enough to make one sick. And have we learned anything from all of it? Do we look at what we have done to ourselves because of this ridiculous fanaticism and call a halt to it? Not at all. It continues today just as it did centuries ago. Bigotry, hatred, persecution, wars, the lot of it. And so has religion been, on the whole, more positive than negative for us as humans? My own private convictions are that we would have been better off without it, at least in its structured form."

"What do you mean by that?"

"I mean, Alfred, that no real harm can be caused if an individual wanted to follow his own beliefs, within his own personal environment, in his own way, as long as those beliefs don't foster violence or abusive treatment of others. The negatives of religion manifest themselves primarily when they become institutionalized.

"These organized religions must sustain themselves: they have temples, churches, mosques, and a hierarchy; they pray in a group in a certain way, on certain days, and at certain times. There are ministers and committees organizing it all, and possibly a management structure on top of that. They need money to maintain themselves, and to get the money they must keep their patrons faithful.

"These organized religions must each proclaim their own belief systems as the one true belief system, or at least imply it. The result is conflict between the belief systems and that is what so often leads to trouble of one kind or another."

"But all religions aren't vertically structured."

"That's true. Judaism isn't, for example. The structure is spread horizontally. But it is still very much an organized religion with the same kinds of needs and the same sorts of problems. Even in Israel today you can have an Ashkenazi synagogue right next to a Sephardic one and likely as not, the people will snub each other. The prejudice exists. They probably won't shoot each other, thank goodness, but the conflict in beliefs between the two sects can cause mental anxiety and frustration.

"Look at India. When the English left they had to partition the country, creating two Pakistans, to keep the Hindus and the Moslems from killing each other. There are no great hierarchies in these two religions either. Nonetheless, they are organized."

"Maybe it's time for a little tea."

"Good idea, Alfred, this is getting me all heated up."

"I noticed."

"It's not good for me to get all heated up."

"Who is it good for?"

"Another good question. You make the tea, I'll warm some biscuits."

The two men entered the cottage and busied themselves in the kitchen. Andrew brought the tray to the porch.

"My, what a beautiful day," Alfred remarked.

"It certainly is. Our senses can bring such joy to us from scenes like this, if we can just relax enough to let them."

"Getting back to religion again, Andrew, do you believe the founders of the great religions—Jesus, Gautama, Abraham, Mohammed, for example—would have been so forceful if they could have known of the negatives that would come as a result of their teachings: the bigotry, the wars, and so forth?"

"It would have certainly given them pause for thought," Andrew replied. "What would you do if you came up with this body of great ideas that you fervently believed was a direct message from God, but also could see into the future to know that the conflicts caused by the beliefs would result in a considerable amount of unanticipated murder, mayhem, and hatred, offsetting the goodness that would be derived?"

"I don't know what I'd do."

"Neither do I. Today, if a God figure came down and delivered its message to me alone and asked me to be its prophet for the world, I'd say forget it. The last thing we need is another religious system. I'd also say that if I got up in front of some TV cameras and said I just saw this God and this is the message it gave me, I'd likely as not be locked up. I don't care how good the message was.

"I could even lose my pension. Some young legal counsel for the pension plan would probably find some loophole that denies money to a fruitcake. Because that's what everyone would think I was, a fruitcake. The advantage Christ and the others had is that they weren't covered by TV and questioned by someone on '60 Minutes.' Plus, they had some excellent communicators to spread their gospels.

"No, if God came down and spoke to me and it all sounded good, I'd tell it to wait right there while I called the networks, so it could spout its own message. If it was believable enough for the whole world to understand, it would be the all time God send, if you'll excuse the pun. One world, one religion, no conflict, what a magnificent thought."

"Except, Andrew, what language would God speak during the telecast?"

"Perhaps all of them at once," Andrew chuckled.

"You asked," he continued after a pause, "if the religious founders would have carried on had they known all of the results of their works, good and bad."

"We did get off track, didn't we?"

"But it was enjoyable. And to answer the question, I don't think all the great religious teachers foresaw the negatives that would result. For the most part, their teachings focused a good deal on the concept of love and the neutralizing of our evil tendencies, which we know today as our leftover, limbic animal instincts. They were showing humans a way out of the torment that results from life in a structured society, contending with evil or animalistic emotional drives revolving around sex, materialism, violence, power, social status, prejudice, and so forth.

"They weren't aware of the limbic area of our brain that was causing this animalism. Life for most people was pretty brutal when those men developed their thoughts. What they taught, for the most part, was excellent. If their followers through the years, including those today, understood their teachings and attempted to put the most positive and practical of them into actual practice, then the conflicts between all religions would be minimal."

"An excellent point, Andrew."

"Thank you. The problem has been, Alfred, that the best of the teachings have gotten lost in the human condition. This is perhaps what the founders never realized would happen."

"I would also seriously doubt that they had the slightest idea that structured organizations would result from their efforts."

"That's true. But this kind of organization is also part of the human condition. Our brains initially accepted these belief systems. We gradually became convinced of their rightness. Our natural drives then impelled us to spread the word so that others would be similarly enlightened. To spread the word and keep new recruits in the fold, we needed to organize. Then, as part of the organizational process, we developed top-notch communicators to go out in the world to get the job done. Places of worship were erected and people flocked to them. They heard fine and noble messages; they prayed, but most never got it.

"When the workweek started they were back in a survival mode, fighting and kicking and doing just the opposite of what their religions taught. To make matters worse, they looked down at those practicing other religions, generating abuses that would never have been condoned by Jesus or Gautama, or most of the other founding teachers. By the way, this same general process still happens today with new religions and cults."

"And that's what you mean, Andrew, when you say the founding teachers never took into consideration the human condition."

"Yes. Maybe they saw the problem. But I'm sure they never envisioned the depth of it. Karl Marx made the same mistake with his *Communist Manifesto*. He envisioned a utopia, an impossible dream, given the human condition. More precisely, this human condition boils down to the structure and operation of the human brain. It could very well be that the founding religion teachers envisioned the same utopia that Marx did. They might have believed that if a feeling of religious euphoria enveloped them, why couldn't it envelop everybody through their teachings. Then we'd all be happy, loving, and accepting. The world would be utopian.

"But when you look at the world realistically and the operation of the brain specifically, it's obvious that there is nothing that we know of, no specific set of ideas, that can be universally accepted. Then or now."

"Andrew, aren't you overemphasizing the negative side of religion? Religion has done an awful lot of good for the world, too."

"It has. No doubt about it. There are probably hundreds of millions of people in the world who follow the basic precepts of the best religious thought and lead exemplary lives. They are loving, accepting of all others, and feel a oneness with their God. That alone can do much to create order in one's life and in society on a more consistent basis.

"There are two major points to consider in relation to that. First, not enough people who believe in a religion follow on a day-to-day basis the very basic and most important precepts of their religions. Second, religion, in my opinion, isn't always necessary if we are to feel loved, accepted, and experience oneness with some supreme being."

"Explain that last statement."

"Well, look at me, Alfred, if you can stand it. I have no religious beliefs of any kind. I was brought up in a religious household and held the beliefs I was taught for many years. Even at the university, when I began to suspect the speciousness of those beliefs, I held onto them, because I am also superstitious.

"I felt that if I said certain things to myself or to others, or to my God, some ill luck would befall me. But then slowly, I took the risk of alienating myself from this God, only in the sense of not following a religious regimen. For example, I haven't stepped inside a place of worship for almost thirty years, except to attend a funeral or wedding or what not. I have, in other words, no structured beliefs.

"And yet I do believe in a God figure of some kind. I have no idea what it is, where it is, what it looks like or what it wants. But I do believe that this planet, this universe, the other universes, our bodies, and the thousands of living things we know about could not have been some mere accident, although there are people who believe that. Things are much too complex for that. Something had to be behind all of this. Whatever that is, is my own personal God figure.

"When I am late for an appointment and a bus is nowhere to be found, I'll beseech my God for a break. Or I'll talk to Him when a loved one is in danger. It's a marvelous comfort. I also consider myself loving. I don't know of anyone I hate. I consider myself accepting. I've been able to eliminate all prejudice from my life. I am not greedy, nor envious. I still have some negative emotions I'd like to get rid of. I have them pinpointed and am working on them. So I'm not perfect. For goodness sake, you're not even perfect, Alfred."

"And I thought I kept my little emotional problems well hidden," Alfred chuckled.

"The point is, I feel I lead a more exemplary life within the society we are caught up in than most religionists I know. What that means, at least to me, is that being part of an organized religion isn't essential. Nor is it necessary to go to the extreme of atheism. The most important thing is to recognize that we must follow the rules of whatever society we're in or somehow escape to a society we like better. We must love and accept all others because that is how they were born and later conditioned to be."

"Which is what religion is supposed to help us do, Andrew."

"When it accomplishes that, let it be, Alfred. When it turns fanatics into outlaws and persecutors, we don't need it. The problem is we don't have a referee or an omnipotent person—at the center of earthly wisdom—who can make a decision and enforce it regarding religion or any other worldwide concern that has a potential for threatening human life and serenity. Those of us who people this planet are left to our own devices, to sink or swim, and maybe there is some purpose in that. If so, we may be part of an ugly experiment, and I don't like it."

"And so we live with a little uncertainty and fear."

"Yes. Fortunately the brain shields us from a lot of it. The brain keeps most of us from thinking too much about the uncertainties, which can be very frightening."

"How about walking down to the hotel to eat tonight, Andrew?"

"A marvelous idea. Tomorrow we leave for home. Tonight we have a banquet, just the two of us."

"Without speeches."

"Not one."

"Just a little small talk."

"Between two great old friends."

The two men stood up, took a last look at the beach, and walked inside their cottage.

THE POINT

There has been speculation that the capacity for ritualism is wired into the limbic areas of our brains. And why not? If you were in charge of designing the human brain to live on planet Earth without definite answers, wouldn't you build in a capacity to quickly absorb some ritualistic, structured religious belief? As long as we have this capability, why not use it and enjoy the security and feelings of serenity that a good religion can bring to us?

But at the same time, we need to view religion as a vertical part of the purpose program that is running in our brains. We must see that our religion is just one of hundreds and to accept those other religions as equally viable belief, or nonbelief, systems.

If we have erased our need for a structured religious belief, we still need to respect those who find their religions a comfort.

When it comes to religion, we simply need to unlock our thinking.

19

What's Important

It was the third week in September and Elliott Simmons and Art Meyer were at a campsite near Durango, Colorado. Elliott, the former school teacher, and Art, the former bank officer, were still traveling around the country on a three-year sabbatical, enjoying the respite from the lives they had known. They called it their "step-out adventure."

This was now the second year they had come to Durango. They had found a relatively secluded campsite for their tent about two miles from the city limits. This was their vacation within what had been a working vacation of odd jobs, mostly waitering at restaurants. They walked into town practically every morning to play tennis at a city park. The afternoons were spent exploring the many mountainous trails that surrounded their campsite area. They had come to Durango from Chicago and intended to leave for San Diego by the middle of October.

It was late in the day and although it was warm, they had started a small fire. The two canvas chairs they sat on were among the camping items they had stored the year before in a lock-it-and-leave-it warehouse in Durango.

Art pushed a long branch into the fire and said to Elliott, "You know, last night after we went to bed I just couldn't sleep. So I brought my sleeping bag outside and I must have spent an hour just staring at the stars. The night was remarkably clear. I suppose you're wondering what I was thinking out there?"

"I am practically having an anxiety attack waiting to hear."

"Yeah, I knew it," Art said sarcastically, knowing that he could always pique Elliott's interest in opening their discussions.

"The first thing I thought about," Art continued, "was how are we ever going to get a grip on this galaxy thing? There are billions of them out there, each with tens of billions of stars, and to get from one to the other, a family might have to fly at least two million years at the speed of light."

"I see," Elliott said with his usual opening response of feigned interest.

"So I thought to myself, what is the idea here? If the creative force behind all this wanted to keep all the stars and their planetary systems separate in the universe, why did it go to such an extreme? Why do we have to be so far apart that there is practically no hope of ever seeing each other, assuming that at least a small percentage of the trillions of stars in the universe have planets like ours?"

"And what did you conclude?"

"The only thing I could think of was that this creative force probably doesn't want the planets to communicate with one another. This would be practically impossible if Einstein was right and the speed of light is as fast as anything can go."

"And why do you think it doesn't want us to communicate?"

"That one has me really stumped. Maybe all the planets with life on them are in some kind of contest with each other, some kind of scientific experiment, and it would spoil things if we could compare notes. Maybe that's why. What possible reason could there be?"

"Hey, don't ask me. I slept in the tent last night."

"Then another question altogether sprang into my mind."

"Go on."

"I began to wonder: in terms of this galactic viewpoint, with the trillions of stars in this enormous universe, what is really important in our lives? What *should* be important in our lives?"

"Okay, I see where this is going. A subject of enormous interest. So if you don't mind, I'll make some coffee to help me through it."

"I'll help you, despite your rudeness."

Art stoked the fire while Elliott brought out an old, enameled pot. He filled it with water and sprinkled coffee grounds on top of the water. He then set the pot down on a small grate that Art had placed on the fire. When the water began to boil, Elliott looked at his watch. After 110 seconds elapsed, he removed the pot from the fire with a hot pad and began pouring the coffee through a strainer into two large cups. Art picked up his cup and took a sip.

"Your ability at making coffee in this highly unorthodox manner is absolutely fantastic," Art said.

"With this subject, we're going to need it. Now, where do you want to start?"

"Let's start with winning and losing. In other words, how important is it for us to always want to be winners? Is this desire genetic? Is it something we learn? What is it and why do we need it?"

"Oh boy," Elliott said stifling a yawn.

"Yeah, I know, this subject isn't getting you excited, but it should. Look at all the unhappiness that this winning concept gives to us. Every time there is a winner, there has to be a loser, so fifty percent of the participants are always unhappy with the result."

"You never bring this up when you beat my ass at tennis."

"Can we stay off ourselves for a moment, Elliott, and concentrate on the concept?"

"Fine, that's just fine."

"To start with, look how strong our 'want-to-win' trait is. We want to win things desperately. But goddamn it, what is so important about winning? I mean let's really get into what happens when opponents win or lose. Let's use football as our example, but the same thing would probably apply in most other win-lose situations, like lawyers in a courtroom, people in a beauty contest, or one architectural firm pitching its design against another, and so on. It's all the same thing.

"Now take the losing team of persons first. What do you see? The first thing you see is their sad robot-like state as they walk off the field of play. The final moment has just passed, the score or decision has been inputted in their brains, and bang, the loser program is triggered. What's the loser program? It's a feeling of being demeaned. It creates sad, long faces. Losers who are into winning are emotionally upset. Among other things, they feel frustrated that they did not get what they wanted. They didn't win. They might be embarrassed or ashamed. They kick the dirt as they walk. When they get home they might take their frustration and other negative feelings out on family and friends. It's all part of the loser program.

"People don't know what to say to losers. It's hard to talk without some artificiality to a person who is into winning and has just lost. You can't say, 'But wasn't it a neat experience even though you lost so lopsidedly?' Can you imagine an innocent, but ratings-driven television sportscaster thrusting a microphone into the face of a top football coach whose team just lost by a big margin in the major bowl game of the year and asking a question like that? Instead of getting a lighthearted, witty answer in return, he'd probably be punched in the nose.

"There is a definite set of emotions that combines to form a robot-like loser's program and it can only be neutralized if we balance the importance we place on winning by trying to comprehend that within the perspective of this planet of ours hurtling about in space within a galaxy that is one of billions, all of which are part of infinite and eternal space and time, winning this game, or any game, isn't all that goddamned important." He drew a breath.

Elliott chuckled.

"A very cogent viewpoint, Art. But what about the winners? They *feel* they should be rewarded. How do you handle that?"

Art stood up again, stretched, put his arms behind his back, and instead of pacing, just started walking slowly around the small clearing.

"The contrast, of course, *is* incredible," he began. "While the losers are kicking the dirt and are in other ways experiencing unhappiness in their robot-like loser's syndrome, the winners are all clapping each other on the back, offering compliments, and giving credit to everyone they can think of for the victory—including fathers who gave them endless encouragement, and mothers who worked overtime in a factory. Everyone can talk to a winner. You know what to say automatically: 'Nice game.' You can even ask: 'Tell me your most important moments of the game in minute detail.' You can ask winners anything. But what did those winners *really* accomplish? The only thing they achieved is a euphoria, which will quickly pass. There is the trauma of tomorrow yet to come. Nothing special will be done that we know of for even the most consistent of winners when they die. There will be no special celebrity waiting lounge in the sky. From our perspective of hurtling planets, stars, galaxies, and multiple universes, winning is no more important than losing. As a matter of fact, the whole concept is total crap, but we seem to be stuck with it."

"Yeah, so?"

"So if this is a programmed attitude in our brains and it causes fifty percent of the participants to be unhappy, we should probably do something about it."

"Like what?" Elliott asked.

"Like overriding our programs with reason and teaching ourselves that it isn't so important to win. The important thing is to play hard, to try hard, to do the very best you can. If you win, it's no more important than if you lose. Maybe the contest is judged not by the result, but by the overall performance of the teams. The only losers would be the ones who fell below a line of minimum acceptable performance. Mr. and Mrs. Skill, with their leadership abilities, intelligence, and energy who usually win would still win, but they wouldn't be paraded around. They scored more points. That's fine. What's next?"

Again, Elliott stared blankly at Art.

"If you don't mind, I'm going to have more coffee," Elliott said.

"Fine."

Elliott stirred the fire, set the pot down into its center, and watched for the water to reboil. Then he refilled their cups, performing the same ritual as he had before.

"Okay, let's get back to it," Elliott said suddenly. "How do you feel about the professions people are in, their occupations, in terms of this same subject of what's important? Aside from winning and losing, a lot of people think that just what they do in everyday life is tremendously important."

"You're right." Art sat back in his chair and thought for a moment. "You know," he continued, "there are problems with that, but only if one assumes that what one does is *more* important than what anyone else does. When this happens it creates a division, a separateness from others that in my opinion is not good for those assuming a superior 'look how important I am,' attitude. Nor is it good for those who feel that what they are doing in this world is of lesser importance."

"But surely, Art, when you get down to basics, a world without brain cassettes, you have to feel that some occupations are more important in this world than others."

"Not at all. In the real life we've been speaking about, the world of billions of galaxies and the concepts of eternity and infinity, why should any one thing we do be more important than anything someone else does? All any of us can hope is that we find things to do that we *feel* are rewarding, that keep us happily occupied, and allow us to cherish the experience. Why place a scale of importance on it?"

"I'm not sure I go along with that real-world perspective or not. I think that people must have a feeling of self-importance in their work, to feel pride, a sense of identity, and achievement."

"Wait a minute, Elliott, I'm not saying that a person shouldn't feel self-important. I'm saying that the person shouldn't feel *more* important than anyone else. Let's all have a very high level of self-importance. But let's all keep it on the same general level. That's what I'm saying. There is no occupation you can name that in my opinion is more important than any other."

"I think you're nuts."

"I think we're both nuts," Art replied immediately.

"You're right. Okay, I'll name a few occupations and you give me your comments on them."

"Fine."

"Let's start, then, with artists, a sculptor or a painter or a violinist. They bring their talents to the whole world. Surely, for the sake of argument, they deserve a higher rating on a scale of importance than, say, a night watchman."

"Why? It's nice for them if they enjoy it, but I don't think it has any more importance than anything else. Creating a beautiful painting, in other words, is not any more important than someone guarding a factory or you and me just sitting around at this campsite."

"It's hardly in the same category, Art."

"I don't agree. View the importance of art against the mystery of a galactic perspective again. How does it stand out? It is nice. It is a good thing. But what has the great artist really done? To be great in the first place he or she had to have some genetic predisposition for it."

"Maybe or maybe not, Art."

"So then how did Mozart write a great symphony at age seven? Why are there genius piano players at age ten? Or to go to an extreme, if you are born without fingers and retarded mentally, you can hardly figure to reach artistic heights. The genetic material must be there. Any good teacher or coach will tell you that. The artist had nothing to do with creating his or her own genetic material."

"I suppose I really have to agree with you there," Elliott said. "I always wanted to be a painter. Not even a great one. I just wanted to paint. At a relatively early age, I believe fourteen, the art instructor at my high school said I was hopeless, that I should try something else, that I just didn't have the eye for it."

"Did you give it up?"

"Not really. I still thought I had it inside me. I kept taking the courses but I couldn't get anywhere. Then when I became a high school English teacher, I worked with every art teacher I could find. All of whom told me it was hopeless. The innate ability was not there or maybe it's there and I can't find the code to unlock it."

"So there you are. Whether that genetic material is wired into place at birth or created or introduced by conditioning or trauma soon thereafter makes no difference. The point is that the artist had nothing much to do with the initial capacity. Nor did he have much to do with the skill levels of his early instructors and coaches. Nor did he have choice over his guardians, who probably gave him encouragement and paid for all or part of his training. So instead of an artist patting himself on the back and feeling smug and self-important, he should merely be grateful that Nature and luck teamed up to give him the brain programs that worked together to create the artistic ability. He should also be grateful for the chance happenings that allowed them to be recognized. An artist who has reached the top of his field should think nothing of walking into the cafeteria at his local sewage works and having lunch with the boys. What *they* do, what their role here is on Earth is no less important than the artist's. I might add that that single fact is reinforced by the fact that none of us knows what our role should be here, anyway, or even if we are supposed to have a role."

"Okay," Elliott said. "Let's forget artists and go to something far different. Let's go to generals and admirals, military leaders. How do you feel they rate on the scale of importance?"

"The same way. They are equal. What is a general doing anyway? What he is doing is madness. If the people of the world could find a way to trust each other, we wouldn't need generals. But we have them. With their authority over life and death and the command of others, they have this sense of self-importance. Like most corporate and other civilian leaders, generals even dress themselves to reflect and reinforce the authority of their role and their importance. A general wears a uniform with stars. A civilian chief executive officer of a large, publicly held corporation more often than not wears a dark, striped suit, starched shirt and tie as reinforcement. This dress ties in with a demeanor that shouts: 'Boy, do I know what I'm doing.' Now these leaders do play a part in society by using their respective skills. But that's the long and the short of it. Ask any of them why we weren't born with a third eye in the back of our heads. They can't tell you. Nobody can. Against the reality of billions of galaxies and so forth, they are simply equal to you, me, and everyone else except they may not necessarily know that, they haven't got it all figured out."

"Are you also saying, Art, that a general and his civilian counterparts should be humble? That they can lead being humble?"

"No, I think in that sense it's the wrong use of the word. You can be imbued with a sense of inflated self-importance and still act humble. What you actually have to *feel,* under a real-life perspective of hurtling galaxies, is that what you are doing is not any *more* or any *less* important than anything else. I keep repeating myself on that point. Humility then is automatically real; it won't negatively affect your performance. If you know how to do something well, you'll still do it well. You can still be a respected leader while feeling a deep sense of humility."

"Okay, what about comedians, to go to another extreme? They are in the business of making people laugh. How do you perceive their sense of importance?"

"I don't think comedians or actors in general are that much different from a general, a brick mason, or anyone else who has some special knowledge or skill, although most think they are. You know the story. They can be on stage one minute making you fall down laughing; the next day you spot them in the hotel coffee shop and they won't even nod their heads or sign an autograph for your kid. Many of them think they're that important. After all, their names are known. They are seen in movies, on TV, and on the stage. Like a lot of other celebrities they think this is really some big deal. But it doesn't mean anything. To make things worse, some of them will even *dramatize* how important they are. A comedian's mother might be dying from terminal cancer, his son a hopeless drug addict, his finances in ruin because of a crooked manager, but the show must go on. There he or she is on stage doing their important role act.

Please spare me. Comedians, like anyone else, need that real-life, galactic perspective. What they do is great. But it's no more important than what the fellow who guards the stage door does."

"What about journalists, Art, your favorite people?"

"Oh, we can't leave them out can we?"

"I didn't think you'd want to."

"We're not trampling on people are we?"

"No, Art, I think what you're just trying to say is, that what you do is okay, it's fine, it's great; just don't get carried away with it. Now tell me how that applies to journalists."

"Well it's true, journalists do play a significant role in our lives. Again, speaking in generalities, many do tend to look at themselves as all-important. In particular, I love the TV journalist who is covering a war or some other form of violence and is reporting to us on the spot with bullets flying over his or her head. The reporter usually reflects a false sense of dedication, which translates into 'look at how important what I'm doing is. And how brave I am.' Now it's nice to know that bullets are flying somewhere so that we can avoid the place, but please spare me the dedication and the inflated importance. The same holds true in so many of the other professions and occupations: teachers, historians, ship captains, politicians, foremen, managers, maître d's. Too many of them are obsessed with this sense of role importance."

"By that last statement I take it you believe that there are some people in this world who have this real-life, galactic perspective you have been describing."

"I think there are many, quite definitely."

"Just as a matter of curiosity, you mentioned historians as being imbued with role importance. How is that?"

"Oh brother," Art replied rather excitedly. "These people think that chronicling every little event in history is one of the most important things we can do. But why? What the devil have we learned from history? The human condition remains a sour one. Let them collect their facts. Let them record history, but it's no more important of a profession than carpentry or lanyard-making. I sometimes think we'd all be better off forgetting history. Simply look at reality as it is today and start fresh."

"All right," Elliott said. "Let me throw you a curve ball. Tell me that you don't think mothers are important."

Elliott had a whimsical grin on his face.

Art smiled as well.

"Well, that is a tough one, but let's look at it. The experience of being a mother can be wonderful. But it's not an all-important experience. You can have a perfectly wonderful life and never be a mother or a father. There is no overwhelming reason that we know of why we have to reproduce to perpetuate humanness on this planet. If we all died off during the next generation instead of 4.5 billion years from now when the sun goes out, what difference will it make? To whom will it make a difference? And speaking of mothers, I'd like to get one more thing off my chest. I dislike it personally when a mother looks at a child as her creation. Not unlike the great artist, she was only a part of the process. Sperm was released, an egg was fertilized, and through some process, the reasons for which we have absolutely no knowledge, a life was begun and nurtured in a womb that was already there. In other words, the only thing that mother had to do to have a child was have intercourse at the right time. Everything else was done for her. All the organs to nurture the growing fetus were there. Mothers, in fact, don't have a say-so in anything creative regarding their babies after the right sperm cells hit the egg, unless they are into drugs or an artificial process. The most that mothers have done during this initial process was go through discomfort. Now I'm not downgrading that. It is all very nice being a mother, a satisfying experience that is certainly equal to being recognized as a top-notch bowler. However, it is not something that is more important than other services one can perform."

Elliott got up from his chair and rinsed his coffee cup with some water from a large thermos. As he turned back to where Art was sitting, he said, "Now let me get this straight again. You're not contending that a person shouldn't work hard at what he or she does— being a mother, a football coach, an artist, a general, a corporate leader—simply because each is no more important than anyone else?"

"No, I'm not saying that at all. You can work as hard as you want at something. You can be as driven as you want, if that makes you happy. Be a perfectionist if you want. You can actually do all those things and still not have an inflated sense of importance. You can be the head of a ten-billion-dollar corporation and still not feel any more important as a person inhabiting this planet than somebody on welfare or in prison. And if you achieve that way of thinking, you'll find life more rewarding because you have eliminated the separateness between you and others. In order for all people to feel some reasonable degree of contentment, the first things we have to achieve are attitudes that allow all of us to feel equal with one another. Aren't you getting hungry?"

"I am."

"What do you think we should eat tonight?"

"We have some hot dogs in the cooler. We could hike down to the store to get buns and all the fixings for a first-class weenie roast before it gets dark."

"My mouth is watering already. Let's do it," Art said.

"Great. Except one last bit of conversation before we leave."

"What about?"

"It seems in our little conversation today we dwelled more on importance as it relates to our roles in life, our occupations and experiences. Now surely there must be things in life against this great real-life perspective you refer to—us versus the planets and galaxies—that are more important than other things."

"Well there are, Elliott."

"What are they?"

"To take the most obvious, it's more important to love people than to abuse them. Along that same line of thought, it is more important, in general, to fine-tune and focus on the more positive emotions and characteristics with which we are or can be imbued."

"Like what?"

"Like love, kindness, generosity, acceptance, trust, consideration, sensitivity, politeness, respect, and so forth—the greater use of which would make life here a much more pleasant experience."

"And what else is important?"

"Making an attempt to determine what you like to do in life, what will make it a more meaningful experience for you, and then making the attempt to do it. That's important. One should attempt to do so with a perspective that will not cause wild leaps of euphoria or disappointment based on the result. The attitude should be, 'It was something to try, it didn't work. Let's try something else.' Or, 'it did work and isn't that nice.' Period. Not worrying about, 'Gee, with what I've got going for me I can only be a draftsman, not an architect, and architects are more important.' It's valuable to realize that we are all equally important in just the fact that we inhabit the Earth. Don't worry that what you are doing isn't perceived by others as important. If they don't see your importance as an individual, then *their* heads are in the sand, not yours. Avoid them. Just making it through this life with a reasonable level of relatively consistent and positive emotions is an important achievement."

"And what else is important, Art?"

"You're dragging this out. You don't taste the hot dogs?"

"Keep going."

"All right. There are certain other things that are very important. Like attempting to reprogram your brain if you have violent or angry tendencies. For example, rage is abusive, so pinpoint those tendencies in yourself and watch them. Then work to get rid of them. Just the gesture of attempt will help ease the plight of those around you. I think it's also very helpful to take responsibility for what is happening in your life, even though your circumstances might render you helpless. The mental exercise of taking responsibility for everything that happens to you regardless of what you think might be the truth, will make you less likely to blame others, to generate anger, to be abusive to others. While I am at it, I think it is critically important that you keep your word. If you shake hands on something, if you promise something, then do it, no matter what. There is nothing quite so mentally therapeutic as being honest and feeling that you can be trusted to keep agreements. If the whole world could be more trusting on even simple oral agreements, we would be so much better off. There would be so much more harmony."

"What else?"

"I'm sure there are other things, but that's enough for now. So let me get my boots on and we're off."

The two men went into their tent, took off the sneakers they were wearing, and put on hiking boots. Then, after carefully putting out the fire, they started walking down one of the trails leading from their campsite to the convenience store.

As they had done weeks before in Chicago's Lincoln Park, they began discussing the merits of various brands of hot dogs. They could never agree. But it wasn't important.

THE POINT

The purpose program we have running in our brains will frequently cause us to view the things we do with an unbalanced sense of importance. We then begin to see ourselves as important in comparison to others, whose work we perceive as less important. The result is arrogance and snobbery, which cause pain to those who become victims of our actions and innuendo. We all know what it's like to be around people like that.

Under Art Meyer's galactic viewpoint, it's fine to feel that what we are doing is important at the moment, but only insofar as giving the job our total focus. In terms of being important to the future of the Earth, what we are doing, even as a government leader, has no real significance in a galactic time frame that spans billions of years and more.

I have known many men who have been corporate leaders, CEOs who have understood this quite well. They worked their tails off. They were tough when they needed to be. They watched the details, but they never got carried away with their sense of importance.

On the other hand, we have all dealt with people at the lowest levels of authority, who thought the world started and stopped with them. So this purpose program, which can create an inflated sense of importance, can reach into all areas of life. For those who are in the vicinity of these people, it can be one of the most discomforting brain tricks of all.

20

The Flawed Brain

Ed Sanders was sitting alone in the basement Rathskeller located in the union building at the University of Wisconsin. It was a Sunday afternoon and he had called his brother, Roy, a neuroresearcher employed by the university, to meet him for a beer.

Ed's home was in a suburb of Madison, so he decided to drive over early. It was cold and snowy outside; Ed had to park a few blocks from the union. The Rathskeller was a famed meeting place for the college crowd. It's decor was part German, part collegiate. Large round tables were interspersed with smaller ones. The floor was inlaid with slabs of tile. Dark walnut wood covered some of the wall area, which was decorated with round, brass, teutonic plaques. At the far end, a sweep of windows overlooked an ice-covered Lake Mendota.

The area was broad and bright, but it was rather empty today. There was a handful of student groups conversing quietly. Others were sitting alone reading or studying.

Ed was facing the broad, open entrance to the Rathskeller and soon saw his brother slowly sauntering up the hallway, gaping up at old, black plaques that hung high near the ceiling. The plaques dated back to the turn of the century and carried the names of senior men inducted each year into the university's Iron Cross honorary society.

Roy entered the room, walked to Ed, and saw that he already had a beer. He walked to the long refreshment bar to order one of his own and then sat with Ed at one of the large, round tables.

"What took you so long?" Ed asked.

"What do you mean?" Roy replied, looking at his watch. "I'm only two minutes late, for pete's sake."

"Oh, come on," Ed said. "I saw you looking up at those old plaques, trying to find your name."

"I see. This is your way of reminding me again that my name is up there and yours isn't. I just hope that that doesn't lead to your usual reminder about me being a big-time scientist, while *you're* just a low-life insurance man—at least not until I've had a couple of beers. Then maybe I can handle the usual guilt trip."

Ed laughed.

"I think you're beginning to catch on."

"Beginning? Hell, I caught on when I was 10 and you were 7. You did everything possible to hassle me then and you still haven't stopped."

"Yeah, well look what a tonic that's been. By being hostile to you, I have a happy home life."

"What a break for you," Roy said, grinning., "And forgetting that, I'm happy you called. I felt like getting out."

"Me, too."

They sat in silence for a while, watching the students at other tables.

"So tell me, Roy, what did you think of that last article in the newspaper about Ilyich Barkeloff?"

"I thought it was great."

"I hope I can be that sharp at that age. Hell, I'd just be happy to live to that age."

"I know what you mean. But what really interested me most was a tangential statement he made about the brain being flawed."

"I don't think I remember that."

"It was there all right. He claimed that the brain is defective, as he called it, for twentieth-century living.

"But you study the brain everyday, Roy. That's your business. So why should the idea that the brain has defects come as any surprise to you?"

"Because the defects Ilyich talked about haven't anything to do with brain disease, like some malady affecting cellular structure or the connecting devices and so forth. The point he touched on is that it's the basic *design* of the brain that's defective. In my work we haven't been looking for that. We've focused on studying what makes the brain tick in general."

"So then, what concerns you?"

"Well, first of all, it never dawned on me that the brain might have natural defects. Second, I think there might have been some oversight here."

"What do you mean?"

"I think what Ilyich was driving at is that our brains today are betwixt and between. We have the rationality that the lobes of our cerebral cortex give us—something that grew as we emerged from our animal-like states—but rationality can be overpowered by the limbic programs that remain: the drive for power, territory, and so forth. I think this might have been an oversight, something the Creator or whatever just overlooked or never thought about. Maybe it's just part of some process. Since reading that statement by Ilyich, I am becoming convinced that we do have brains that are flawed, though I hope only temporarily."

"I don't know, Roy, I'm not sure I like that idea."

Roy smiled at Ed, thought a moment, and stood up.

"All right. Let me just see if I can find a copy of today's newspaper."

Ed looked surprised as he watched Roy push his chair back, rise energetically, and start to walk through the Rathskeller looking at the tables as he searched for a Sunday paper that somebody might have left behind. Ed saw him ask a group of students for permission to take a paper resting on a chair. They nodded and he returned. The paper was thick and the sections were out of order.

He began thumbing through, looking for the first section. When he found it he said, "Okay, let me read just a few headlines to get this discussion in perspective: 'Kidnapped Americans Released in Colombia.' That's a good start. Now why, Ed, should anyone's rational brain impel them to kidnap someone? Here's another article." He read, " 'Picture Clears on Life of Girl in Custody Fight.' This is about two divorced parents fighting over the custody of their child, who the mother has hidden away in another country. The father is described as being despondent, in mental anguish." Roy looked up. "The picture I'm trying to paint here Ed, is of things we hear about and experience every day but that just don't make rational sense. These have to be the limbic drives at work. Like this next

article, 'Black South African province is battling the enemy within.'
Let me read a paragraph, 'In this bloodied eastern province of Natal,
blacks continue massacring each other, mutilating each other, and
torching each other's houses.' You see what I mean? Power and
territorialism."

Ed looked quizzical as Roy turned more pages.

"How about this? 'City Police Ranks Hit 20-year Low in Chicago.'
This article says that Chicago is only operating with 11,657 policemen,
about 1,300 fewer than it should be. Now, why would an up-to-
date brain system drive us to require that much protection from
one another? Oh, here's another good one. 'Because of the 1990 Census,
Political Rivals Have Been Secretly Mapping Strategies on Redistricting.' It says that millions are being spent by our two major political
parties to make sure they don't lose power in a legitimate redistricting.
Tell me, Ed, is that the right thing for people who are governing
us to do? Why weren't our brains modified to lower our limbic power
surge so that we could always identify the right thing to do and
then do it? Here's another qood one, dateline Cincinnati. Let me
read the first paragraph verbatim, 'A hospital here has paid $2.3
million to settle all lawsuits filed by families of 26 patients who a
former nurse's aide has confessed to killing.' I mean, first you have
some random, real live nut doing all that killing, then the families
of the victims hire lawyers to sue and collect from the nut's employer.
Is that what we are supposed to expect from ourselves as correct
behavior? Why not just make sure that nuts are safely removed from
society and be done with it? On the other hand, why does the brain
design in general even allow for the emergence of nuts? How much
adjustment would that have taken?

"Here's another one from Africa, dateline the Ivory Coast. Let
me quote an actual paragraph again, 'Anti-government demonstrators
stoned buses and cars in this capital and demanded freedom for
students who were beaten and detained after ending a church sit-
in.' It's hard to believe. And here, 'Lebanon Christians now battle
each other.' The story, as you must know, points out how dozens
of innocent people have been killed, hundreds wounded. And . . ."

"Wait a second," Ed interrupted. "Tell me what this is all saying."

"This is just one Sunday newspaper on one day in a rather small
community like Madison. All over this world, hundreds of millions
of people are reading newspapers similar to this one or watching

TV news, absorbing stories like those I just described. But yet none of us are really surprised by these events. Once in a great while something happens that is ghastly, so we might be shocked for a few moments, but for the most part we accept all of it as part of our normal lives. We watch movies and soap operas and read books where people are doing horrible, unkind things to each other and we accept it. We don't seem to question it, because we have these limbic drives ourselves and under certain circumstances can feel them driving us."

"I'm not sure about that, Roy. I think we question these drives a lot. As a matter of fact, I would say that most religions focus on it. They've come up with answers that have satisfied millions of people. And that's not to mention probably hundreds of millions of peaceful individuals who constantly question the violence they see or read about."

"I suppose we do question it in general. But when I read all those terrible things to you, you didn't blink an eye. Maybe if you were actually witnessing the scene, you might have, but just hearing about it didn't alarm you. Do you agree?"

"You're right, most of it was old hat."

"Being a neuroresearcher, I look at the horrors we commit on each other from the point of view of three pounds of brain, which is not what your typical theologian does. While I personally believe that there must be a God or Creator somewhere, I don't need to be guided by the viewpoints of any religionist, although I would respect those viewpoints. In other words, I can step back from it all and ask 'What exactly are we dealing with here? Is there any way that a brain scientist can explain the obviously twisted phenomena of life better than a theologian?' Do you see what I mean, Ed?"

"Yes, I think I do. So go ahead."

"To get off on a tangent for a bit, a well-known anthropologist was recently lecturing on campus and one of the points he made was that evolution does appear to have been random. Of all the millions of living organisms on Earth, it appears they could just as easily have been something other than what they turned out to be. In other words, we are the result of random forces."

"Does he know that for sure?"

"Nobody really knows anything for sure."

"So then what's your point?"

"My point is that this randomness also seems to be in conflict with the disciplines we've come to expect from the mechanical laws of science, which replicate themselves time and time again. Drop dozens of balls of the same weight from 100 feet in the air in a vacuum and every ball will hit the ground at precisely the same time."

"So you're saying that the mechanical laws of science should have applied to how we evolve."

"I think so—or the quantum laws—because things can be designed around the uncertainties. The only law that seems to apply in human life is that when a man and woman conceive as a result of intercourse, we know that a child is going to emerge from the womb and not a duck. Everything else is random: how that child will look, grow, and what kind of brain it will have. Now, what this does is inject a strong element of chance into the entire human process. In other words, because there is nothing mechanical about it, things can go haywire: obvious physical deficiencies, physical deformities, retardation, or disease immediately after birth or thereafter. There are literally thousands of physical and mental diseases we can be subjected to right in the womb or during the course of our respective lives. So the point is this: maybe it's not just the brain that is the victim of an oversight, but the process of creating random human bodies. Why couldn't this have been considerably more precise given its importance and the fact that we are often taught to see the Creator's precision in so many other things around us?"

"Yes, but it could be that we are a perfection of our own, with a purpose outside of anything else we know."

"That could be, Ed. Who can argue with that? That's why a religionist's or anyone else's viewpoint will always have some credence until we are given final, irrefutable answers. In the meantime, the fact is that we are all the result of a random reproduction process that can generate some very bad results and it is perfectly permissible, in my view as a scientist who likes things all buttoned down, to be curious and confused about it. You'll go along with that?"

"Yes, of course."

"Okay, so let's assume that there is some purpose to everything. The slow, evolutionary process we have observed on this planet has some purposeful ending to it. There might be countless other planets within the universe where our experience has been duplicated or where something else altogether is going on. Because we're not part of the big picture—we're not in Management, so to speak—we aren't being made privy to the total purpose of our universe or other universes or whatever it is that we as human beings on this very tiny planet are part of. As part of this purpose, human reproduction, including the development of the brain, is random and subject to error. Whether it's that way on other planets we have no way of knowing. But for us it's a given.

"Some of us are more imperfect than others. One person might live to the age of 60 and never have more than a cold or two. Another person might spend half his life in a hospital fighting one malady after another. Someone else might live sixty years and never do anything more violent than lose their temper occasionally. Another person might become a cold-blooded killer.

"You see what I mean, Ed? All this random imperfection is right in front of us. It's what I just read from the newspaper. It is part of the human condition. We are all imperfect. The only thing that varies is the depth."

"I don't think what you said is any great shakes, Roy. Again, let's look at religion. I think most religions have accepted our imperfections. They don't view the body as any piece of cake. There's a definite body of thought that says we are going through some trial by fire down here and better things can happen to us in another life."

"Which of course might be true. Where the study of the brain seems to take its own course is in our findings that what we think in our minds is created by the computer-like nature of our brains. For all we know, there might not be any light at the end of the tunnel, despite what some religionists contend. That thought might be just an idea we've invented."

"You mean no salvation?"

"Maybe there is, but from the viewpoint of a cold-blooded neuro-researcher, there probably isn't."

"So what does that add up to?"

"It means we have to be more concerned about our imperfect bodies and specifically our defective or flawed brains, the ones we have in our heads, which at the moment appear to be betwixt and between the animal state of our past and the supposed totally rational state of our future. Maybe there are some Eastern religionists whose members can float free of their bodies at will, up there on what they call the astral plane, but I haven't been able to do it."

"You mean that you've tried?"

"A long time ago. I bought some books written by people who belonged to the Theosophical Society. According to them they've actually traveled together on the astral plane chatting about this and that."

"And you believe it?"

"Let's say I don't disbelieve it even though I couldn't make it work."

"If you ever figure it out, Roy, why don't you book the two of us passage to Hawaii in the ether. Don't forget my wife, Evelyn, who I'm sure would go for it in a big way."

Roy laughed. "I'll keep that in mind."

"So where are we?" Ed asked.

"I think we got off on a tangent."

"You're right. Go ahead, put us back on the straight and narrow."

"What I think we lose sight of is that while most of us will freely profess that the *body* is imperfect, we've never really included the *brain* as part of the body. You don't see in the scriptures or in the writings of philosophers any mention of the flaws that exist in the brain although some philosophers have focused on mind-brain identity. That's probably because only until recently we didn't have an inkling about the brain's physical role in generating our intellect and triggering our emotions. I think most people just thought that some type of spirit or soul entered the body sometime after conception and proceeded to make up who we are. Now we know that the brain controls our minds; we need to be aware that this controller can be flawed."

"Again you're talking about design flaws, not the problems our brains share with other parts of our bodies: cancers, tumors, and such."

"Yes, we're back to the natural flaws, the limbic programs, which in some of us can be off kilter and make us do unkind or even horrible things."

Lost in thought, Ed paused and then said, "I think you were implying before that there might be a purpose for these flaws simply because, with a little effort, God could have fixed them to begin with."

"That may be true, yes."

"So, what are your thoughts on that?"

"Let's assume that our leading anthropologists, including Charles Darwin, were all absolutely right: we have evolved into humans from other life forms, perhaps as a result of random action. I can tell you, Ed, that I myself don't believe in absolute randomness. I look around me, I observe who we are and what we have done, and I can't convince myself that this was the result of purely random action, some ugly form of natural selection. I feel that a program existed to guide our evolution, at least as far as human beings are concerned. What steps took place between the time we were in the slime and where we are today was guided somehow. But whether you or I believe that this was totally random or preordained doesn't make much difference.

In what we perceive as Earth time, nothing much was done in a hurry. We are literally talking millions of years here to get from one step to another. For example, it took the Earth about 4 billion years to produce the first animal-like human, then millions of additional years to grow the extra brain cerebrum for humans to evolve as they are today. There were a lot of giant steps involved here, but the evolutionary program was in no rush. During most of the 500,000 years that Homo sapiens as we know them have existed, the brain's design was perfectly suited to its task. All the limbic, genetic drives that protect the higher animals like gorillas and help them propagate were ideally suited for man as well. Let somebody of a strange color enter the territory our prehistoric ancestors staked out and they were limbically triggered to dislike him and harm him if he didn't leave. Tribes were organized by limbic power thrust, often called the pecking order: usually decided by eye stares and perhaps some brief physical displays or scuffles. Sex was automatic, even when early humans didn't know that it produced babies. Men and women engaged in intercourse because they were triggered to do so. And it went on and on. Most of our triggered actions appeared to have been designed to help us survive and flourish in a wilderness environment. Are you following me?"

"I'm following you."

"Good. What happened then might have been a miscalculation. All of a sudden humanity began to take giant steps forward in its ability to create new and exciting things. Beginning about 12,000 years ago, in several parts of the world there was a movement out of caves and into community environments. While life was still quite physical, there was obviously greater mental activity, and as we have found in the laboratory, the brain reacts to mental stimulation. Stimulate the brain and more connections will grow. Stop using it to think and those connections begin to atrophy. So it's not unreasonable to assume that humans have made great strides in adding either connections or nerve cells or both to the brain in a relatively short period of time. But the older limbic system that kept us alive in the caves remained in the brain.

"If you look at history over the past 4,000 years, you see a lot of stops and starts. In most of the world, civilizations flourished and then were wiped out in cyclical patterns, right into the twentieth century. Look at what we humans did to Europe only 50 years ago. If the brain has an *independence* of its own, if it's an independent observer of events, as Ilyich Barkeloff pointed out, there has certainly been no good reason for it to believe that it could safely do away with its animalistic thrusts. The problem is that our civilizations and cultures are not deep. Newspaper headlines about the mayhem taking place in our cities and between countries we consider to be natural. We took great technological leaps forward since we emerged from the caves, but our brains observing our experiences independently appear to be following a slower and safer evolutionary process."

"So how would you account for it?" Ed asked.

"Who really knows? It could have been a miscalculation that wasn't supposed to have happened at all."

"What do you think was supposed to have happened?"

"Who knows? But some of our best anthropologists have pointed out that we are definitely evolving. Our very shapes have changed in just a few tens of thousands of years. We appear to have grown more cerebrum, as I said. Perhaps the miscalculation might have been in the evolvement of the brain itself. Maybe the Planners didn't really know that we would move as rapidly as we did into civilized cultures with laws and governments and morality. We might be a few thousand years ahead of schedule, which in anthropological time is like nothing. So maybe the state of our brains is indeed a temporary oversight, something that Nature itself will step in and take care of, if we don't learn to fix the problem ourselves. In other words, our brains might be slowly evolving to rid us of the drives and impulses that aren't needed in a civilized, cultured society. But in the meantime, as a species, we are still partially a throwback."

"I see." Ed was looking blankly at Roy.

"You don't think that makes any sense?"

I haven't gotten far enough with you to know if I think it makes sense or not."

Roy, who had been tense during the whole discussion, relaxed his shoulders, looked down at the floor, and laughed deeply.

"I know this all might sound a little crazy when you first hear it," Roy continued, looking up at Ed, "but the more you think about it, the more sense it can make—at least if you're open to new ideas."

"Oh, I'm open to this all right. I'm sure when I go home tonight and tell my wife that her brain is all flawed and a temporary oversight, that will go over real big."

Roy smiled again and then turned serious.

"But what if she read it in the newspaper, Ed? What if a special symposium on the subject was conducted, say at Oxford in England, with scientists like me in attendance from all the major countries of the world. Say that for weeks scientists from practically every specialty reviewed and heard papers focusing on the mayhem that humans cause one another. Asked to come to just one conclusion, a Pulitzer Prize winning scientist stands up and announces that it is very possible that the brain is flawed and might just be a temporary oversight. Would Evelyn believe it then?"

"You know, Roy, she probably would. Any time anyone with a lot of authority says something, she usually gives it some credence."

"So there you are." Roy became lost in thought for a brief instant, recovered, and then continued. "On the other hand, Ed, maybe there was no oversight. Maybe the brain has an independent sensing mechanism of its own to observe what is happening and changes accordingly in its own good time. As I mentioned before, what it has seen in the last century alone is not enough to convince it. From 1914 to 1990, it has observed nearly 92 million people murdered as the result of one war or another. The brain isn't convinced that it's time to give up its caveman characteristics."

"So you're saying that the brain might be designed to change on its own?"

"It's one thought," Roy replied. "Obviously changes in any part of our bodies have to be caused through some change in our genetic structure. But how can a gene sense anything? The brain must be tied in with some part of the process. On the other hand, if the brain is a magnificently sophisticated instrument with an independent, sensing intellect of its own, why can't it just see through the problems that our limbic, cave-dwelling drives are causing us here in a twentieth-century environment and work more quickly to neutralize these drives?"

Roy paused and then quickly answered himself.

"You know, there are a lot of possibilities here. Maybe the brain hasn't taken action on its own, because it simply requires decades or centuries of intellectual sensing, that something is wrong before a message is delivered to the genetic structure. If this is so, you have the problem that the vast majority of humans have no idea that their brains are imperfect, that something is physically wrong with the present design. There is no intense awareness that something needs to be changed, and no safety mechanism built into the brain that would allow it to see beyond this masking of the intellect. Maybe that's the problem. Or maybe it's something else. Who knows? The upshot is that we have to live with a brain design that, for some, might have been the result of problems in the Creator's workshop. I would hate to think that all this madness was not the result of some innocent miscalculation of our progress, that we as humans were meant to live absolutely forever with these raw, twisted drives."

Ed pushed his chair back and again stared blankly at Roy.

"I sure hope this building has lightning rods."

Roy smiled, relaxing a bit. "Oh, I wouldn't worry about that. Ilyich has had thoughts like these, he said, and he's going strong at 110."

"Yeah, but we may not be as lucky. I'm not sure I agree that something has to be changed in our brains before we can live peacefully. There have always been communities that have lived peaceful and gentle lives by controlling these negative emotions and feelings on their own. Take the Amish communities we see when we drive to mother's. You look at the way they live together, the way they think and share with one another. I don't see any brain flaws or mistakes in that."

Roy thought for a moment, "Yes, but look at how the Amish and similar cultures have to work at it, Ed. It's not a natural phenomenon. They isolate themselves, refusing to assimilate into the societies that surround them. They fear unleashing the limbic drives which they are trying to keep under control. The repression impacts not only their lifestyles but the depth of their religious beliefs. Such groups force enormous disciplines on themselves to keep these emotions in tow. In this sense they are very much like the cultures of the Middle East, particularly those in fundamentalist states, whose members frown on any contact with Western cultures, believing that they will become tainted from this contact, thereby unleashing the limbic emotions they've done so well to control. I happen to think that some of these fundamentalist cultures have a good point. They see that freedom of thought, speech, and expression allows violent, sex driven, wildly acquisitive, and generally bad elements of society to emerge. Strong discipline is used to keep members' brains from wreaking havoc. Strict fundamentalist cultures don't require the vast law enforcement structures of free societies. You're right, Ed. It's possible to have peaceful communities without any neutralization of the limbic drives. But look at the cost in freedom, isolation, or assimilation. Look at how much easier it would be for the world to live peaceably if our brain design or its evolutionary program were such that these limbic drives would be dampened if not totally neutralized as our general world culture, civilization, and awareness of our brain functions rose to higher levels."

"I suppose you're right," Ed said. "Under present circumstances the human brain certainly requires strong, rational disciplines to keep the limbic drives under control."

"Yes, but not everyone has that kind of strength, upbringing, or training to control the drives. Today the result continues to be the bigotry, hatred, war, and the like."

The two brothers began to look around the room. The Rathskeller was almost empty now. A clean-up crew was already at work in a far corner. Ed got up and walked to the long bar, where he ordered two more beers.

When he returned, he asked Roy: "So what's the answer to all this?"

"Who knows? And thanks for the beer. I guess the point is that we just have to be more careful. If our brains are all a bit defective, flawed in some way, temporary or not, we have to live more cautiously, paying greater attention to what we say and the actions we take. We must be more forgiving of others."

"Easy to say, Roy."

"Yeah." Roy turned away and began staring out the windows facing Lake Mendota, twisting his beer glass. Then he looked at Ed abruptly: "Damn it, Ed, maybe what we need is some world-wide regulation that makes every human being wear a badge every-day that says, 'Beware. My Brain Is Flawed.' Look at what that would do."

"Wait a second," Ed broke in. "You mean a badge that you wear on a lapel? Who would wear it?"

"Well, say it was designed to be unobtrusive. Or maybe there were several designs and variations you could choose from. The point is that you'd be required to wear it during all waking hours, and you wouldn't mind."

"I see," Ed looked at Roy as though he were a lunatic on the loose. "A badge that says 'Beware, My Brain Is Flawed.' "

"Exactly." Roy thought a moment. "Come on, let's look at what that would do for us. We would know, for example, why our mothers or siblings are sometimes irrationally mean to us, or why our fathers are abusing us. We'd see their badges that say their brains are flawed, implying a temporary oversight plaguing the world. We would know why some people cheat on their taxes. Or why some politicians will do practically anything to save their jobs. We would know why the person we work for, or the guy working next to us, is some kind of jerk. We would understand why we might have to go through the pain of a divorce if we can't get along with our spouses. We could finally fathom why murders and rapes occur. Just look at their badges. We would know why we endure the stupidity of a sexual mating dance: even in a singles bar everyone would have to wear their badge. Given the international circumstances, it is quite natural for one country to want to war on others and massacre them. Then, of course, there is bigotry and greed. Every time we would be faced with a situation where there is no justice, no fairness, we would understand why. Everybody involved would be wearing the badges.

"We would know why going on a diet is often so hard, and why some of us become addicted to drugs, alcohol, or gambling. We would understand why strong caste systems still exist in some societies. We would know what drives corporate raiders and people who are simply into buying and possessing. Even big shots would have to wear those badges. We might better understand why our sons and daughters aren't doing well in school and why we can't handle it. Many of us would be better able to accept the faults of others, no matter what those faults were. We would understand that we're not perfect, that our brains are flawed and tricking us and that we have to be careful. It would be like knowing we have a broken foot. If you know your brain is flawed, you'd be more careful about what you say, what you do, how you act. No matter what you said, you would know inwardly that you might be wrong.

"One quick look at our badges every day and we would never be sure that what we say or do is right. You'd take your best shot at everything, but now you could always see the other side. In any event, we need most of all to convince people that they are walking around with a flawed instrument. The brain doesn't want them to know that, which is probably the greatest brain trick of all. And so to remind us everyday, we have that damned badge. If we don't wear a badge as a constant reminder, the brain will snap us immediately back into thinking that we are okay, totally rational without any caveman drives. We would have other forms of communication, complete with billboards all over the world to reinforce the whole idea. The copy could read: 'Don't forget. Your brain is flawed.' "

"And if somebody would point out," Ed said, "like you did to me, that our brains have something like 1,000 trillion connections that all grow out of a fertilized egg you can't even see, then it shouldn't be any great surprise that there are a few flaws. Just look at all the defects we have in our automobiles and other products; we don't grow them from some tiny eggs. We stamp them out of metal and plastic and other things so we can double check and triple check them. Still we have flaws."

Roy chuckled.

"Who knows," Roy said, "maybe if we had these constant reminders about our flawed brains, we'd have more incentive not to wait for Nature to fix the problem. We could fix them ourselves. We're not really that far away from correcting a lot of our physical disorders with changes in the genetic code. There is this enormous genome program going on that is intended to map out the entire code. That will be the start. It will be like uncovering the tip of an iceberg, but it will allow us to begin to think about how we might change ourselves both physically and mentally. At some point, we might have the tools to fix our brains, if we can agree on what to fix and how to fix it. Literally, we could redesign our brains ourselves to assure that those limbic drives are no longer troublesome, so that we can live in peace and harmony while still enjoying the positive emotions of life."

"If that's possible."

"Oh, I think it is. Look at Barkeloff. He has worked hard at transcending the limbic emotional thrusts and impulses that have caused most of our problems. He's not going to start any wars or cheat or lie or get into some power game. Yet he seems pretty happy. You see? This concept can be the start of true worldwide democracy. The whole human race is flawed with a brain that is still part primitive. Everyone remains equal in the human experience."

"But some people are more flawed than others. You'd have to admit that, Roy."

"Well, just look around you. Someone who is out there maniacally seeking power and physically abusing people is more a victim of these throwback brain programs than you or me, at least in that vertical sense. But that person, on the other hand, might not have some other addiction . . . like having ten locks on his front door."

"Locks?"

"Some kind, older gentleman living in a peaceful suburb is frightened of people around him. He has a high security program. And so he has locks everywhere. But it's driving his wife nuts because of all the keys she has to carry."

Ed chuckled and said, "Let's say that some of the results of the throwback programs are more abusive than others."

"Depending on who the victim is. If you find yourself working for or living with a real jerk, that isn't as bad as being physically abused, but it's certainly a form of torture."

Roy turned to the window again as if Ed weren't present. After a minute or two he turned to Ed, who was still looking quizzical and said:

"What do you think of the badge idea, I mean seriously?"

"Roy, I think it's one of the greatest ideas ever conceived. I hope it works and I'll support you if you decide to quit your job and travel the world to try to get the thing done. In the meantime," he looked at his watch, "Evelyn is roasting a chicken for the family and while I'm overwhelmed with your badge idea, my flawed brain is creating a fear that if I'm late, Evelyn will say some negative things and I will feel depressed. So with that as an excuse, dear brother, I will leave you now to give you additional space to think about how you can get everyone in the world to wear that badge."

Ed got up, shook Roy's hand, and left.

Roy spent some time staring out the wide windows again, watching the iceboats sailing by. Then he took a pad of paper and a pencil from his pocket and began designing the badge.

THE POINT

Most of us will admit that we aren't perfect. After doing some asinine thing, we'll say, "Who's perfect?" but we usually say it tongue in cheek.

Yet, if we pick up one Sunday newspaper, as Dr. Roy Sanders did, and read about all the miserable things we're doing to one another in a single day, we don't need to be rocket scientists to conclude that the brains that impel us to do these things must be flawed in some way. Not only with serious physical imperfections that might cause some of us to exhibit high levels of violence and sexual perversion, but with limbic wiring that makes all of us react to certain circumstances with irrational attitudes.

These irrational attitudes are brain tricks. Our spouses might have to work late, night after night, and our brains might provoke us to begin thinking that our spouses are unfaithful. A family of a different race moves next door to us and our brains launch into unthinking hatred. Another driver accidentally cuts in front of us and we begin yelling out obscenities. Our father tells us we'll never amount to anything because he might be envious of his own offspring.

We all have flawed, throwback brains, but because each brain is different, the limbic drives exhibit themselves differently in each of us.

It is hard to admit to ourselves and to others that our brains are flawed. I wore a replica of Dr. Sanders's proposed badge to a casual dinner party to gauge the reactions to it. When people saw it, they would stare at it and for the most part, say nothing. When I asked others to put it on, they refused, except for a close friend who is a Number Three on Ed Grogan's scale of humanity (described in another chapter). He had no problem wearing it. I even had trouble getting it back.

We must fight any urge not to admit that our brains are flawed. Make up a stick-on badge that says "My brain is flawed" and wear it around the house when no one is home. It can do wonders for your humility, which you'll need when you attempt to trick your brain into being a positive force for you when it counts.

Ultimately, you need to be able to say to yourself: "My brain is flawed, it can use some fixing, let's get to work."

21

The Human Genome

Carl Ullman looked over his notes as he readied himself for another interview. He was in Studio A of radio station WCRK in San Francisco. His program, "Unlimited Reality," was syndicated to dozens of public service radio stations throughout the nation.

His guest, once again, was Henry Heiman, whose offbeat views received an unusually high listener response on two previous interviews.

Part of WCRK's revenues came from the sale of program tapes. The station manager informed Ullman that his last interview with Heiman—on the scales of time, space, and size—had set a station record in tape sales. Ullman had already decided to bring the odd little man back.

Not long ago, Ullman received a postcard from a regular listener asking him if Henry Heiman could be interviewed on the subject of mapping the human genome, that schematic blueprint that determines the makeup of the entire human body, including the brain. Perfect, Ullman thought. He had wanted to do something on the genome and had already made some casual inquiries at Berkeley about locating a geneticist who could make clear to his lay audience what this whole thing was about. In 1990, Congress authorized a fifteen-year allocation of $3 billion to map the human genetic system. Publicity for this was scant despite the amount of money involved and the enormity of the effort.

Ullman looked up at the clock, five minutes to show time. This appeared to be Heiman's habit, to arrive just when Ullman began to think which program he could re-run if his guest failed to turn up.

251

Two minutes later, the thick, insulated studio door opened and Heiman walked in. Ullman stood up to greet him.

"Just in the nick of time again, Henry."

"Oh, you never have to worry about me, Mr. Ullman. The Union Street bus I take at this time of the day is very reliable. I take a lot of buses in this city and I can tell you almost precisely how they'll run at which hour. Just last week . . ."

"Excuse me, Henry, but we only have a minute and I wanted to run through this genome subject, some of the questions I intend to ask."

"That won't be necessary," Henry replied as he sat down opposite Ullman, the microphone between them. "I know quite a bit about the subject and I'm sure we'll have no problem."

"Well, that's great Henry," Ullman responded, trying to hide his skepticism. "And I must tell you that you should be proud of yourself. That last interview we did set a record in tape sales."

"What do you mean?"

"We tape all of these programs, and listeners who want copies write in and order them. Your last tape set a record. You should be proud of that."

"I don't know why, Mr. Ullman. I only said what I thought."

"But people really liked it."

"Look, Mr. Ullman, a lot of people liked Harpo Marx. I try not to be swayed by what other people like. I know what I like and in this world of violence and selfish-minded thinking, that's really all I can cope with."

Ullman could see that Henry was getting warmed up. The timing was perfect. Out of the corner of his eye he saw the engineer through the control room glass begin to count down.

"We're about ready to begin," Ullman said.

"That's fine."

The opening music filled the room. As it quieted, Ullman began.

"Hello, this is Carl Ullman with another edition of 'Unlimited Reality.' Our guest today has become a favorite with many of our listeners. He's Henry Heiman. Usually when I introduce guests on this show, I have to spend some time reading off their credentials. But Henry has no official credentials to speak of. As he told me on a bus when I first met him six months ago, he reads a lot. Those are his credentials. But I might add that Henry seems to interpret what he reads in a rather unorthodox way, which I think makes him perfect for the subject we're discussing today, the human genome project. Henry, why don't you start by describing just exactly what the genome project is."

"The genome, Mr. Ullman, is the genetic system. And the human genome is the human genetic system, versus the mouse genome, for example. Genome is a label that scientists have put on all this and so we all go along."

"And my understanding is that this subject has only been studied for a relatively short time."

"That's true with respect to its technical workings; for example, what a DNA molecule actually looks like and all that. But the subject of genetics and heredity goes back a hundred years or more. Gregor Mendel, the nineteenth-century botanist, came to some very interesting conclusions watching plant life and such."

"Why did it take so long to get to the technical workings?"

"Because we are dealing with some incredibly minute things, here. Let's start with the fact, Mr. Ullman, that you cannot see a single cell with the naked eye. Go ahead, look at your hand."

Ullman did.

"Can you see a cell, an individual cell?"

"No, I really can't say that I can, Henry."

"But if we had a microscope here and you were peeling from too much sunburn, and we put a sliver of that skin under a microscope, you could see a cell."

"Yes, I imagine I could."

"Now if we had a really strong microscope we could see that this tiny cell, not visible to our naked eye, is like some factory machine with a number of different components, all working at their specific job."

"Yes, I've seen photographs of cells."

"And with that same microscope we could see the nucleus. Inside what scientists call its envelope are where the chromosomes are located—all 46 of them. They make up the human genome, but that's just the beginning."

"What do you mean?"

"I mean it takes an electron microscope, our very strongest, to begin to make out the DNA coils that make up each chromosome. We can make out these coils because they are so thick. If you stretched a coil out, its thickness would be three or four billionths of a centimeter. You can't see that with any microscope we have."

"I see."

"You see, Mr. Ullman! You see what?" Heiman suddenly stood up, agitated. *"How can you see, Mr. Ullman? How can anyone see? Do you realize how small these things are that we are talking about?"*

Henry stared at Ullman for an instant and took his seat, quickly calming down.

"Please forgive me, Mr. Ullman. You know how I get with these matters. I find them all utterly amazing and yet when I talk to you or anyone about them it is as if no one really wants to comprehend the miraculous nature of the technical workings we are discovering. It's as if we are programmed not to want to work to comprehend them. Even scientists who deal with these facts every day seem not to comprehend the enormity of what they are dealing with."

"I heard what you said, Henry. I'm just trying to follow you." Ullman had felt his pulse rate speed up when Henry started to shout. But seeing Henry quickly get a grip on himself helped Ullman do the same.

"Now, Henry," Ullman appeared to be talking with exaggerated calmness, "you were talking about the fact that we can't make out an extended coil with our best electron microscope. I'm assuming it's our DNA coils that the world is currently trying to map. So how are we going to do it?"

"Very good, Mr. Ullman. That has been the problem. Over the past forty years or so, the problem has been solved with some complicated x-ray procedures, which first allowed Nobel laureates, James Watson and Francis Crick, to figure out the DNA's helix shape. Today's x-ray procedures are really sophisticated."

Heiman began staring to his left. Ullman looked where Henry was looking and saw nothing. He quickly realized Henry was simply lost in thought.

"Ah, so what's the upshot of all this?" Ullman blurted out.

"Oh, yes, the upshot."

Henry, alert now, paused as he fished around in his shirt pocket and pulled out a piece of thread about two inches long.

"This is the upshot, Mr. Ullman."

"That piece of thread?"

"Yes."

Ullman quickly described the thread to the audience.

"Now tell us, Henry, why that is the upshot?"

"If we were to take all the DNA coils out of the chromosomes in just one of our cells and fully extended them, then attached them together, they would be about six feet long.

"The DNA from each chromosome is about two inches long and there are 46 of them. So what I did was take 46 tiny fibers and twist them together to make this two-inch thread. The result is a replica of the DNA from just one cell. Of course, you couldn't see a real DNA thread because its diameter is so incredibly thin."

"That's extremely interesting, Henry. Please continue."

"Well, let me tell you what's involved here. Let's really make an effort at pretending that this piece of thread is actually DNA from one cell, all woven together."

"That's fine, Henry, we'll visualize it as DNA."

"What you have on this thread are about 100,000 genes and maybe a lot more. Now the word 'gene' is simply a label given to a small section of a DNA coil, or thread as we're now calling it. I respect scientific labels, but I like my own as well. They are only all words. Of course, not everyone feels the same way . . ."

"I agree," Ullman interrupted. "Call anything you want whatever you want."

"Thank you. What's critical here is that this two-inch thread has about 20 billion bits of information on it. If you are into computers, you know it takes about 6 bits of information to form a single letter or number. So what we really have on this thread are 3 billion letters. But there are only four letters. In other words there are 3 billion copies of four letters in a jumbled type of sequence. Are you with me?"

"Yes, I think so."

"Each letter represents one of four different proteins that, when combined in certain proportions, can create thousands of other proteins that form the workings of our body. Something similar might be a four-color printing press: with subtle combinations it can create thousands of different colors. Now I'm not going to go through all the math for you. Suffice it to say that it would take about 300,000 pages set in the type style of a standard encyclopedia to record all the letters on this thread I'm holding between my fingers. And that's what the mapping of the human genome system is all about. In a sense we are taking something the size of this thread, but in a diameter that is totally invisible to our strongest microscopes, and copying the letters. We will literally end up with about 300 volumes of letters, each about the size of an encyclopedia volume. It will in fact be a book of life."

"Fascinating."

"I should say so," Heiman said, still staring at the piece of thread.

"Somewhere in those 300,000 pages," he continued, "will be the coding for the human eye, in another part the heart, the liver, the leg, the elbow, the thumbnail, the teeth, the nasal passage, the ear drum, the spinal column, the cheek bone, the stomach, and . . . the human brain with among so many other things, its hard-wired, limbic program all ready to be sprung on society. Mind-boggling as this fact is, all that coding, all those 300,000 pages, come out of a thread that's probably smaller than this, when you consider that not all of the DNA is useful."

"That's not only incredible, it makes life sound sort of mechanical."

"Not just mechanical, but embarrassingly unfocused as well. After all, there is a thread just like this one in practically every cell in our bodies. For example, in every cell in our heart, there is DNA coding that can make a brain. In every DNA cell on our fingers, there is coding that can make a heart. Is this unreal? Most of these cells can reproduce within 24 hours and with some types of cells, much faster. Can you imagine how it's possible to duplicate 300 encyclopedia volumes that quickly inside something as small as a cell?"

Heiman continued to stare at the thread.

"This thread is you, Mr. Ullman. When your mother and father had intercourse, a thread in the one sperm cell that penetrated your mother's egg literally combined with a similar thread in that egg, which became the first cell. Just one cell, Mr. Ullman, that's all you were. Those two threads combined, were broken up into 46 different chromosomes or sections, and made ready to do their work. How your dad's sperm and your mom's egg had only 23 chromosomes each to form a new cell with the correct sum of 46 is a miracle of technology all its own."

Ullman looked a bit stunned as Henry fished through another shirt pocket and brought out one more thread.

"Here's your mom's thread and here's your dad's; all they did was combine to create you." Heiman began twisting them together.

"So you ended up having half of your dad's genetic letters and half of your mom's. This section down here . . . ," he pointed to the end of the thread, "determined whether you would be a boy or a girl. This is what the scientists in effect call the 'X' or 'Y' section. That's all the difference it was. All this fuss about being a boy or a girl, all this fanaticism about sex, and all it derives from is a little section of the DNA thread. That's the human genome in a nutshell, Mr. Ullman. If that doesn't make you feel meaningless, nothing will. Think about the fact that every living organism—from a rat to a tree to a potato to a mosquito to a snake—has this same piece of thread in every cell. It may not be as long, but the same four letters are there in different arrangements. Everything comes out of that same book of life. That makes us all no better than a potato, if you get the idea. Your origins are about the same."

"So that's the genome," Ullman said weakly.

"That's the genome."

"This is difficult to comprehend."

"What's even more mind wrenching is the fact that the x-rays of a section of DNA look like a bar code, almost precisely like those codes that companies put on their products to be scanned at checkout counters. In fact, it is the same kind of system. What that means is that the human body and the organisms of the world are somehow coded like a can of tuna."

"This is hard to believe."

Henry reached in his pocket and pulled out some sheets of paper.

"I carry these with me, from time to time, Mr. Ullman. They are copies of photos from a book I was reading about this subject. These are reproductions of the DNA x-rays. Look at them."

Ullman took them and described them to the audience.

"They certainly do look a lot like bar codes," he said.

"They do indeed. You can imagine how many of these x-ray reproductions will need to be studied to track the 3 billion letters."

"This is incredible," said Ullman, staring at the bar codes.

"I have trouble absorbing this information myself, Mr. Ullman, and I've been following it quite a while. As a matter of fact, many of the geneticists who have been uncovering all of this haven't really absorbed it. You would be amazed at the jealousies among them, the competition to be first with an announcement. I mean here we are doing probably the most important work on this planet and these people can't rise above it. They are making these absolutely marvelous discoveries, but they haven't digested how the very genetic letters they are studying are impelling them into these jealousies and all the other stupid things our genetics give us a predisposition for. So don't feel bad, Mr. Ullman, if you can't comprehend all this. You are in good company."

"Thank you, Henry."

"Do you know what one of the telling arguments was that influenced the Congress to appropriate the $3 billion for this research, which is less than the cost of one space shuttle and all the support apparatus? I mean this absolutely enormously important work?"

"No, what was it?"

"It was that the Japanese might do it before we do. *Do you believe that?*" Henry started to rise excitedly, then quickly caught himself and calmed down.

"Excuse me, Mr. Ullman, I almost went off again."

"That's okay, I understand."

"Thank you. The point is that here we have discovered this remarkable genetic system, something the entire world needs to know about, something the entire world should work on together, something that eventually will do the entire world a great deal of good . . . and we need to resort to a limbic-based power argument about which country is likely to do it first! The scientists who appeared before the congressional committee went right along with it. 'Oh yes,' they said. 'The Japanese are already at work on this.' Of course anything the Japanese do terrifies our leaders. I saw this testimony on a cable station I watch and I found it nauseating. It was all I could do to refrain from using my remote channel switcher. All I could conclude is that our scientists are going about this by the numbers and this work is doing nothing to neutralize their competitive and petty attitudes."

Ullman saw how upset Henry was becoming and decided to steer the interview in another direction.

"Tell me, Henry, how should we feel about this genome project? What is it supposed to mean to us?"

"It means basically that we have discovered what all the great philosophers, scientists, and religionists throughout history could only guess at, namely, the secret of life. Amazingly enough, in our generation, Mr. Ullman, we have discovered that the secret of organic life is the result of what happens with this thread."

Henry held up the two threads that he had twisted together.

"That is life?" Ullman asked with bemusement.

"This is it. Pick up an ordinary book on sexual reproduction, even a Time/Life book, and in it you will probably see a four-color reproduction of a fertilized egg, just one cell invisible to the naked eye. What follows are photos of how this single cell divides, then divides again and again, and in a matter of weeks the form of a future human is apparent. But it starts with that single cell. Inside that cell is a microscopic facsimile of this thread that makes it all happen. We know this. Moses didn't know it. Aristotle didn't know it. Jesus didn't know it. Roosevelt didn't know it. Hitler didn't know it. But we, Mr. Ullman, our generation, is fortunate to know it. And now the question is obvious: what will we do with this knowledge? Will we allow it to lift us above our narrow and bigoted attitudes?"

"I certainly hope so, Henry."

"I haven't seen it yet, but of course we are only at the beginning. The credentialed scientists in charge of the human genome project estimate it will take about 15 years to track, to get all the letters written down, so to speak. The next step will be to determine precisely which letters control what and how they act to produce an organism. In other words, Mr. Ullman, how does this thread come alive? How, for example, can a relatively little section of it produce an organism as complex as the human brain?"

"And you think we'll be able to do that?"

"I think that 200 years from now we'll not only have it all figured out, but we'll be able to manipulate the coding to create a society that makes a good deal more sense than it does now. I'm confident that by that time or even before, we will be free from disease and from the flawed mental, limbic drives that make the society of the world the abomination that it is now."

"What do you mean, free from disease?"

"Well, for starters, there are about 3,000 known hereditary diseases and probably a lot more we don't know about. Even with the little knowledge that geneticists have, they have been able to find the tiny sections of the genome that cause a number of them. For example, they have found the genetic letters that cause Huntington's disease. They are working on schizophrenia and manic depression, and as we sit here, they might have already found those genetic sections. They have already found sections that can lead to cystic fibrosis and those which are responsible for colon and breast cancer a high percentage of the time. It seems that each month there is a new discovery."

"Yes, I've read about Huntington's at least and muscular dystrophy. And after listening to your description of the genome and its three billion letters, the wonder is that they were able to locate these genes."

"It is a wonder. Are you aware how they did it?"

"I haven't the vaguest idea."

"They did it by tracing the histories of these diseases through families where they were prevalent. They compared the DNA from various chromosomes of family members with the same disease and noted slight variations that were similar. Then with what can only be described as hard detective work, considering the hundreds of millions of letters involved, they found the DNA section or genes that only appeared in victims of Huntington's, or whatever disease they were focusing on. I imagine, Mr. Ullman, that as these researchers proceed with their work and this line of research, they will find the DNA sections that make a person a great pianist or a painter or gymnast or what have you. It will undoubtedly all come out in the end. With genetic testing at birth or even before, our life's story will pretty much be laid out. As genetic engineering improves, our abilities—our intelligence level, for example—might be dramatically enhanced."

"Incredible."

"It is, isn't it? There is already considerable controversy over prebirth genetic testing. What do you do if you discover, for example, that the child will have an awful disease for which there is no cure? Do you allow the child to emerge or do you abort it?"

"How do you feel about that, Henry?"

"That's a whole issue by itself, isn't it?"

"Yes, it is."

"And you want to discuss it now?"

"You don't have to; we can do it another time."

"Thank you, I would feel better about that. Let me say now, however, that I believe putting a decision like this in the hands of parents is foolish. Parents have children for the most selfish of reasons . . . to keep the marriage together; to have something more than a dog or cat to love; to continue the family name by thrusting one's genes into the future; to have an object over which power can be easily exerted; to have something to show off to relatives, friends, and strangers; I can go on and on. There is hardly a reason you can think of, Mr. Ullman, that isn't selfish. And supporting this selfishness is a tremendously strong, programmed *genetic* impulse to procreate. Nature plays every conceivable trick with our brains to impel us to reproduce. And that's what we do, just like moose. So, surely, the child who might have a long life of suffering and deprivation hasn't very good odds with a parental decision. No, eventually society will have to make that decision. But it will be dozens of years, maybe even hundreds, before our global society is sophisticated enough to truly face the problem, to rise above the fanaticism and emotion involved with this entire issue. However, I hope by that time we'll have the genetic engineering skills to restructure errant genes in utero so there won't be any decision to make."

Henry looked down and began playing with the two strands of thread he had twisted into one.

Ullman had a glazed look, but quickly caught himself and said, "Yes, Henry, we'll have to get you back sometime to talk more about that. You mentioned before that by discovering the genetic system, we had found the secret of life. Do you really think we have found the whole secret?"

"I'm sorry, I didn't mean to imply that. The secret we have found in the genetic system is what creates and propels all organic life. What we haven't learned is who developed the system."

"You mean who God is?"

"Yes, exactly."

"So you believe in a God."

"Absolutely, yes. Look at just the breathtaking nature of the genetic system I've been describing. This must have been an invention of a Higher Being. I probe my mind constantly for some concept of who this Higher Being might be, our God of all religions, if you will."

"And have you come to any conclusions?"

"Well, I have to some degree."

"Then please, Henry, tell us about them."

"You're sure I won't offend anybody."

"I don't think you're capable of purposely doing that. So go ahead."

"Okay. Well, first of all, I can't really believe that God was working alone on this. If there is only one extreme Higher Being, our God figure, then He must be supervising quite an organization of super intelligent beings of some nature."

"I see." Ullman sounded hesitant. "Go on."

"Just look at these threads, for example. Look at them very closely."

Ullman stared at the two threads Henry had twisted together and described that he was doing so to his audience.

"Okay, Henry, I looked at them."

"Well, now say that you, Mr. Ullman, were in a position of very high authority and you went to our nation's Pentagon, where the secretary of defense was meeting in an auditorium with all of his top research and development people, and with them were the best genetic scientists in this country as well as from other countries. Say you went up to a podium and held up this thread and said that it was absolutely critical for some reason, say the survival of Earth, that we design a duplicate of this thread . . . a genetic thread that is so narrow it cannot be seen by our electron microscopes and which can replicate itself in a few hours. When present in the chemical environment of a human egg the thread can direct the billions of cell divisions that can create a human body or a stalk of celery. You ask everyone present what kind of resources they would need to get the job done, regardless of whether or not we presently have those resources. Then you cap it all off by asking for a report on everyone's best stab at the idea within a week. Now what do you think that report would say?"

"That it's all impossible, of course."

"No, no, we only asked for their best stabs at it."

"So what would they say?"

"They would probably say that we would need to accelerate considerably the tracking of the human genome project and after that the techniques could only be guessed at. But to complete the tracking process and what follows would require immense laboratories and tens of thousands of skilled scientists and engineers working on the project night and day. Now what does that tell you, Mr. Ullman?"

"I really can't guess." Ullman sounded perplexed.

"It tells me that our God figure required laboratories of His own, for one thing, and that He directed a crew of Super Scientists and Engineers who worked to create this thread, with all its potential coding for the tens of millions of living organisms on Earth and probably trillions of other planets. And then packaged it so it could be shot into the enormous space of our universe with the mind-boggling intensity of the 'Big Bang' explosion."

"So you're saying God or His Subordinates were scientists and engineers," Ullman interjected weakly.

"As a very minimum, of course. Who else could have done all that? And further, it also makes sense that God and his workers are somewhere outside this universe. In other words, these people are outside what physicists call the 'singularity,' that point before the 'Big Bang' when the mass of the universe and its concept of space-time were infinitely small. They had to be outside it to create it. And let me tell you, it would take some big-time Scientists to create the concept of time alone, which as I mentioned when I was last on this show, Einstein found to be relative, of all things. In other words, its pace is different depending on where you happen to be in the universe and how fast you're going. The point is, that as immense as the universe is, what's beyond it could be even more mind boggling because the inventors are there or maybe somewhere beyond that. All I can tell you is that God and his people must have known what they were doing to create us, the other living organisms on our planet, the nuclear concept of the stars, the concept of gravity, and so on. And this gamut of invention runs from the smallest of things—the quarks and other sub-atomic particles—to the immensity of the universe. I would give everything I own just to meet these People. Talk about detail and scope."

Now it was Ullman who found himself staring beyond Henry. He found himself transfixed on the studio door knob. The silence jolted him into his next question.

"Eh . . . do you think we'll ever be able to meet these People, as you call them, Henry?"

"I would say that's a real long shot. There is obviously some reason the Creator and His Team are not in contact with us. It hasn't happened yet in this rational sense, some event that the whole world is able to witness at one time and then agree that it happened. But that isn't to say it couldn't happen tomorrow. If we have no idea what we're all supposed to be doing on or off this planet, what the ultimate purpose of our lives is, then we can't accurately predict anything. This revealing of the God figure is only something we can hope for, pray for, really. There is another thought I've had from time to time in this regard."

"Yes, what is it?"

"I've often had the feeling that we are limited in our view of anything we can sense beyond our real world, limited by something that has been coded into or left out of this genetic thread."

Henry picked it up from the table where he had put it and held it up again.

"In other words, the Creator simply didn't code in the genetic capability for intelligence that would allow us to figure it all out. Now I pride myself on following physics and mathematics rather closely, even though I feel I am somewhat genetically impaired in understanding the subjects anywhere near as well as the credentialed scientists who are discovering and then reporting on them."

"Excuse me, Henry, I don't want to break your train of thought, but what do you mean by genetically impaired?"

"I mean that I simply can't think through many of the concepts and some of the equations I read about. Yet I see some children of 10 do it without any struggle whatsoever. I can only conclude that I am genetically impaired in dealing with this type of vertical intelligence, while those casual 10 year olds, and others like them, are not."

"And you don't think you can overcome that?"

"I don't know if I can or not. The brain is a remarkable and mysterious instrument. There are things I thought that I could never do, but woke up one morning and was able to do them."

"Like what?"

Henry paused for a moment and looked somewhat sheepish.

"Come on, Henry, like what?"

"Well, like harmonize, for example."

"Harmonize?"

"Yes, harmonize. I like to sing with old tunes on the radio and for more than 30 years I would try to harmonize, but couldn't. Then one day, out of the blue, I broke into such clear harmony, it actually startled me. So I don't think that I am totally beyond being able to think through the concepts and equations of physics and mathematics. It could happen, and if it does, then I can only think that the genetic impairment was resolvable. For most people to whom I talk a lot about this kind of thing, the impairments they experience don't improve very much, if at all."

"So, what was your original point before we brought up genetic impairment?"

"Oh, yes. The point was that even the very finest minds among our credentialed scientists cannot get beyond the point of what they call the 'singularity'; in other words, the point before the 'Big Bang.' All the current theory that our best minds have been able to generate breaks down at that point. These scientists are as much in the dark as we are about where we all came from and why. They, as much as we, are victims of a genetic coding system that doesn't allow us to understand our very beginnings and our purpose. I believe I talked about this once before on your show."

"Yes, I think you did touch on the fact that nobody, no matter how well credentialed, knows why the universe and everything in it was created."

"Now that's not to say that we don't have coding on our genetic thread that will someday allow us to have this understanding, or the genetic engineering ability to create the capacity for this under-standing ourselves. We don't know where our evolution or technology will take us, what we are ultimately supposed to become, and so anything is possible."

"What are we supposed to do in the meantime, Henry?"

Henry paused for an instant.

"I think the best thing we can do is make some attempt to get people off their high horses."

Ullman looked puzzled.

"Their high horses?"

"Yes, exactly. Turn on your TV any night and what you see primarily are people on their high horses—in neat suits or clothes that make some ridiculous statement or in uniforms of one sort or another, all out there trying to impress us with what they know. They are so serious and smug about it. One of the greatest inven-tions of all time was television, Mr. Ullman. It could ultimately be one of the greatest forces for peace in the world, because for the first time in the history of the world we can see that most countries are made up of ordinary people, most of whom want to live in peace. Wars will still be possible, of course, but they won't be as easy to start as they were before television gained such a grip on our lives.

"But as great as television is, the invention of the remote channel switcher is even better because as soon as you see those smug, know-it-all people talking or in other ways reflecting how knowledgeable they are, whether on the news or being interviewed or in a movie or whatever, you can switch immediately away. Someday I would like to walk up to just one of them, pull out my genetic thread and say: *'You fool, you darned fool.'* " Henry suddenly rose to his feet and was waving the thread in the air. *"Don't you know you come out of this little thread? You are nothing but 3 billion letters. That's all you are. Three billion letters made up into a bar code, the same bar coding that creates asparagus. You don't know how this thread was created. You don't know how it could be made to produce the body you're inhabiting. You don't know a darned thing, no more than the rest of us. Do all of us a favor and just shut up until you fully realize your ignorance. Then and only then can we relax together, have pleasant talks about how we don't really know much of anything, and have some fresh lemonade."*

Henry sat down. Ullman looked stunned.

"Believe me, Mr. Ullman, I've made that little speech many a time to somebody on my TV set. I hope to do it someday in person, but I don't want to be arrested because the holding cells they use in police stations are usually a little damp and they would probably aggravate my asthma."

"I don't think that talk would be cause for arrest," Ullman replied, trying to regain his composure.

"Well, I'm sorry, Mr. Ullman, but I'm just not sure about that."

Henry paused to look down at the thread he was now twisting between his hands. Then he looked up startled when Ullman touched him and pointed to the studio engineer, who was giving Ullman a two-minute signal.

"Before we close, Henry, I'm sure I echo the feelings of our audience when I say that you not only have described the human genome in a way we can all understand, but you've given us quite a lot to think about as usual. Now is there any last comment you'd like to add?"

"There is one thing. And I'm not unhappy we're ending now,

Mr. Ullman, because I'll just be able to make the next bus home. It stops just a few doors from here."

"Yes, I know that, Henry. I take it myself from time to time, as you know. So go ahead, give us your final thought."

Henry looked sheepish again.

"Well, you've read this book we're in, I'm sure."

"Absolutely."

"And so you remember the chapter previous to this one when Dr. Roy Sanders was designing the badge that read 'My Brain is Flawed,' the one he suggested that all human beings wear to remind them of our biggest problem . . . the fact that we don't know or refuse to recognize that we are all victims of flawed brains in one way or another—brains that are still a partial throwback to our caveman days?"

"Yes, of course I remember that."

"When I first read it I recall saying to myself that this was the ultimate identification for the human being. For after all, as we've talked about today, we know absolutely nothing about why there is a universe and what our role is supposed to be in it from a strictly rational point of view. And to blunt what should be an overwhelming curiosity about it, our genome appears to be programmed or coded to blot it out of the thought processes of our brains. Now, there are some obvious advantages to this, particularly if we tend to see these ultimate truths as being frightening. But an unfortunate result of this lack of curiosity is that it allows our lives to be influenced by petty and selfish things that should be meaningless to us, in light of the stark realities our scientists have already discovered. That badge, if we were all compelled to wear it, would remind us to rise above this coded blotting out. Do you agree?"

"Without reservation."

"Well then my idea, Mr. Ullman, which only came to me recently, is to redesign that badge ever so slightly."

"Yes, go on."

"Here, let me show you."

Henry reached for a pad of paper on the table, took a lead pencil from his shirt pocket, carefully adjusted the length of the lead and began sketching a badge with lettering on it. In the meantime, Ullman was working to describe Henry's actions to his audience and recounting again how he first met him on a bus.

"There."

Henry turned the pad around so that Ullman could look at the new badge design. Ullman smiled and said: "Henry, that is tremendous. Let me describe it to our audience. What Henry has done is draw on the badge the thread he has been using to describe our genetics. Underneath the thread he has in small letters the words: 'This is my Genetic Thread.' And next to it he has larger lettering, a line that reads: 'My Brain Is Flawed and This Is What Caused It.' "

"Of course I intend to work on it a bit more."

"I think it's great just the way it is. I wouldn't touch a thing. Now, Henry, one last question. Do you think anyone would ever wear it?"

"Not if they want to find or keep a job, Mr. Ullman."

"Wonderful. Henry, I expect we'll be inviting you back again."

"That will be fine with me. It's really a very pleasant bus ride, except on Fridays during the evening rush hour . . . if we can work around that."

"I'm sure we can. Goodbye, Henry."

"Goodbye, Mr. Ullman."

Ullman signaled the engineer and the closing music filled the room. He shook Henry's hand and watched him leave. Then he picked up the pad of paper, tore off the page with Henry's badge design on it, rummaged in the drawer of a nearby desk, found some tape and used it to paste the page to the wall behind his studio chair. He stared at it for a moment, turned off the lights, opened the heavy studio door and left.

THE POINT

We are coded human beings. We come out of that tiny bit of DNA, a thread, as Henry Heiman calls it, that contains four letters that combine in different ways to create the proteins that build our brain, eyesight, hearing, bone, heart, reproductive organs, liver, everything.

It took more than six months of reading technical material before I could explain parts of it, through Henry Heiman, in everyday language so that it would be as easy as possible to comprehend.

In working through this powerful subject, my purpose program was running at full steam. This might be one of the most important pieces of writing ever done, I believed. Finally somebody was taking the time to tell the world that we all emerge from a biological version of the kind of bar code found on a can of tomato paste. Our DNA coding is found in exactly the same format in every other living organism, from trees and elephants to bats, carrots, dandelions, and the lowest form of bacteria. We all evolve from the same basic molecule. The only difference is in the length and configuration of the letters.

The knowledge itself wasn't new. Scientists have been talking and writing about it since the double helix was discovered. But they weren't communicating what it all meant in language the rest of us could understand. And so I thought that what I wrote was a tremendous exposé. Who are we, after all? How can we think we are above the animals? Who is the Super Genius that managed to encode us on a thread we can hardly make out with our best microscopes? Why aren't we demanding some answers we can sink our teeth into?

But it didn't work out. An associate of mine asked a highly credentialed writer in Chicago to look at the first draft of this chapter. This writer came back with lots of positive comments about Henry Heiman as a character and he thought the style of writing wasn't bad, it did need some polishing and so forth. And then he concluded by saying: "Thanks for the lesson on genetics."

Most people would probably say much the same thing: "The information is really interesting." What Henry Heiman and others in this book have said about our brains being designed to mask this information from our conscious minds is probably true. It is a built-in brain trick that causes an irrational attitude about ourselves. We simply do not accept the fact that we are the result of some thread. We are so much more, or so our brains lead us to think. If we are in a room where someone is being born, we will say to ourselves, this is some kind of miracle, this mind-boggling thing. But what's a miracle?

The real miracle is the fact that we come out of this ultramicroscopic thread we call DNA and we aren't more flawed than we are. The miracle is that we can hit a baseball coming at us at 90 miles an hour, or create a magnificent painting or symphony, or drive a car, or write a letter, or walk without falling down. So how can we fault ourselves when we aren't what we think we were supposed to be? Take a thread out of your coat pocket. That's what we started as, except our thread is much too microscopic to see.

Think about that for a minute. Pick up something small: a coin, a paper clip, better yet, a piece of lint from your clothing. Now try to visualize what it would take to produce a human body from that. It's impossible.

The masking program of the brain is strong. So how can you trust it? How can you know that it is really working for you? How do you know you have wrung out every last bit of its capacity for intelligence or memory? How can you feel assured that it will be there to support you in moments of emotional turmoil or in pressure situations?

What you really have in your brain is a stranger who is sometimes helpful and sometimes not and it doesn't want you to know very much about it. We have thousands of scientists studying it, experts who have created wondrous things in this world, but they haven't as yet figured out how the brain remembers things. What's the big secret? Worse, they have to kill rats and other animals in droves to see if they can find some change in the brain connections that a trauma prior to death might have created. This is what we're reduced to.

So begin to look at your brain as something other than the center of who you are, something that you need to regulate to give you more moments of peace and contentment than you're getting from it right now. Open yourself to this possibility.

22

The Numbers Scale

It was almost 2:45 A.M. as Ed Grogan sat with Essie Beecroft in the basement recreation room of the Sunnyday Home. They had just watched a press conference in Moscow that featured Ilyich Barkeloff. Ludmilla Denisov had worked with TASS and the government to transport Barkeloff from his mountain home to an old auditorium just outside the Kremlin, where he answered questions fired at him by an international gathering of reporters.

During the 90-minute press conference, Ilyich touched on a number of his ideas ranging from the transcending of emotions to the brain tricks Nature plays on us in order to keep the planet functioning and reproducing.

His comments had stunned the audience. As he and Ludmilla were leaving the stage, the audience sat in a hush. Ilyich was saying something to Ludmilla that couldn't be overheard. It appeared that the press conference was already out of his mind and he was simply intent on strolling with Ludmilla to the side entrance where the special two-car train that brought him to Moscow awaited to transport him home.

When he and Ludmilla disappeared from view, the journalists began straggling to their feet and gathered in small groups. The TV cameras continued to pan the audience. There was no narration, nor was there any sound other than the soft patter of talk echoing through the auditorium.

Ed Grogan stood up and looked at Essie.

"You know I really do like that guy," he said.

271

"Yes, he appears to be a remarkable individual," Essie replied in a tired voice.

"I think I know and agree with what he's really saying."

"I thought I did, too."

"Are you kidding? He covered a lot of territory with the idea of brain tricks and how we need to reach toward higher perspectives of humility."

"I know."

"But you and I have talked a lot about the same things, maybe in different terms, and you weren't always so agreeable with what I had to say."

"That may be true, Mr. Grogan, and perhaps the problem is that when you talk with me, you're always telling me things. When I disagree with you, then you get mad. Mr. Barkeloff said things, but always in a way that implied it was just his way of looking at things and if you had different opinions, it wouldn't bother him."

"You're saying he is more diplomatic, that's it. That I'm opinionated and he's not."

"Yes, quite frankly."

"So you're telling me, Essie, that you are swayed more by someone who is a smooth talker?"

"Oh, Mr. Grogan. Maybe we should just go to bed. It's late and I'm tired."

Grogan cupped his hand over his mouth and said in a feigned whisper: "I don't suppose you're hinting at anything, if you get my drift."

Essie gave him a nasty look.

"I quite get your drift, and as you must know by now that is definitely not what I had in mind. I can't imagine why at this hour of the morning you should still feel so wide awake?"

Grogan leaned back in his chair.

"Maybe because what that Russian had to say stirred my blood a little." He leaned forward. "I have to admit that he put into much better words what I've been trying to talk to you about these past months. I just thought you and I could talk about it a little. Kick it around. But hey look, Essie, if you want to go to bed, be my guest. I can think about it myself."

"You mean you'd really like me to stay down here with you to talk about this?"

"Well, yes, goddamn it."

"That is very sweet of you to say. And if I'm not mistaken, Mr. Grogan, this may be the first time you've actually issued a direct invitation to have me in your company."

"Aha! You see! That Russian isn't the only one who's a sweet talker."

Essie chuckled and visibly brightened as she saw Grogan was struggling in his way to convince her to stay.

"I'll stay for a little while. Where would you like to start, Mr. Grogan?"

"All right!" Grogan slapped his knee with enthusiasm. "What do you think about the idea of brain tricks? Let's start there."

Essie reflected briefly.

"Well, I thought it was an interesting term to use for some of our irrational emotions and feelings. But I don't believe we can use the fact that our brains are imperfect and play tricks on us to avoid responsibility. In other words, I don't think someone who abuses another person can use his problems with his brain as a cop-out."

"So what are you supposed to blame?"

"You blame yourself. You take responsibility for your actions."

"Yes, but it's the brain, Essie, that is doing all your thinking and creating all your actions for you. That was the Russian's point."

"Yes, but you can control your brain. You can discipline it if you work at it."

"Well, I don't know if I'd go that far," he paused. "But at least you feel that the brain is your control center, so to speak, whether you're able to steer the thing or not?"

"Yes, I would say that."

"What about the thought that the brain is defective, flawed? What do you think about that?"

"I'm not sure I would agree, Mr. Grogan."

"So then, Essie, you believe that your brain is designed perfectly? That it won't trick you into doing things that may not be good for you?"

Essie thought briefly.

"Well, it is very difficult for me to stay away from the dessert pies they serve here. I feel a real hankering for a slice when everyone else is eating it, even though my doctor says I should stay away from pies."

"That is unbelievable."

"What is so unbelievable about it?" She looked irritated. "I thought you'd be pleased that I thought to define what I might feel as a brain trick, to use that phrase."

"What's unbelievable is how you can have a hankering for the muck they call pie around here."

"Could it be, Mr. Grogan, that in all your wisdom you might have missed the fact that all of our brains are different and they all trick us a little differently? And mine tricks me into wanting the pie they serve, however you regard the taste?"

Grogan, who had been casually looking down, suddenly twisted in his chair and stared at Essie with a stunned look.

"Christ, I can't believe you said that."

"Why, don't you agree?"

"Yes, I agree, it's just that . . ."

"You don't think a woman of my age, and I emphasize *woman,* can accept a dramatically new thought."

"Aw, Essie, we're getting off the track here."

Essie could see that she was beginning to get Grogan aggravated. She liked it, even though what had suddenly come out of her mouth about brain tricks was as shocking to her as it was to Grogan.

"Okay, Mr. Grogan, why don't you get us back on the subject."

Grogan got out of his chair and began pacing.

"All right, let's move on to another thing the Russian hit on and that was what he called our humility perspective. What I took that to mean was that we all seem to have a different level of it. We can't reach the higher levels until we understand how much we don't know. Did you get that?"

"Yes, that sounds about right."

Grogan stopped pacing and faced squarely toward Essie and gestured with his finger.

"Then let me put it to you, Essie, my dear, that I very much believe I have a higher level of that perspective on humility than you do."

Essie looked annoyed.

"Well, really. I don't know how you can say that. I pride myself on my humility."

"Yeah, but you're thinking about how kind and sweet and unassuming you are in public. That's one kind of humility and it's not at all what I mean."

"Then please enlighten me as to what you do mean?"

"Okay, then. Do you think you are some kind of piece of dirt?"

"In what sense, Mr. Grogan?"

"In the sense that you don't know shit when it comes to the really important issues."

"Like which issues?"

"Like the issues that go beyond our everyday lives. Like why we're born, why our parents screwed on the particular night we were conceived, why sperm were invented, why the design of conception was invented the way it was, why our brains can be replicated out of the DNA in any of the trillion cells in our bodies, why the Earth is round, what's it doing where it is, why we are floating alone in a space that appears to be infinite, and for a period of time is supposedly eternal, whatever infinite and eternal really mean? Like those issues just for starters."

"I'm afraid that what you say certainly makes it appear that against all of that we are nothing more than pieces of dirt, to borrow your phrase. But all of it is also far beyond my control and certainly not on my mind."

"It's hard for you to say it, isn't it Essie?"

"What is hard for me to say?"

"That when it comes to the really important things in life, the large-scale things, you don't know shit. That's what's hard for you to say."

"First of all, I refuse to use that vulgar word. And second, I feel that I am knowledgeable enough in things that are within my control."

"But don't you see, that's why I have more humility than you do."

"No, I don't see that at all. You are down here haranguing me with theories and I sense no humility in your presentation."

"But goddamn it, Essie, it goes beyond presentation, it goes smack dab into the fact that you won't admit you don't know diddley and I will come out without the slightest hesitation and in front of any audience and gladly admit that I do not know shit. And not only that, I will also quite willingly confess that my brain is defective and is as screwed up as can be. And, that it has played tricks on me everyday of my life that I can remember, from the first days of kindergarten . . . resulting in the creation of vast amounts of torments I could have done without."

Grogan paused and looked at her, then continued: "And so to my way of thinking, Essie, that makes my perspective of my humility higher than yours. I know I am being dumped on. You don't. And as one result of that, I am open to more new ideas than you are. I am more humble in the face of all that."

"You make an interesting case, Mr. Grogan, but I'm sorry I don't agree with you." She knew she was being defensive, but she really didn't agree with him.

"Jesus."

Grogan looked dejected as he took a seat a few chairs down from Essie. He became lost in thought and then snapped out:

"Okay, Essie, how about trying something to get rid of the little brain trick that makes you want that repulsive pie when you know you shouldn't be eating it."

"Like what, Mr. Grogan?"

"Well, you remember when that Ilyich fellow said that when you get feelings you don't want, like jealousy or hatred, or bigotry and such, when your brain tricks you into getting those feelings, you should try to transcend them. You remember that?"

"Yes, I think so."

"All right then. The problem is that that's pretty damned hard to do. He probably got that idea from the Indian philosophers and some gurus who say in their writings you can transcend your emotions, but they admit it can take years of training. I came across a shorter method, a more mechanical method and you might want to try it with your pie."

"What do I have to do?"

"Well now, this isn't as simple as it sounds. I read it in a book written by a fellow named Ken Keyes, called the *Handbook of Higher Consciousness,* a sort of New Age book. There's a whole process involved, but the first thing is to recognize something as an emotional addiction that you find is upsetting you. And what he meant by addiction is that the same upsetting emotion is triggered time after time under the same circumstances. In other words, you're stuffed, you see pie in front of everyone and boom, you still get a craving for the pie, even though you rationally don't want it because your doctor tells you it may eventually kill you. And that happens every time. You have an emotional addiction to a pie you neither need nor want. I once had to deal with a guy in business I couldn't stand.

Every time I would hear his voice on the telephone I would feel anger and jealousy. At the first sound of his voice and it was automatic, probably because for years this jerk was not only doing better than me, he kept telling me what I was doing wrong and in a way that just plain pissed me off. So hearing his voice and feeling automatic anger regardless of what he wanted to talk about, was another form of triggered emotional addiction. You follow me so far?"

"I think so."

"Well, you really have to read the whole book and go through a number of steps, but one of the most important is to come up with one sentence that would work to neutralize the addiction. For example, you see that pie in front of you and you say: 'I will *not* feel a craving toward that pie.' You see what I mean? This is after you've had a full meal and there is no reason in the world why you need to eat that pie."

"Yes, I follow you. Then what do you do?"

"As I said, there are a lot of steps to take, but basically, the final one is to put your head in a wastebasket at the exact time you are feeling the emotion, in other words after you've eaten through the main course and you're stuffed and the pie is now in front of you. At the first feeling of the emotion, you scream out that sentence at the absolute top of your voice four, five or six times. On subsequent days, you repeat the process under the same circumstances and eventually the addiction begins to go away."

"Mr. Grogan, that sounds like absolute, utter nonsense." She threw up her hands as if to wave Grogan away and meant it.

"Aha. There you have it. I knew it." He slapped his knee gleefully three or four times. His face looked like the cat that caught the mouse. "You're not open to the idea, I didn't think you would be. But I was open to the idea, from the first instant I read about it. And you know what? It actually got rid of some little addictions that were bothering me. Of course, you have to try the technique in some privacy. I'm not sure others at the dinner table here at Sunnyday would appreciate you picking up a wastebasket some Saturday night and screaming into it. On the other hand, most of them can't hear even if you scream. So maybe you could try it."

He paused, looking down at his feet. Then he looked back at Essie and continued, "Aw, forget it. Let's get back to my point: I *really* know that I don't know shit. So if some fellow out of the blue comes up with a way to make my head feel better, even if it means shouting into a wastebasket, I'm going to try it. I mean a fellow like this could end up knowing how to fix some mental part of your brain as much as some credentialed fool with a bunch of initials after his name. You think you know it all, Essie, or you believe that some person in authority knows whatever you don't know, so you aren't into trying something out of the blue. In my book, that makes my humility perspective higher than yours."

"I hate to disappoint you, Mr. Grogan, but I don't see it that way at all and I daresay most people would not see it that way, either."

"But don't you see, Essie? Say you were the official representative of the Canadian government. You were to be at some worldwide meeting of similar representatives to work out some way to get rid of the disparity of wealth between nations. If you went into that meeting thinking that you knew something and everyone else thought like you did, you'd never come up with any solutions. You wouldn't be open to every new thought that comes up."

"I disagree with you entirely, Mr. Grogan, I would go into such a meeting with quite an open mind."

"Oh sure, you'd *think* you'd have an open mind, and so would the others. Most people do think they have open minds. But it's not true. Not unless you'd all be willing to try screaming into a wastebasket. That would be one acid test. Can't you see that?"

"I'm sorry, but not really."

"Oh, Christ. All right, hold on a minute. My thoughts don't run at their fastest at this hour of the morning."

"Take all the time you need, Mr. Grogan." She folded her arms in a gesture of patience.

Grogan got up again and started pacing. Essie could see that his mind was working furiously. After about two minutes of walking back and forth, he sat down next to Essie.

"Now look, Essie, this goes back many years. Maybe it will help get my point across. Anyway, I used to hang out in a very sleazy saloon some years ago. For fun all the regulars who came in called themselves the 'Asshole Society.' "

"I'm afraid, Mr. Grogan, that this doesn't sound very promising."

"Look, accept the word 'asshole' for a minute, will you? It's important. I mean, for Christ's sake, we're not sitting here in some church."

"Well go ahead, but you know I don't like it."

"Thank you for not letting one word prejudice your whole, god-damned thinking." Grogan stood up, began pacing again. "Well anyway, I personally came up with what we called the 'Scale of Assholes.' "

"Are you being serious, Mr. Grogan? A *scale* with that awful name?" Essie now had a teasing look on her face.

"Serious? I am goddamned serious."

"Well then, by all means, please proceed. This scale sounds absolutely ingenious."

Grogan thought to himself that at that particular moment he wanted to kill Essie. He calmed himself when it quickly came to him that it was nothing but a brain trick caused by his power program.

"Okay, then, here's the scale and I'd appreciate it if you'd listen carefully."

"I promise."

Essie made an obvious effort to look serious and interested.

"Well, a number-one asshole is one who doesn't know he's an asshole. This is the worst sort of person—like a corporate raider or a congressman—the kind of person you would want to avoid at all costs.

"Now, a second-level asshole is a person who *suspects* he or she *might* be an asshole. You could probably spend an evening with this kind of person and get through it. Next is a third-level asshole: a person who thinks in the back of his or her mind that it is very *possible* they might be an asshole. They think, as a matter of fact, that it's quite likely. You could go on a trip with this person and actually enjoy it a little."

Grogan was pacing faster now.

"A fourth-level asshole is quite an achievement. This person actually *believes* he or she is an asshole. You could spend a lot of time with this person. Now we are getting up into the big time because to be a fifth-level asshole is one of life's greatest achievements. This person *knows* he or she is an asshole. Two fifth-level assholes, if they are married, would have the greatest potential for being on a constant honeymoon. You have almost reached the point of nirvana, which, by the way, is what a sixth-level asshole has done . . . reached the ultimate in humanity. That's because a sixth-level asshole *absolutely knows for a fact* he or she is an asshole. This is like a saint or a guru or a god-like figure. This asshole can accept anything said to him, can be kind under the worst conditions, will give you the shirt off his or her back. This is the ultimate."

"That is a very interesting concept, Mr. Grogan, but I'm afraid I haven't the vaguest idea of what it all means."

"Oh, no." He stopped pacing and looked at her. "You mean you don't get it?"

"I'm afraid not."

"Well, when you get down to the nitty-gritty, the real difference between all those asshole levels turns out to be the depth of their humility. Don't you get it? Just like that Barkeloff fellow said. The first-level asshole doesn't know he's an asshole. That's the worst. In other words it would be like spending time with someone who thinks he or she is important and powerful. The sixth-level person absolutely knows for a fact he is an asshole, a total piece of dirt as measured against the scales of the universe. In other words, an extremely pleasant person."

"Perhaps, Mr. Grogan, it is the use of that word. I find it offensive and like so many things you say that include profanity, the point gets lost. Perhaps if you thought of another word . . ."

"Ah, no, that's the word all right. That's what we used to use. It makes sense to me."

"Maybe it might give me some frame of reference if I knew what level you considered yourself at."

"Me? Well, I'm just barely a Three-and-Three-Quarters. At one time I considered myself a full-fledged Four-and-One-Half, but I got into a serious fight with a cousin of mine about some stupid thing and after I thought it all over, I had to conclude that I didn't have enough perspective to control my anger and so I demoted myself back to barely a Three-and-Three-Quarters."

"And what do you think I am?"

"You Essie? I'd peg you at a Two-and-a-Quarter."

She looked relieved.

"Really. I thought you would think of me as a Number One."

"Number One? Are you kidding? Do you think I would want to spend all this time with you if you were a Number One? Christ, you must be nuts or something. I wouldn't spend ten minutes with a Number One. I mean now, do you understand what I've been saying? There are differences in the levels of humility we can achieve, the perspective of it, call it asshole or whatever. I claim I'm a Three-

and-Three-Quarters and you are only a Two-and-a-Quarter; that's pretty good and it gives you something to work on."

Essie chuckled softly.

"Well maybe I do see it. But it would certainly be helpful if you came up with a more delicate name for your society."

"One time I did, but I thought it was too mild."

"What was it?"

"The Nothings Society."

"The Nothings Society?"

"You got it. A first-level Nothing is someone who doesn't know they are a nothing. The worst kind of person. A second-level Nothing is someone who maybe suspects they are a nothing. A third-level actually thinks it possible he or she might be a nothing. A fourth-level believes it. A fifth-level knows it. And a sixth-level Nothing absolutely knows it for a fact."

Grogan and Essie looked at each other full in the face for what seemed minutes, but was only seconds.

Essie then started chuckling. The chuckling grew into spasms of laughter Grogan had never heard from her before. She turned away from him and reached into her purse to find a tissue. Then she brought herself under control.

"Jesus, Essie, I didn't think it was *that* funny."

"What was funny," she was still giggling, "is that I think I finally understood what you have been saying."

"No."

"Yes. That there are levels of humility perspectives and you being a number Three-and-Three-Quarters Nothing means you have a higher perspective of it than me. You are much less prideful; I will agree with that."

"Well thank you, Essie, and now that we both know we are nothings, how about a little tumble in the hay?"

"Mr. Grogan!"

Grogan could see right away that he might have said the wrong thing. This time he wasn't serious in his statement; he was using it to see if he had really broken through.

"Why is sex your common denominator?" she responded angrily in a sudden shift of mood. "Why, in your state of such humbleness, do you have to look at me as some sex object? Is this some trick of your brain, you little man? You are no level Three-and-Three-

Quarters, just because you are a profane individual. I would put you just above me, perhaps at a Two-and-a-Half. And now you have something to work at, yourself."

She began to sniffle.

"Oh, Jesus, Essie." For an instant he reached out to touch her, to comfort her, but drew back almost shyly. "Please . . . cut out that crying. Christ, you know that it's just my brain tricking me into saying stupid things like that. I mean, my body is tired but my brain ignores it, that's how fucking defective it is. So please . . . if you keep that up I'm going to have to demote myself to a Three-and-a-Quarter and that will ruin my day." He paused. "I'll tell you what. I won't ever make another pass at you."

Essie looked up at him with her tissue at her nose, looking at him with questioning eyes.

"Well, not again this month, anyway."

Now she was both spasmodically laughing and crying. Grogan watched her as his look of agony turned into puzzlement. He took a seat almost directly across from Essie.

"No wonder I could never stay married," he said. "What man can, who is uncouth and not even a Four?"

Essie was now giggling more than she was crying.

"Now that you mention it, Mr. Grogan," she said sniffling, "I really can't imagine the hardships you caused those poor women you were married to."

"Hardships would be a merciful description. I would say that I was barely a Number Two when I was married both times, which means that any criticism directed my way would set my clock off immediately. Now that I am almost a Four it is much harder for a person to do that to me, even though I was on the edge a few minutes ago. Actually in the back of my mind I have been thinking about whether the fact I got so goddamned mad at you is grounds for me to demote myself to a Three-and-a-Quarter."

"And yet you call me a Two-and-a-Quarter and I rarely get mad."

"Yes, but you get upset in other ways. Like you got upset when I told you about the wastebasket."

"But that is nonsense, screaming into a wastebasket."

"And right there you have it. You, a Two-and-a-Quarter, think it's nonsense. But if you were a Number Five, you would say right off: 'Oh, so you think a wastebasket might work? Do you have one I can keep handy until I feel the addictive emotion?' Do you see what I mean? The higher you are on our so-called Nothings Scale, the higher your humility perspective and the more you understand how little we all really know. The more you understand that, the more open you are to both people of all sorts and their ideas even though they may sound wacky to begin with. Do you see that?"

"I'm not sure."

"Damn it, Essie, you just go in and out. One minute you say you have it and the next minute you're not sure. And now maybe you see why I am under a Number Four. A Number Six would have said to you: 'Have patience, Essie, it will come. And if it doesn't come, it doesn't really make any difference.' " Grogan looked away from Essie as he briefly reflected. "Can you figure this? I can act out a Number Six, but my lousy, defective brain is keeping me from being one."

"Please, Mr. Grogan, don't shift the responsibility of your mental problems to your brain. That's letting yourself off too easy."

"Oh, that's great, that's really good, Essie." Grogan was getting excited again. "I mean just what *is* responsible for what I say and think if not my brain? What is it, my foot? Or my hand . . . or my lung or liver? No way. The screw up is in my brain. And if my brain isn't defective, then no one's is."

"So you think that just by passing the responsibility to your brain you are off the hook for your actions."

"Who is off the hook, for Christ's sake? As I'm sitting here talking to you, who is doing the talking? It's my goddamned brain. Don't you get it? The only responsibility involved is whether the rational side of my brain is strong enough to take responsibility over the emotional, caveman side. But even that may not count when the emotional, caveman side is simply overwhelmingly stronger, no questions asked."

"Well, however you want to put it, Mr. Grogan, someone or something, if you insist on blaming the brain, must take responsibility."

"But damn it, sometimes the emotional side *is* stronger, period, like when you see that miserable pie they serve here and on *certain days* your emotional feelings override your rationality and you eat it, even though your rational side says you shouldn't."

"Don't you see, though, that when I eat that pie I personally take the responsibility for my weakness. I don't get myself off the hook by blaming my brain."

Grogan put his head between his two hands as he looked at the ground.

"Good Lord, tell me why I am putting myself through this at this hour of the morning."

"You are absolutely right," Essie snapped. "We should go to bed right now."

Grogan quickly looked up.

"Now, now Essie. We've both been living here at good, old, stagnant Sunnyday so long, we can't be sure anymore when we're having a good time. I put it to you that what we are doing down here in this dreary, basement recreation room during the wee small hours of the morning, even when our little discussion gets a bit heated, is as close to a good time as you can have at Sunnyday."

Essie softened. "Oh, it isn't that bad. I rather enjoy it here."

"Well if you like it here, you'd really love a Siberian gulag."

"Oh, Mr. Grogan." She smiled wistfully at him.

"That's better. Now let's get back to the responsibility issue. Of course we can't do mean and vicious things and simply blame it on our brains. And then let it go at that. The point is that we should be able to see these things in the context of brain tricks and then work to do something about it."

"Like screaming into a wastebasket, I suppose."

"If that works for you, then try it. The first thing to recognize is that something is wrong. Okay, I get mad at you for not seeing things my way. That is a brain trick, it's irrational. My brain is probably driving me to have power over you . . . to place you under me in the pecking order, while in fact we should be equals. The point is my brain is driving me, whether it's for power or something else I don't understand. When I spout my drivel about the brain and you don't agree, all sorts of bad switching takes place in my brain and I get upset. I say hurtful things to you as a result. But at the same time, while it's all happening, I actually *see* it as a defect or brain trick. When you're able to do that, it's like a third person watching over you. If what you are saying and doing is really bad, then that third person is telling you, if you are above a Number Two that is, to try to do something about it. In other words, it is appealing to your rational self to take command. It might be saying, 'that is a very bad brain trick, sucker, you'd better damn well do something about it.' "

"And so what do you do?"

"You try to work on it. Maybe it's time to see a shrink, or read some good self-help books, or meditate, or I try the wastebasket. But this is the real problem, don't you see? We have limited means to neutralize a serious brain trick. It's each person for themselves. The idea is to first recognize your brain tricks. That's the most important thing of all. And then to try to strategize against them. But I can tell you, just as that Russian did, just recognizing the problem as a brain trick, as a quirk of your brain, can go a long way toward eventually finding a solution. The recognition itself, over time, may be enough. But let me add this. By recognizing the brain tricks, you are also taking responsibility for them. You are taking responsibility for having a fucked up brain. And that's a big step. A Number One Nothing, I guarantee you cannot recognize that anything about him or her is messed up—most especially their brains—so they can't accept the responsibility either. A Number One will always blame someone or something else. A Number One cannot say, 'Oh gee, I fucked up. or, 'Oh gee, my brain fucked up.' You can see that, can't you?"

"I would prefer the term messed up. And yes, I can see how certain people blame everything but themselves."

"Okay, then. Now I will ask you, Essie, how does this concept of the Number Ones apply in everyday life?"

"I don't understand what you mean."

"How does it apply between children and parents, to take one example."

"In what way?"

Grogan paused briefly as he thought.

"What does a child do if one or both of his or her parents are Number Ones?"

"Make the best of it, I suppose."

"That's absolutely right as an answer, but it's also a very big wrong that has been foisted on this crumby planet. On the one hand, a kid is told father knows best. But the guy in reality may be a Number One. What happens is that the kid is not only confused, he or she has to suffer. There is no bill of rights for children, unless they are being physically abused. And we're not talking about that here; we're talking mental abuse only. What we probably need are some gentle Number Fours on television telling the kids, say on programs for those 10 years or older, 'Now children, some of your parents are Number Ones. If you have one parent who is a Number One, that is bad. If you have two, that is just awful.' And then that person on TV tells the kids how to identify a Number One. 'Now if you have one or more parents who are Number Ones, under the law there is nothing you can do unless they are banging you around. So I would just try to recognize what is happening to you, ignore the abuse as best you can, and know that you've had some really bad luck, but also know it won't last forever. Before you know it, you'll be an adult and you can leave that hornet's nest you probably feel you're in.' That, in my opinion, is the right message to deliver."

"Oh really, Mr. Grogan, I can't understand how you can say that. All you'll do is get the poor children confused."

"Maybe so, but that's what I would tell them. I would also tell them that nobody's perfect, including them. That we are all walking around this rotten planet with defective brains and that all of us who understand it are just trying to make the best of a bad situation."

"Oh, please be serious."

"I am serious. There have been plenty of times when I've seen parents mentally abuse their kids and I was tempted to put a note in their pockets telling them that their parents were nothing but true blue assholes. That they shouldn't be taking what's happening to them personally. It was their parents who deserved harassment, not them."

"I certainly hope you never did that."

"No, but next time I see it happen I think I'm going to try it. And I'll tell you why. Parents just come to us out of the blue. Kids don't get a chance to vote. But even worse, human nature being what it is, not *all* parents are decent people. As a result, you've got some truly terrible people as parents, probably in the millions throughout the world, making their kids feel awful for no reason."

"It's true that we've all seen people who don't do very well as parents for whatever the reason."

"Well, I see the reason for the Number Ones as being obvious. Would you like to hear it?"

"Go ahead, Mr. Grogan. You can let your brain trick you one time into believing you have something important to say."

Grogan broke into a laugh.

"Good grief, Essie, you are certainly making a fine attempt to climb up our Nothings ladder."

"Thank you," she said with feigned modesty.

"I think that Number Ones view their role as parents from a position of power rather than love. A Number One simply isn't capable of loving very deeply. For the rich or famous Number One, parenthood probably becomes just one more extension of the power they work so hard to build in other areas of their lives. For the not-so-well-off Number Ones, it is a way to create power. They treat their kids like dogs to establish the fact that they have power. It is my suspicion that among the poorer to middle class Number Ones there is a higher incidence of larger families primarily because it gives them more kids to lord over or to use economically or both."

"That's an interesting theory, Mr. Grogan, but I'm afraid it will be difficult for you to prove."

"Hey, who wants to prove it? It's just you and me talking down here. But I've seen it enough to know it takes place. I once knew a woman with two sweet little daughters. She treated them like it was a commando training exercise, getting them ready for a landing on the Normandy beachhead. When her kids reached their teens and were becoming independent, this woman was immediately thinking about getting pregnant again. In my opinion she needed another little one to continue her commando exercises. She was the victim of a merciless, power program brain trick to pour on that kind of abuse."

"But you can't know that for sure. The children might have needed a lot of discipline. She also might have been a very loving woman, deep down, and simply wanted another child to continue expressing that love."

"Hell, you may be right. But that's you, always looking at the brighter side, while I probably focus more on uncovering the Number Ones and their trails of crap."

"I think, Mr. Grogan, that you not only try to uncover them, but you are attempting to learn how to deal with them."

Grogan gave Essie a stunned look.

"By Jesus, Essie, that was very thoughtful of you to say. Very thoughtful. I have done a lot of thinking about it, not with our Nothings Scale, which I am beginning to like, but with its predecessor, the Asshole Society Scale. I've thought long and hard about how to deal with the Number Ones in the business world, particularly if you find yourself working for one."

"And what did you conclude?"

"You really want to know?"

"Yes, I'd be interested."

"I'll be darned. Who knows, Essie, our Numbers might cross yet."

Essie got a little red in the face as she quickly looked away from Grogan, who didn't notice. For the first time she felt on a par with him.

"Well the first thing I concluded," he continued, "is that there are a multitude of bosses who are strictly Number Ones, because unfortunately, the business world rewards a lot of Number Ones, who also have street smarts, by promoting them. Odds are you are going to be confronted by them from time to time in the work place. Now as I pointed out before, there is no way you can walk up to Number Ones, tell them that they are Number Ones and what that all implies. Typical Number Ones cannot see beyond their noses. If you want to combine the concepts of brain tricks and Nothings, I suppose you can also say that Number Ones cannot see their brains pulling tricks on them as easily, for instance, as a Number Three might see them. It is at that level, a Three, in my opinion, that a person can begin to grasp the principle of brain tricks."

"You are implying," Essie interrupted, "that because I am only a Two-and-a-Quarter, going on a Two-and-a-Half, that I cannot grasp the concept?"

"Now look, Essie, I don't want to get you mad again, but I wouldn't be down here all hours of the morning trying to reason out this concept with you if you were a Number Three or above. I am trying to get beyond your problems with pies."

"Please continue, Mr. Grogan."

Grogan looked at her closely, but couldn't figure out if she had gotten mad again or not. Then he *noticed* himself being interested in whether she was mad or not. A change in his way of thinking, which immediately led him to the next thought of whether he should begin considering promoting himself to a full Four.

"Gladly," he went on. "I concluded that as soon as a person finds that he or she has a Number One as a boss, the person should immediately decide to look for another job, even if under the circumstances it might take quite a while to pull off. There are two reasons for making the decision and then not rushing into it. First, as soon as you make the decision, a lot of the frustration of working for a Number One is removed. You already know that this isn't going to last a lifetime. You can do your job as best as you can knowing that your suffering is only temporary. The second reason for not rushing into it is that there is a chance that the Number One you're working for may be fired or transferred and you might luck out with a successor who is a Two or above. You can work for a Two. It's not easy, but you can do it. Working for a Three can be quite satisfactory and working for a Four can be exhilarating at times. Working for a Five can be exhilarating most of the time, and if you work for a Six then you might as well shoot yourself because life will not get any better for you. The upshot is that by mentally freeing yourself from the Number One you are working for, you are giving yourself the space to find yourself a Two or above. Committing yourself to a One for a long term relationship can make you very depressed and particularly surly at home. Once you've made the decision to leave, you might still be depressed and surly, but to a lesser degree."

"I think, Mr. Grogan, that I also agree with you on that."

"No."

"Yes, I believe so."

"All right, Essie, my dear. Then let's go on to one more everyday application of the . . . what shall we call it . . . the Nothings Principle, for right now. You get married and after a period of time you find to your chagrin that your mate turns out to be a Number One and you're not. What do you think you should do?"

"I'll leave it to you to tell me, Mr. Grogan."

"Very well. I'll tell you. If you are a Two or above and if after all the passion of the romance is gone and you wake up one morning to discover that the person you are sharing your bed with is a Number One, you should immediately *decide* to get a divorce."

"Excuse me, Mr. Grogan, but isn't that a bit abrupt? What if there are children?"

"So what? If you find that you are married to a Number One . . . a person who can't take a needle, a person who thinks he or she is always right, a person who doesn't even *suspect* who he or she is, a person who distrusts you, who tries in every way to outpower you and you can't take it, then it's time to decide to get a divorce, whether there are kids involved or not. I put in two conditions. First, that you can't take it. There are some very fine Number Threes, for example, married to Number Ones, who are very happy. They have learned to take it, might even enjoy taking it, for one reason or another. In other words, they have given up their power to their spouses. Some people do that and enjoy it, even love it. They are the compromisers in the marriage, as the psychologists might say. But if you can't take it, if you find that being married to a Number One has become repulsive to you, then get the hell out, the kids be damned. When the kids are fifty years old, it won't be a central issue in their lives.

"The second condition in this whole thing is that you *decided* to get divorced. There is a difference between deciding and rushing into it. You might decide to get a divorce and then take five or ten years to actually do it. But the actual decision can give you a little immediate mental release, similar to the decision to quit a job. Every time you are up to your ass in misery with your spouse because of some inane thing you're fighting about, you can think to yourself that it won't be for much longer.

"What you are doing is tricking your brain into giving you a bit of relief. Your brain wants you to hang in there with any relationship. It's not fussy. It just wants you to screw and have kids and doesn't really care if you are happy with your spousal sex partner or not. So you've got to start tricking it to get out of the deal with the least amount of pain to yourself. As far as I'm concerned you need to, at all times, view your brain as a Republican, a conservative. The normal brain doesn't like a lot of change in your life. You've simply got to fight it tooth and nail when you are considering a change."

"I'm afraid, Mr. Grogan, that you are oversimplifying the process of divorce. You aren't taking into consideration the feelings of obligation that parents have toward their children. Or the sadness and guilt that develops during the process of divorce and afterwards."

"Oh hell, Essie, that's just part of the price. The Number Twos or above who want to get out of their marriages or serious relationships have to understand the lousy tricks that are thrown at them by the brain to keep them coupled to their spouses: the feelings of obligation, sadness, and guilt to begin with, then the feeling of jealousy when you begin to suspect that the spouse you are separated from is see-ing someone else. You've just got to grit your teeth and go through the process. And know why you're going through with it. You have to keep reminding yourself at all times that you have *discovered* a Number One next to you, that you never saw this to begin with, that this is a new insight for you, that you've now determined the necessity of getting out of the relationship and that it will cause some temporary pain because your brain is defective and refuses to recognize the situation you're in.

"Barkeloff, I thought, made an interesting point on this very subject. He pointed out that when you are divorcing, the brain throws feelings like guilt at you. Ilyich said you can go to see a shrink or save the money and live with it. Let the guilt be in your head and eventually it will go away, he said. I really agree with that, to include not only the guilt, but the sadness, jealousies, and other things the brain throws at you. Emotions are like waves. They come and go. When you are being overcome with guilt and sadness, the right approach for a Number Two or above is to watch them as just more brain tricks. I mean really observe them. If you keep your eye on them long enough, they will just go away. Faster for some people than others. The point is that when you are going to do something that is contrary to a basic program in your brain . . . and coupling is a basic program, it's going to be emotionally painful. The brain has little mercy in this regard. It is worse than breaking your leg. The idea, then, is to observe it and work through it. That usually ends up including the finding of a new Mr. or Mrs. Right while you're in the process of separating."

"What do you mean by that?"

"I mean Nature wants you to couple with someone. That's got to be a very deep brain program. So the minute you have physically made the separation from your spouse or your significant relation-ship, the old fire bell rings and you're out looking for someone new, when you should really be learning to live all by yourself."

"Well what on earth is wrong with wanting to be with someone?"

"What's wrong with it is that if you don't learn how to live independently, I mean really take the time to go through the mental pain that that requires, you could be right back in the soup with a new Number One. Romance has a great masking effect. When you're kissing, having sex with someone new, and such, you begin to believe that this is really it. And if you are just plain lucky, it might actually be that way for you. But without taking the time to learn to be independent, you'll never know for sure. I mean how many times have you heard a divorced person or someone just out of a relationship talk about their new find? 'Oh, he's so unlike Fred. This man really supports me. He sees things my way. We go out for dinner. He loves my folks. He adores my children. He talks to them. We read the same books. We love the same art. He simply is crazy about the ballet. He is everything that Fred wasn't.' How many times have you heard something like that, Essie?"

"Well, I must admit, Mr. Grogan, it does sound familiar."

"You're damned right it's familiar. And so this new couple gets hitched and after a year the magic vanishes and she finds she has a new Number One, who in actuality hates ballet, but probably was so lonely or horny or both during the courtship, he would endure practically anything if only that night he could be with her. So this is just one more drive, one more feeling you have to go through during this process of separation. The difference between this drive to couple and the feeling of guilt is that the former can get you right back into the soup. The guilt will go harmlessly away."

"And these are brain tricks that cause all of that, I suppose?"

"Let's call them brain tricks in series."

"Tell me, Mr. Grogan, what happens when two Number Ones are married to each other?"

"Hah! I'm glad you asked that. I'll tell you what happens. They are probably blissful. They are both so into themselves that they hardly notice each other. I mean I'm sure you've seen a Number One couple. They come to the party late and in their best duds so that people can see how really great they are. They like to paw each other in public so that they can show everyone how much in love they are. They will find ways to abuse their help. They make mistakes, but nothing is their fault. They'll build some garish new house, not for their own comfort, but to impress everyone else. They give a lot of money to their church or charity, but they'll make damned sure everyone knows about it. They'll kiss their kids in public and fondle their dog to make sure everyone knows how caring they are."

"But surely all married Number Ones aren't rich."

"Good point there, Essie. The rich Number One couple is more noticeable, of course. But you don't have to be rich to be a Number One couple. You can have a Number One couple living in a public housing project and they'll find ways to make their neighbors feel dumb. Number Ones permeate all levels of society."

"I see."

Grogan could see that Essie was thinking hard. It looked to him as if they were two ships crossing in the night. He was beginning to feel bone tired and she was getting her third wind. For the first time all night, he was beginning to think about bed.

"You know, it seems to me, Mr. Grogan, that we have a Catch-22 situation when it comes to your Number Ones."

"What do you mean by that?"

"I mean that Number Ones, according to your descriptions, have the most problems. They have the worst perspective on humility, of all humanity, but yet, according to you it is impossible for them to recognize it and do something about it."

Grogan thought about what she said. "By gosh, I think you hit on the crux of it, Essie," Grogan said brightening.

"Do you really think so?"

"I do. To illustrate it, let's look at some of the Number Ones in history who really caused the world its greatest problems. Hitler, for example. This guy had to be your all-time Number One. Enthralled with himself, he had some grand vision for the planet. Hitler couldn't see that he was wrong even at the very end. He was distrustful of almost everyone. You couldn't walk up to Hitler, slap him on the back, and tell him what an asshole he really was and that he didn't know shit. That would be like committing suicide. Hitler might have even been a Minus One.

"Then there was Napoleon, another classic One. He was not only surly and into self-aggrandizement, he couldn't care less how much misery he caused. Nothing made any difference to him because he actually thought that he was born to fulfill some great destiny. There was no convincing him that the only reason he was around was because his mother and father had intercourse one night. Or Genghis Khan, who didn't give a damn what his soldiers did to the families in the cities he conquered. Another Number One. . . ."

Essie interrupted. "I think I get your point, Mr. Grogan. You probably mean that most heads of government have been Number Ones."

Grogan rose from his chair, his tiredness seemed to be gone for the moment. He began pacing again.

"Not necessarily, Essie. Not necessarily."

"Well, then who wasn't a One?"

"Probably the classic example of a modern leader was Jack Kennedy. He didn't take himself too seriously, he seemed to have fun whenever he could. I would say the guy was just short of being a Three. That probably had a great deal to do with his popularity. People like those who can make fun of themselves, who can take a needle from someone they can relate to."

"I always liked JFK."

"And how many other presidents did you really like?"

Essie thought briefly.

"I really liked Franklin Roosevelt. And even Harry Truman, now that I think about it."

"I would say that both of those boys were above a One. Maybe One-and-Three-Quarters for Roosevelt, a Two for Truman. Do you see the pattern? Reagan was probably a Two, and so was George Bush. Carter was probably a One-and-Three-Quarters, bordering on a Two. Johnson definitely a very basic One, as was Herbert Hoover and Richard Nixon."

"Goodness, Mr. Grogan, you could probably patent your Nothings Scale and sell it to the politicians."

"That would be a good idea, except for one thing."

"What's that?"

"The Catch-22 situation you mentioned before. It's like pulling teeth by hand to artificially get Ones to upgrade to Twos. It's the stuff of literature. Look at what Charles Dickens put that poor Scrooge through to get him from a very hard core One to a passable Two. He had to scare the hell out of him with ghosts, threats of death, and the like. Before his conversion, it would have been nuts for one of the book's characters to walk up to Scrooge and tell him he was lower than whale shit. He would have hired someone to steal the guy's Christmas tree. But after he went through his conversion it would have been almost natural for some little kid to walk up to him and say: 'Gee, Mr. Scrooge, my father says you are a victim of your brain tricks,' with Scrooge replying, 'Indeed, sir, indeed.' "

"An excellent example, Mr. Grogan."

"Okay. Next look at how tough things are for the evangelists, guys like Billy Graham."

"What about them?"

"Well, aren't they trying to do the same thing?"

"I really couldn't tell you."

"I think they are. Look at how hard these guys work to have a relative handful of people give up and come to Jesus. What they are really doing is appealing to all the Ones in their audiences. Asking them to put aside their pride and arrogance, their self-interest, their distrust and smugness and give up themselves to Jesus. As far as I'm concerned, anyone who truly gives themselves to Jesus, I mean from the bottom of their hearts, has to be an automatic Two."

"It's hard for me to believe, Mr. Grogan, that you, of all people, believe in evangelism."

"Hey, I believe in anything that gets the job done, to get the Number Ones upgraded, so to speak."

"I would never have thought you would feel that way."

"Look, Essie, it's almost 3:30 in the morning. Any thought is possible."

"Do you have any more examples of this conversion process, of upgrading your Number Ones?"

"Aren't you getting tired?"

"I was, but I think I'm getting my third wind and so you can give me another example."

"Okay, and this is an interesting one. I have an old friend who became a born again Hindu, of all things. He really got into it, gave me a bunch of books to read authored by Hindu gurus. I read them all, but deep down they upset me because the first thing these gurus wanted was for you to plaster their picture everywhere, including wearing a locket with their picture around your neck. I never said anything to him at first. Then one night we were having dinner together at one of his favorite vegetarian restaurants and he gets into the guru stuff right away. I felt myself getting upset, angry, as a number Three-and-Three-Quarters still does, because of the picture thing. So I decided to confront him with it. I told him that as far as I was concerned, these gurus were nothing more than press agents because they wanted you to carry their fucking pictures around your neck. That I just didn't like the smell of it. Well, do you know what he came right back to me with?"

"Please, Mr. Grogan, tell me."

"Without a second's hesitation, he said that the reason they want their picture all around you and even around your neck is that they want you to lose your identity in their's. Do you get it?"

"I'm not sure I do."

"Well, it hit me like a ton of bricks. It was the same thing as giving yourself to Jesus. The same process. Instead of giving yourself to Jesus, you give yourself to your guru. The same thing would happen. Giving up your pride, your self-interest, your smugness, your very identity, and in effect pushing yourself up from a Number One to at least a Number Two. You see what I mean? These guys have the same basic idea as the Christian evangelists. Both recognize the problems of the Number Ones and how to get them upgraded, except they use their own terms to describe the process."

"You do raise an interesting point, Mr. Grogan."

"You think so?"

"Yes I do."

"I like you at this hour of the morning, Essie. Maybe we should do this every night at 3:30 A.M."

"I'm afraid not, Mr. Grogan."

"Well, I was only kidding, anyway."

"I thought so."

"So you want to hear one last example of the conversion process?"

"Please."

"Okay, back in the late 1970s, there were all these higher consciousness movements. EST was the big one. There was even a movie about it. Anyway, the basic process for all of them was to sit in large groups for hours at a time while the leaders tried to convince you that you were nothing but 'assholes.' That was the very word they used. A person would stand up in the group and practically no matter what you said, the leader would state that you were some kind of asshole. Well, a lot of the people at first couldn't understand what this process was all about. But goddamn if it didn't turn out to be the same thing that the evangelists and the gurus were trying to do. When these leaders called you assholes, what they really meant was that you were Number Ones. The minute you stood up and said 'yes indeed, I am an asshole,' they knew that they had upgraded you. It was a rational road to the conversion the religionists were trying to achieve. Do you get that?"

"Yes, I think I do. I remember those movements and at the time I thought they were rather silly and even cruel. They wouldn't let you go to the bathroom, I heard."

"I know, but it was no more cruel than what Dickens put Scrooge through."

"Mr. Grogan, I do believe I've lost my third wind. It's time to go to bed. I must say I enjoyed myself tonight, despite our earlier disagreements. Perhaps I'll wake up in the morning a Two-and-a-Half."

"There can be no nobler aspiration, Essie, my dear, than to rise up on our little Numbers Scale."

"That is ironical, is it not? Here we are, Mr. Grogan, taught all our lives to become as smart as we can and through the Numbers theory we appear to be contending that we should attempt to become as dumb as we can."

"Aha, Essie, you really shouldn't get that confused. It takes some real smarts to know how dumb you are. Some of our best scientists have understood this quite clearly, as they've begun to uncover the tremendous scales of the universe, from the complex coding of a DNA strand to the incomprehensible distances to other galaxies. No, the real dummies of the world are the Number Ones. They see only themselves as the universe. They have no interest in the workings and mysteries of the brain and our lives in general, except to have enough knowledge to talk authoritatively at cocktail parties. The most intelligent of humans are the Number Sixes, and I guess that Barkeloff fellow is one of them, because they not only can see how ignorant we all really are, but they can put that ignorance into practical application in their everyday lives. They see quite clearly the tricks of the brain and they humor them. When their brains call for rage or anger or jealousy or hatred or bigotry or power or unreasoned lust, they immediately recognize this for the tricks they are and ignore them or in other ways deal with them. They see their brains as some kind of mistake. Me as a Three-and-Three-Quarters, I see that, too, and the tricks as well. But I can't humor them as yet. Somebody gets me mad and I get angry.

"I see you, sometimes, Essie and plain lust overtakes me, although until tonight, I never let on. I don't see you as the real friend you can be to me. I see my own frustrations and hostilities, so out comes the word 'fuck' time and time again, even though I know it offends you. And I just sit here helpless and watch it happen. But at least I'm watching it so maybe someday it will go away. I get word that a relative I don't like has made a million, and I get envious and jealous, even though I know I should be wishing everyone well in this vicious and violent world.

"As a Three-and-Three-Quarters, what happens is that I can see my brain victimizing me, but I can't do much about it. A Six can and that's what I want to be. I don't know how to get there for sure, except to keep my eye on it and to try to understand it, and maybe that's the key. All I know is that I'm not too old or too far gone to give it a shot. As far as I'm concerned, wherever we are on the scale, we should be working on moving up a notch while dealing as best we can with the miseries that the imperfections and defects of our brains are causing us. End of speech. It's been nice being with you, Essie."

Essie stood up, picked up her purse, and looked at Grogan.

"Perhaps I *will* wake up a Two-and-a-Half, tomorrow, Mr. Grogan."

"I hope you do, Essie. Goodnight."

"Goodnight, Mr. Grogan."

He watched her walk toward the stairs. Then he turned his eyes back to the TV set, which was still carrying the transmission from Moscow. The journalists had remained gathered in small groups, talking quietly. A soft murmur could be heard. None of them as yet had left the auditorium.

THE POINT

You might not have realized it, but one of the primary objectives of this book to this point has been to get you up to at least a Number Two-and-One-Quarter or above, if you weren't already.

I have thrown at you fact after fact to make you feel as meaningless as possible in the grand scheme of things. If you still feel you are some kind of hot shot, some know-it-all with all the answers, a Number One, then there is probably nothing that can be done to get you out of it. You might find some contentment being just the way you are. Nobody knows anything really important.

Those of us who are Number Two-and-One-Quarters and above

have sensed that something is fishy. We have been guided by authority figures all our lives, we have tried to do the right things, but we have known that something is wrong. Guideposts that we have lived our lives by, the certainties we have believed as truths, we have felt deep down might not be everything that credentialed people told us they were.

This book exposes many of the questions that would be uppermost in our minds, if our brains weren't designed to mask them out so that we can more readily absorb the belief systems of our cultures.

The higher we are on Ed Grogan's Numbers Scale, the more humility we have and the more open we are to pure rationality and concepts that might help us live our lives with less aggravation and anguish.

So if you're ready, on we go to the last chapters, which contain the only real answers we need to worry about.

The Answers

23

Getting Down to Basics

It doesn't require an extraordinary leap of faith to realize that our brains are the driving forces of our lives. As part of the process, they trick us into doing what we've probably been programmed to do genetically.

As this book pointed out time and again, its most imaginative trick appears to be the one that lulls us into focusing on our lives on this tiny planet that floats within a gargantuan universe, without ever giving the slightest thought as to what our rational purpose is supposed to be. Instead, our brains appear programmed with predispositions to believe what authority figures tell us or to dream up purposes of our own. It rarely strikes us to view our everyday lives against the dumbfounding scales of time, space, and the genetics that Henry Heiman described for us and be satisfied with that.

The chapters of this book might have opened a door for you as they did for me. If so, the possibility exists that eventually that door might open wider. If the door is still closed for you, give it more thought.

Why, you ask? Because it is critical to our survival to realize that our brains are indeed chemical computers containing genetic and conditioned programming that can lead us into chaos. Until the world begins to comprehend the often vicious nature of the brain, progress toward making this planet a better place to live will be at best marginal. More important, without knowledge of the brain's trickery, we won't have the slightest clue how to guide ourselves toward leading a more trouble-free life.

We need to accept that our emotions and thought processes

are controlled by drugs excreted in our brains which work in micro-seconds to restructure their connections. We need to comprehend, for example, that when we look at a child and feel a deep love, the cause is a drug, a narcotic of sorts, being emitted to restructure our brain connections. We need to know that when we feel anger, bear a grudge, or are gripped by a driving ambition, it's the result of this chemical/electrical process. Whatever the emotion or thought, it originates within this computer chemistry.

Everywhere we look, we see evidence of life manifestations of the chemical nature of our brain. In 1992, *Time* magazine featured a cover story detailing the frightful experiences of manic depressives and how new drugs attack the brain processes at fault to help neutralize the problem.

It is not very romantic to think that our brains are chemical computers, whose drug dispersions through trillions of neural fibers control every aspect of our lives. It goes against the grain of what we've been taught and what most of us think we have discovered about ourselves. We consider ourselves as something special in the universe. We sense the very special nature of our minds. We know that our minds (it doesn't bother us that we can't grasp exactly what the "mind" is) can create great art, erect magnificent structures, write great literature, uncover marvelous mathematical concepts, develop the law and its processes, build great religions, launch sophisticated systems of education and a myriad of other things we deem to be extraordinary. We allow ourselves to soar, awed by what we are achieving.

It is little wonder that the concept of the brain as a chemical computer dispensing drugs that drive us into doing the things we do each day is basically a repugnant thought. Who likes to think that we are so utterly controlled by some form of chemistry?

However, the brain's design doesn't allow us to dwell on the thought. The feeling of repugnance is not a sustained condition. Stop reading now, start doing something else and within minutes you'll be back in your reality.

I have been absorbed in this subject for a number of years. Yet my mind continues for the most part to be fixed on other things. I think about it most when my mind is upset about something. Some mistake that I made, for example. I now find in the middle of the upset, whatever the negative emotion I'm experiencing, that I begin to think about what my brain is doing to trick me into the feeling, and why. Which of my brain programs is running? Is it my sense of power that is being threatened? Is it my sense of social self-esteem? Is it my territory that's being invaded? Is it a fear of the unknown, my sense of security? What in my genetics or conditioning, in other words, is causing me to react? When I initiate this thought process in the middle of the emotional upset, nothing much happens immediately. I am still feeling the emotion, but at the same time I can see the rational irrelevance of it. Years ago this anger would stay with me for a day or two or even more. Now I can be done with it in an hour.

What I've learned firsthand is what gurus and the more saintly among us have known for centuries, that you can't force a strong, unpleasant emotion to evaporate quickly. Maybe the Indian philosophers can do it, but then they are near a Number Six on the Ed Grogan scale, while I am a mere Three-and-Three-Quarters.

It took years before I was able to inject a rational thought about the trickery of the brain during an emotional upset. The brain, it would appear, would like you to play it out or if you have been trained to do so, to bear the anguish internally. It takes some effort to remind yourself that your brain is not always your best friend, that it is dispensing drugs within the labyrinth of its connections for its own purposes and that we haven't the vaguest rational idea of what those purposes are.

As Henry Heiman pointed out, the program in the three billion letters that forms our genetic code might have been purposely constructed to keep our intelligence at a below-discovery level, thus preventing us from figuring this whole thing out. A key question to ponder is whether in 1,000 years or in 10,000 years—an instant in anthropological time—chemistry and electronics will ultimately redesign our brains, allowing us to unlock the secrets of the universe and the roles we play within it.

In the meantime, we are programmed genetically to focus on the moment, to be concerned about our lives and those we love within our life spans of 60 to 90 years, if we're lucky. As part of this inward, genetic focus, we are obviously programmed with a drive to think of ourselves as important, the reasons being inputted to us by others at an early age or from rationales of our own. If we discover that we are left out, that we are absolutely unimportant, many of us will step outside the bounds of civilized living to create power centers in other ways. Others might become despondent. If we are a Number Three on the Ed Grogan scale, we'll learn to live with it. A Number Four will live happily with it.

If you were the Designer—assuming there was one Designer— if it were up to you to create an Earth and other planets inhabited by humans to whom you gave enough brain structure to think, you would undoubtedly include a genetic program proclaiming the importance of human existence and man's overall role in the scheme of things. Andrew Hill, the philosophy professor who retired to India, conjectured that we are programmed with predispositions to create reasons for purpose, religion, and death, therein providing us with a comfort level while we lead our lives.

It is probably within the predisposition to believe purposes that we are led to believe that we are an important link to a better future. A friend of mine, the head of a large corporation, is absolutely convinced that we are important because our purpose is to improve life just a bit for the next generation. An interesting thought, but we don't know it for a fact.

Richard Dawkins, a highly credentialed biologist, makes the statement in his book *The Selfish Gene* that our genes are preoccupied primarily with propagating themselves into the next generation; that we as humans are simply a means for accomplishing this; we are genetically programmed by our genes to assure survival; and that Nature is not necessarily concerned with our happiness or well-being.

The mayhem we see in the world at any given moment gives us a better insight into what Dawkins is saying in his book. Nature has obviously not been concerned with creating a peaceful world. He blames religionists and others with tightly constructed views for not allowing the world to comprehend what is being uncovered through the study of genetics. If we were all equally enlightened with this understanding at this time, he implies, we might be able to better our lives in some way.

In the meantime, the people of the world in general lead a dog-eat-dog life, as we allow genetic programs for social power, territorial protection, and the like to make life miserable for so many. The point is that nothing we have done so far has created a totally peaceful and harmonious society where free enterprise, which gives free rein to our impulses for social power and wealth, and free immigration, which unleashes our hatreds against aliens, were allowed to flourish. Our brains have never allowed us to view who and what we are in a rational and objective way, even as the study of genetics and the brain begins to uncover all of it for us. We are programmed for this kind of ignorance and our only weapon against it is the freedom of thought with which we were also programmed.

Until more of us allow ourselves to unleash our potential for free thinking, to move beyond what we've been conditioned to think, we will continue to create havoc in some way, unaware that we are blindly following the genetic impulses that Dawkins claims are focused on getting our selfish genes passed onto new generations. Dawkins blames religionists and others like them. I blame it on the genetic predisposition programs we were given that makes this view of life extremely difficult to attain.

For academics, it may take years of study before some of them begin to comprehend their ignorance. I had originally hoped to make this comprehension easier for everyone by focusing on the shortcomings (which I later found to be trickery) of the brain, not only for the average person, but for those academics who never caught wind of their ignorance even after years of study.

It is impossible at this time to know any ultimate answer. If we choose, we can believe deeply in a religion that lays out some of these answers for us. This provides the degree of comfort that many of us seek, allowing us to still maintain those spiritual beliefs while understanding that rationally we remain at ground zero.

To those who think they have any ultimate answer at all, there are two questions to be asked: The first question, mundane as it sounds and asked before in this book, is: *What's the general idea behind the universe?* We are not talking about the Earth here, but the universe. Go ahead . . . try to think of any answer at all that we can rationally prove. How often I have thought that if only I had a hint, some small clue, at least I'd have a better guideline for directing my life. Even if we learned that our purpose in this universe is to develop a higher grade of sodium, as Elsa Dixon conjectured, that would be better than nothing. At least we'd have an idea of what it's all about. Unfortunately, with the exception of answers provided through faith, we are left absolutely and totally in the dark.

The second question is: *Whose idea was the universe?* Again, outside of religious belief we haven't the vaguest idea. Surely the very creation of the universe, which we on Earth can barely view with our latest instruments, was someone's idea. Some living, vital thing had to create it. As Henry Heiman pointed out, someone had to be smart enough to create that minuscule DNA strand in a bar code format that produces a relatively perfect human or radish practically every time. All we can do, some of us, is believe in a religious answer, facts we have to accept out of faith. And those answers might be correct as far as they go. But they don't tell us where our God resides, or if He has a crew of super-duper scientists working for Him, or what He looks like. Is He three universes tall, for example. The mere effort to create some image of His dimension is a mind-straining activity.

As Andrew Hill stated, the only way the world will ever be able to agree on our purpose or the nature of the Creator would be if a message appeared in the sky that told it all. That message would need to be in a language no one in the world had ever seen before, but which all of us would immediately understand. It would require some trickery like this for even a Creator to pierce the masking, know-it-all facade of our genetic programming. Until that happens, we need to conclude that any ultimate purpose for our being alive today, any of us, will remain shrouded in a mystery.

And if we can't look for answers from above, then we need to find answers to our everyday lives in order to lead them with greater levels of comfort. That process cannot begin until we understand and fully absorb the following facts, which have been stated time and again in this book, but which require repeating to be absorbed:

- We are genetically programmed to be what we are at birth, our very basic physical and mental hardware. We had no choice in this program. It was the result of our mother's and father's sexual intercourse.

- As part of our genetic program we were given a brain, a chemical computer that for scientists remains primarily a mystery. But they know enough about it to understand that it indeed works like some unimaginably complex computer.

- This computer is already programmed with a number of genetic characteristics to guide our lives on Earth. It will trigger fright when we are in danger, pain to tell us we've hurt ourselves, envy to remind us of our social station, love to keep us in nuclear units, lust to make us reproduce, jealousy and the prospect of mental anguish to keep couples together, violence to protect ourselves and loved ones, ethnic hatreds to keep us in the relative peace of tribal units, and on and on as already detailed in the chapters of this book.

- It is also ready to be conditioned with the language, attitudes, traditions, and thought processes of the culture into which we are born. We are not who we are until we are told who we are. If we are up to it and want to do it, this conditioning can be adjusted when we reach a level of rational maturity, at whatever age this occurs for each of us.

- The brain is flawed. Our rationality continues to be threatened by limbic drives that may be out of balance. Further, the brain doesn't come off of a highly controlled production line. It comes from that tiny strand of DNA and the miracle is that it is as good as it is. Each of us is flawed in different ways genetically. Additional imperfections that can keep us from achieving a reasonable level of contentment can be added by our conditioning—from rotten parents, for example.

The first step in seeking answers is to allow these facts to pierce our programmed genetic facade so we can truly absorb them. Uppermost in your mind as you absorb these facts should be a willingness to take a new look at the evidence. Keep an open mind as you begin this new exploration; feel the excitement as you begin to rethink the world around you.

The next step is to begin to recognize that who and what we are today is just a *fluke,* an accident of Nature. Elsa Dixon makes the point that the very fact that we were born as we are is an incredible matter of luck. We were one sperm cell out of approximately 500,000,000 that managed to fertilize our mother's egg. Any other sperm cell would have created a human other than who we are.

Once born, we are either the beneficiaries or victims of our respective environments. If we were born into a family of great wealth, we would have advantages that would not be ours were we born to a single, desolate mother living in a public housing project. If we have the genetic predisposition to become a great singer, we might never have been given the opportunity to do so, having come out of that project. We might have been born already addicted to crack cocaine. Or, we might have been shot dead at the age of ten by one of millions of handguns in circulation. Or, we might not have come in contact with any adult who discovered that we could sing.

We might have been born to great wealth, yet at the age of 14, we are hit by a car and from that time on cannot move any of our limbs. We might have been born to a dirt poor family whose own conditioning saw to it that we had every opportunity they could make available to us. Or we might have been born to a dirt poor family whose father, in a maddening, genetic thrust for power, made sure that none of his kin had any opportunity other than serving him.

The examples are endless. The most we can do is view the whims of fate, luck, chance, destiny—whatever we call it—as something that is absolutely baffling, and hope they will be kind to us.

Some people are often heard to describe luck as something that can be controlled. "Work hard," they say, "and luck will come your way." "You make your own breaks," they say. Most of the people who express this, in my experience, are already successful in reaching some lofty goal. I look at men who are working in car washes, working as hard as anyone, and trying to support a family; if their luck isn't good, they'll be doing labor like that for the rest of their lives.

The odd thing about life is that some people seem to have more good luck on a consistent basis than others. In sports and politics, particularly, we have heard the phrase, "I know how good he is, but how lucky is he?"

We can pray, we can consult psychics, we can squeeze our lucky charms, or do other superstitious things. We can attempt to lead pious lives, or work like the devil, but no matter what we do we cannot consistently control our luck and our destinies. We are who we are, and if we were lucky enough, we were given the genetic programming and the conditioning that allowed us to use whatever combinations of mental and physical characteristics we were imbued with to reach a reasonable level of contentment. The upshot is that we now can view our lives through three basic "rational givens":

- We were born with a chemical computer as a brain. We don't know very much about how it works, but it appears to be flawed.

- We were given no choice about our physical and mental characteristics. We are composed of half the genes of our mothers and fathers, the result of their sexual intercourse.

- Once in the world, we were subject to the whims of chance, which, among other things, accounted for our earliest conditioning and which no one has yet been able to make any sense of rationally.

Considering the fact that we need to lead our lives in the cold light of day revealed by these three rational givens, we should probably be grateful for brain programs that allow us to go our merry way without thinking about them. We are born. The guardians and teachers under whose influence we develop, teach us how to talk, tell us what to think and sometimes how to think, and we go on from there. Only rarely do we concern ourselves with unsettling thoughts of these rational givens, though deep down most of us recognize them in some way.

The only tangible answers we need, therefore, are those that tell us how to cope with our own lives. But what does this mean, in essence? How do we cope with our own brain, our own chemical computer that doesn't have any visible keyboard with command keys that can automatically make our brains think and feel what we rationally want them to?

If you are living a relatively contented life, there may be nothing you want to do with your own brain . . . let it be.

But if there are things that your brain is doing to you, tricks that you can now see it playing, then you can start tricking it back.

It can indeed be a two-way street.

Let's start with the programming that we need to recognize and make use of.

24

Our Six Spindled Programs

The first thing we need to be aware of is the separate, limbic-based programs we have in our heads that are ready to be triggered by the situations we encounter. These brain drives have been called the "dark side" of humans, yet they remain as natural as our rationality. Insofar as the concept of brain tricks is concerned, there are only six of them:

- Our purpose program

- Our social program

- Our power program

- Our sexual program

- Our territorial program

- Our security program

Many of the programs overlap each other: no doubt an entire book could be devoted to delineating each of them. However, the concept needs to be kept as simple as possible because our brains are not cooperative when it comes to remembering things that trick them. I have read dozens of self-help books that seemed very useful at the time. But two or three months later I couldn't remember some of the basic insights that seemed so useful during the first week or two after I read them.

The six programs probably evolve in our head as a result of

both genetics and conditioning. Our brains are presumably wired for them in some way and the input of our upbringing shaped them.

Try to visualize the programs as six stereo records sitting on a spindle in our brains. In a quiet time, when nothing of substance is passing through our minds, the records aren't spinning. But when we move into an active state of mind they begin to spin. Depending on the situation we find ourselves in, they will each spin at varying velocities. A prosecuting attorney making final arguments in court might have the power program spinning at top speed, while total concentration on the case may render the sexual program motionless.

The combination of the speeds of the six individual program records results in the emotions and drives our brains make us feel at any given moment. These programs apparently emanate from the limbic area of our brain, where we have our old wilderness wiring. Our cerebrum, the part of the brain that contains rationality, grew on top of the limbic area and is the few ounces of organic matter that separates us from the animals.

When the programs are spinning, reason feels the emotions and drives that are being created and makes a judgment. Dr. Roy Sanders used the example of the man in the supermarket, who one week couldn't resist the idea of eating ice cream bars, even though he was on a diet. This man had stopped in front of the ice cream freezer; saw the bars; and immediately his security program, which contains the appetite center, started spinning a mile a minute. During the first week, his reasoning ability wasn't strong enough to override the emotional drives, so he bought the ice cream. A week later, either the program spin was slower or the man's rationality was stronger: he overrode the program.

We might also use the old example of being in a theater when someone screams out "fire." Our security program is triggered; we look for the fastest way out and we run for it. But if this happens two or three times during the evening and there is no fire, our reasoning program simply overrides the signal from our security program and we remain seated.

Animals with very little reasoning ability will react to the limbic warnings almost every time. It takes a real effort to teach those capable of it to do otherwise.

Without getting too complicated, let's explore each of these six spindled programs.

PURPOSE PROGRAM

This program contains the emotions and drives that have to do with our sense of purpose, our self-importance and destiny. Our feelings about religion derive from our purpose program, as do our attitudes toward our careers, avocations, parenting, loved ones we feel responsible for, scholastic endeavors, serious athletics, anything we see as a mission in life.

We dream all our lives about becoming a doctor, but we can't pass the tests to get into medical school. Our purpose program will be running at full speed reminding us that we are a failure, depressing us. Then, again, we might be a divorced mother who sends her two kids to summer camp and is separated from them for the first time. Instead of enjoying the time alone as anticipated, we burst out crying and we can't stop. We obviously have a strong purpose program, one that was focused on the kids. When they're not around, then how important are we?

One day we are told we are terminally ill. Aside from the shock to our security program, many of us will begin to question "Why me?" It is our purpose program spinning at this point because we think there is something for us to do in the world and we haven't finished it.

There are many circumstances in which the purpose program can kick in. We retire only to find ourselves feeling depressed. We might get laid off or fired from a job we thought we were good at. We might head a company only to find ourselves making a terrible financial blunder that threatens the existence of the firm. The purpose program is spinning when any of these or many other situations are triggered, often in combination with other programs.

SOCIAL PROGRAM

Our social program consists of all the emotions and drives in our nature that keep us in nuclear family and tribal units, which in the wilderness are essential for survival, sustenance, reproduction, and guardianship.

The emotion of love is critical to our social program. It is the cement in the coupling process as well as in the development of the family. Other emotions that are part of the program include compassion, guilt, anger, acceptance, trust, the things that we need to keep us together in some semblance of harmony, to follow the moral code of the culture in which we were raised and to settle disputes. There are probably dozens of emotions experienced in subtle combinations that emanate from our social program.

We are invited to a wedding and our spouse tells us we have to wear a suit, because that's what is worn at weddings. We really dislike wearing suits, but our social program is strong enough to impel us to go along. We want to be accepted as part of the group, to be liked.

We are not accepted by a country club. We feel dejected, left out. Our social program is spinning together with our power program, which probably emanates from the same genetics that allow for our social program, but it is such a major force in our lives that it deserves its own spinning record.

The examples are many and varied: Your mother-in-law picks on you. You dislike going to her house for dinner because you don't feel accepted. You feel inadequate because you can't make friends, or people at work avoid you. You feel homesick when you move somewhere else. You have a fight with your sister and you feel terribly dejected. This is the social program at work.

Each time our social program spins, we might feel different emotions, each of which is created by electro-chemical reactions in our brains. The same is true of the other six programs. The idea, as we'll see later, is not so much to worry about these feelings, of which we probably have hundreds or even thousands in subtle combinations, but to use our reasoning ability to think through them and determine which of our programs is spinning. It's a lot less complicated.

POWER PROGRAM

Our power program undoubtedly emanates from the strong genetic predisposition we have to climb as high as we possibly can on the pecking order. If our program is exceptionally strong, we will never be satisfied with the power we have, we'll always want more. We have all seen government and corporate leaders who we label as power hungry.

The strength of the power program is different in all of us, as it is with each of our six programs. Most of us have observed husbands who are absolutely dominated by their wives, or vice versa, yet are happy with it. They reached their highest power level on the family pecking order; it was under their spouses, but so be it.

In the wilderness, as Ed Grogan pointed out, one's level on this pecking order is usually established in animal herds with eye stares. There is rarely more than a brief scuffle. The strength of the power program appears to determine whether or not we are happy with our place on the pecking order.

The movie *Avalon* had a scene in which an older brother arrives late at the family's Thanksgiving dinner, held at the home of a younger but much wealthier brother. When he sees that the turkey has already been sliced, he becomes angry, makes some hurtful comments, and stomps out, pulling his wife with him. This older brother now perceives himself as lower on the pecking order because his younger brother has more money. But his power program is too strong for him to accept it.

The family in this movie was oddly aware of this older brother's problem and was obviously working hard to create the perception that his genetic ranking hadn't slipped. But the older brother saw money as the key to the pecking order and he allowed this program to trick him into becoming alienated from his family.

Most family spats, including those between two spouses, take place because of drives caused by the power program, although other programs might be present in combination. We have all seen fathers with strong power programs become jealous of their successful children. The kids, expecting love and approval, get a smack in the face. It's the stuff of movies.

Hatred, it would appear, belongs primarily to the power program. Our hatred of others usually results from disagreements that have something to do with power. The hatred of blacks by many whites is caused primarily by our power program, although our social and territorial programs may also be at work. The whites who feel this hatred usually see blacks as lower than they are on the pecking order. As long as the blacks are subjugated, the hatred doesn't emerge. It comes to the surface when the blacks begin to compete for equal rights and opportunities. The hatred can be intense. This is what a strong power program can do, though it is all part of the electro-mechanical processes of our brains.

Our football team loses in the fourth quarter and we can actually feel some hatred toward the other side. The athletic teams we attach ourselves to are extensions of our own brain programs. What they do affects us in almost the same way as if we ourselves were on the field of play. So we might even feel some mild hatred toward the members of our own team who caused the game to be lost, just as we can hate ourselves when we don't win an event in which we are intensely competing. The depth of the hatred, the depth of any feeling, depends on how strong the programs are that are causing them and how fast they are spinning at the time.

One of the problems with a program that has a capacity for a high velocity spin is that our rationality can never bring it fully under control. We have seen coaches with high power spins who attempt to use their reason to keep their emotions in tow during losing situations. They might do it for a while, but at some point, the lid comes off and the emotions spill over.

Rationality only works when we use it to strategize on how to trick our brains, to sidestep a lousy program.

SEXUAL PROGRAM

Our sexual program, in the context of brain tricks, has only to do with our drive to have sex. This, in turn, revolves around the fact that male and female reproductive organs require sexual intercourse to create offspring. That's the mechanism Nature designed.

The sexual program includes all the tricks that Nature throws at us to impel us to have sex, some of which are highly contradictory and thus cause us to become confused.

It begins with the mating program, the process that determines if two people will end up having sex. Nature here did not treat females and males equally. The female possesses the capacity of between 400 and 600 eggs at birth, which are made ready to be fertilized throughout her lifetime; each containing 23 chromosomes. Each ejaculation of the male produces from 100 million to 500 million sperm cells, each of which is equivalent to the female egg with 23 chromosomes.

The result is that the average female is obviously driven by Nature to be more fussy about whom she chooses as a sex partner. The male can spray away. The contradiction, as Elsa Dixon noted, is that our children need the guardianship of a mother and father, and so while males may be driven to spray away, they are also compelled by Nature into the formation of a family unit. If love is present it can create a natural desire for monogamy.

Yet, it doesn't take much imagination to describe what would happen if our limbic wiring were given free rein. Society would revert to one of dominant males with multiple wives. This is what we see in the wilderness among animals. It was also common in our civilization until just a few centuries ago. In some parts of the world it still exists today.

Against this background, the mating dance continues and fools with our rationality, whether it be a chaperoned walk in an old Spanish village or a singles bar in Greenwich Village.

The sexual program also includes the way we dress ourselves. If we have an extremely strong sexual program, we might wear revealing clothes, heavy make-up, and jewelry—whatever it takes to make us appear more sensual in public. As we grow older, sensual appearances emanate from our power and social programs as well. While we might recognize at the age of 55 that we aren't going to have any more babies, we still might dress like knockouts because we want to maintain our spot on the pecking order or move up, our power program at work. Maybe we simply want to be an accepted member of society, which would mean our social program is at work.

Mao Tse Tung, when he led China, tried to fight through all these programs by making the women wear the same kind of khaki dress as the men. He was trying to create total equality. "Women hold up half of heaven," was the way he attempted to justify it. At least his heart was in the right place.

The sexual program also includes spousal jealousy, the emotion we feel when we fear or know that a spouse is having sex with someone else. Jealousy is such a terrible feeling that it works to punish the victim as well as the guilty partner. We will do everything we can to avoid it. If our sexual program will allow it, we will be monogamous. Our social program also comes into play: we don't like to cause pain to someone we love.

Finally, the sexual program includes the pain of separation. As

Elsa Dixon said, it is Nature's final throw of the dice to keep couples together. I've known several unhappily married couples who remained together not so much for the kids, but because they dreaded the pangs of loneliness and other torments that separation can cause.

All of the six spindled programs being described here can create brain tricks, as we'll describe later. However, some of the unkindest tricks emanate from our sexual program. If we are an unattractive misfit, for example, but have an enormously powerful sex drive as part of our sexual program, we can live with a lot of torture.

TERRITORIAL PROGRAM

The territorial program derives from our genetic predisposition to want space of our own. As Ed Grogan pointed out, Nature probably gave us this program to keep us from getting in each other's hair, knowing the type of humans we would be. By having its own space, each family unit could nurture its young with the least amount of interference and danger from other family units. The same genetic drive for space would then logically extend to an entire tribe, and in modern times to the community, state, and country in which we live.

I grew up in a depression household that at one time consisted of four family units, all living together. At the time I thought this was natural, I couldn't understand how my friends could be happy just living with their parents. But then I'll never forget the feeling of peace, contentment, and security I felt when I finally had my own room as a young officer in the Army.

The territorial program frequently runs in tandem with the power program. For example, at work, somebody might be assigned, against our wishes, to the next desk. Territorial emotions of dislike, distrust, and even hatred can be unleashed. We don't like somebody uninvited, particularly a stranger, invading our turf. That's our territorial program spinning. At the same time, we don't want our power threatened. That's our power program working.

Each of us has the six programs in different strengths, as we'll describe later. But if we have a strong territorial program, we probably also have a strong power program. That's why people who accumulate wealth primarily because of a strong power program want yet another home, apartment, farm, or large ranch somewhere. They blindly follow the drives without recognizing the causes. They think there will be more contentment with the next thing they own. It doesn't work that way.

The real tragedy of the territorial program is the war and death it has caused over the centuries and continues to cause today. Countries that could have peace with one another by trading a relatively few square miles of land don't do so because they believe the land they live on, or used to live on, is some kind of birthright.

Throughout history nations have been victimized because an aggressor, whose territorial program is spinning out of control, simply covets more land.

It is all so fruitless. We do indeed become fond of that part of the world where we were raised. But eventually we become acclimated when we move somewhere else or our offspring do. Look at all the wars fought in Europe in the last three centuries that have been caused primarily by the territorial program. Yet most of the offspring of the people who fought so hard for their lands and then moved to the United States are hardly aware of what their ancestors were fighting for.

On the other hand, we have witnessed dictators with territorial programs spinning out of control, conquering new lands, only to find the experience a temporary high. Soon they are looking for new lands to gobble up.

The greatest thing the world as a whole could do would be to understand the nature of our territorial program, to make sure that our leaders understand it as well. We must work toward rationally overriding it so that we can think through our problems without killing each other.

SECURITY PROGRAM

The security program is pretty obvious: our brains are programmed to keep us alive. Nature doesn't want us to die, if we can avoid it. This is another of Nature's contradictions. We are given this strong program to stay alive, while Nature also seems intent on killing us off so that we don't stay alive too long.

If it were up to Nature, we would probably die soon after we have reproduced and nurtured our young. When we lived in the wilderness, our life expectancy didn't reach much beyond 25 or 30 years. We have extended our life span only because of the formation of our rationality, which has allowed us to develop the knowledge and technology that fights off the diseases and other brutalities that Nature continues to throw our way.

The security program includes our appetite for food. To make sure we eat enough, our brains are designed so that our appetites are not satisfied at the same pace as we consume our food. It can take several minutes before our brains signal us that we are full. Nature would like us to eat as much as we can. This was important in the wilderness, I imagine, when primitive humans couldn't be absolutely sure of their next meal.

Our security program also includes the things we do to assure that we have the wherewithal to lead our lives. The acquisition of money is basically a security program, although the power program can be spinning at the same time. We want to have enough money in the bank so that we'll feel secure. If we have a very strong security program, we might have a million dollars in the bank and still get upset if we are stuck with a $50 dinner check. We have all observed wealthy people who refuse to spend their money. This is their security program at work.

Security programs also emerge when we couple and have a family. The program works hand in hand with our social program. But the security program is there because we all feel more secure when we are part of a unit, whether it be a family, a tribe, an athletic team, a business, or a club. We can sense when we are feeling secure. Our contentment level is generally higher. A marriage can give us a high feeling of security, as can a new job or if we come into money unexpectedly.

The security program also extends to the steps we take to keep ourselves from being victims of crime. If we have an unusually strong security program, we might have locks galore on our front door and we'll avoid walking down darkened streets or talking with strangers.

A former neighbor in my condo building tried to have pizza delivery men banned from our building, even though there has never been a crime in the building during the 12 years I've lived here. The security is very strong. But this fellow's security program was running at full speed and it tricked him into irrational attitudes.

*   *   *

Those are the six programs we need to focus on in determining when and how our brains might be tricking us. Next, we'll look at how we react when these programs run at varying speeds.

25

The Speed of Our Spindled Programs

The speeds at which our spindled programs run depend on what it is we encounter that triggers them. The event might be something traumatic that happens to us during the day, or a thought that passes through our minds.

Most of us have experienced what happens when we are about to fall asleep at night and a random thought that makes us upset runs through our heads. It might have been a recollection of something demeaning that was said to us during the day like: "You keep doing that wrong; you're an idiot." We remember the incident and our power and social programs begin to spin. Before we know it we are wide awake and mad as hell.

How we react to the triggering of the programs depends on their speed and how much in control we are of ourselves at the time. Our brains are electro-mechanical and not designed with the consistency of a computer chip. As a result, we are changeable. It's the stuff that makes athletics interesting. The underdog might be up the same day that the favored team is down.

Years ago, my company handled a very large client, whose CEO had an ultra-high power program. He hired a new vice president of sales and authorized him to make decisions on the road if it meant nailing down new business or the generation of an extra large order. But this poor fellow soon learned that his authority was limited. He would call in and say, "I had to cut our price 5 percent on three products to be competitive, but we got the business." The CEO would always find some reason to blow his cork. "How can you do something as crazy as that? You know our margins are lousy to begin with." Or, "Can't you ever learn? This is not the kind of customer who knows how to represent us in the market."

However, the vice president soon learned that he could do practically anything if he called the CEO first. "Sure, go ahead and do it, that sounds great." The CEO needed to put his blessing on any sales action before a decision was made.

The vice president of sales was the victim of his boss's ultra-high power program, which made the CEO obsessed with keeping his hands on the reins. He had to review every price sheet, every letter that left the office, the color of every new product, the copy in every catalog, the design of employee name badges, the shape of the suggestion boxes, duties that in other companies are relegated to subordinates. The CEO was rational enough to recognize the presence of his high power program—he called it a quirk—and could even kid about it. But he would lash out at any implied infringement of his authority. Yet outside of this one high-speed program, the man was relatively pleasant. He was kind to his family and considerate to his friends. But one bad program can be enough. Eventually he was fired by his board of directors.

PROGRAM SPEEDS

Now let's look at what happens to us when our six programs are running at specific speeds. To keep things as uncomplicated as possible, I have scaled the speed of the spindled programs at the following calibrations:

Barely discernible

Ultra-low

Low

Average

High

Ultra-high

Off-the-scale

Most of us have spindled programs that run between ultra-low and ultra-high. If any of our programs are barely discernible or off the scale, we are probably candidates for immediate psychiatric help, assuming it's not already too late. What the programs and their speeds tell us is why we react as we do.

PURPOSE PROGRAM

Barely discernible:

We are terribly listless. We can't hold a job, we do poorly in school, we have absolutely no sense of mission, we cannot get interested in anything beyond a video game. We have no firm beliefs.

Ultra-low:

We have difficulty in developing any sense of perspective. We try things, but we usually don't do well in them. We have probably lost any religious belief that we had. We have tremendous difficulty making any decision about our future.

Low:

We do have a sense of mission, perhaps in a religion, and we work hard to believe in ourselves. We simply don't go overboard in our beliefs. We won't stand around a cocktail party and argue about them.

Average:

About where most of us are at.

High:

We have definite convictions and believe strongly in a religion or some New Age belief. We have definite political beliefs. We like to tell people what we believe and will defend our beliefs when they come under attack.

Ultra-high:

We are extremely firm in our convictions. We will make sacrifices in our lifestyles to adhere to those convictions. We find it hard to countenance the beliefs of others, and are convinced that we have it all figured out. We are zealots.

Off-the-scale:

Time to check in somewhere. We are ready to shoot people or beat them into submission if they don't believe as we do. We can be maniacal.

SOCIAL PROGRAM

Barely discernible:

We are incapable of forming relationships with anyone else. We have no sense of love, compassion, trust, guilt, or remorse. Depending on the speeds of our other programs, we are candidates for committing homicide.

Ultra-low:

We have a weak family life. We are withdrawn and find it difficult to reach out. We are susceptible to being drawn into fringe groups, gangs, communes, and the like because of the reinforcement they provide.

Low:

We are casual about our relationships: we may love our family and our friends, but we won't sacrifice very much for them. We aren't country club members. We don't like social structure.

Average:

About where most of us are at.

High:

We are fairly structured: we go to church, we belong to clubs, we don't like our kids living with anyone until they are married, we always dress in accordance with the occasion. We are fiercely loyal to our family and friends.

Ultra-high:

We always dress to kill: in fact, we are overdressed most of the time. In business meetings, we wouldn't dream of taking off our suit jacket. We belong to the very best clubs, and we like to be seen with the right people. We only want our kids to go with the best kids. We are known as stuffy.

Off-the-scale:

We are absolutely obsessed with being seen in the right places and with the right people. We don't know what it is to dress casually. We will cut our children out of our wills if we don't like who they've married. Even when alone, we feel more comfortable in formal wear.

POWER PROGRAM

Barely Discernible:

We are frightened most of the time, meek, and unable to hold our own with anyone. We may sense we are being pushed around, but it doesn't register.

Ultra-low:

We may be good workers, but we don't like to supervise. In our family life, we willingly take a back seat to more powerful family members. We like to stay out of the limelight. We are usually pleasant.

Low:

We are not preoccupied with gaining power. In fact, we have difficulty looking people, particularly strangers, in the eye. At home and in the office we are content in playing subordinate roles. When our program is triggered by a demeaning remark, we'll retreat and sulk rather than lash out.

Average:

Where most of us are at.

High:

We are intent on moving upward in our family, business, and avocations. We like being the top dog; when we're not, we feel frustrated. We are constantly thinking about how to get ahead, and often blame others for the problems we encounter that keep us at our current rank.

Ultra-high:

We will do practically anything to claw our way to the top. We will sacrifice family, friends, whatever it takes. Once we reach a position of power, we absolutely dominate it. We are fearful of delegating authority, lest our power base be undermined. Further, we continue to claw upward. We are never satisfied.

Off-the-scale:

We will kill for power. It is the only thing that has meaning to us. We are merciless: wiping out dozens of people, or, if we are a government leader, millions, if it will suit our aims. There is a messianic aura about us that frightens people and molds them to our will. We will kill, imprison, or exile subordinates we perceive as threatening our dominant rank.

TERRITORIAL PROGRAM

Barely discernible:

We are quite content to be homeless, if our social and power programs are also ultra-low or below. We might be possessive of a few material things, but losing them wouldn't disturb us for very long.

Ultra-low:

We could spend our lives "camping out" with friends and relatives. We appear to have no real desire for a place we can own. We're quite content to be renting a small apartment since we just need a place to sleep.

Low:

We might dream of having a home of our own, but it's not a goal we'll fight for. If it happens to us, we'll be delighted, but it won't preoccupy our lives. We won't be doing a lot of remodeling, fixing up. We're just living there and it's fine.

Average:

Where most of us are at.

High:

We are intent on having a home of our own. If we are living in an apartment building that's being converted to condominiums, we'll be first in line. We'll borrow to the hilt to do it. After a while, we'll want a bigger home or apartment. We are acquisitive and protective of our possessions.

Ultra-high:

We will do anything to have our own space, home, apartment, land. We measure our lives by the amount of space we have been able to accumulate. We are never happy with what we have. We will install large fences or walls to keep others out. Our homes will be laden with precious possessions.

Off-the-scale:

We will kill for land. Whether we are a frontier rancher or a government leader, the lives of others have less meaning than our penchant for land. We are clever, ruthless, and will use any excuse to pursue the raw drives of our program. We are never satisfied with the possessions we have and are unmerciful in our efforts to gain more.

SEXUAL PROGRAM

Barely discernible:

We are totally asexual. We have probably never had sex and don't care if we ever do. If we don't understand and accept this, we could look for other, dangerous thrills to give us some satisfaction.

Ultra-low:

We have a sex drive, but sex has no real priority in our lives. We will dress frumpily; use as little make-up as possible; never visit a singles bar; or, if married, never think of cheating on our spouses.

Low:

We may have an active sex life, but sex isn't on our minds very much. If we go without it for a relatively long period of time, it doesn't bother us. We'll rarely masturbate if at all. We may dress fashionably, but not sensually.

Average:

Where most of us are at.

High:

Sex is on our minds a good part of our waking hours. We'll dress so that we perceive ourselves to be attractive to the opposite sex. If we are married, we are ripe for an affair if a discreet opportunity presents itself. We will flirt.

Ultra-high:

Sex is uppermost in our minds. If we are female, we will be into short skirts, heavy makeup, jewelry. If we are male, we'll be into tight pants, gold jewelry, upscale foreign cars. Whether single or married, we are looking for sexually oriented affairs.

Off-the-scale:

We are the nymphomaniacs of the world, whether female or male. We'll sacrifice family and friends to live in a world of sex. We will commit date rape if that's what's necessary. Our dress and possessions will be entirely focused on sex.

SECURITY PROGRAM

Barely discernible:

We are almost totally unconcerned for our own well-being. We don't care about money, but want just enough to get through the month. We'll eat when we feel like it. We rarely lock the door. We are just shuffling through life.

Ultra-low:

Personal security is far down on our list of priorities. We are casual about money, where we live, and what we eat. We are unafraid to take long walks at night. We will take risks with our life. We usually trust strangers.

Low:

We lock our doors at night, may or may not have a deadbolt, but we don't think about it much. We accumulate money, but we're not obsessed with it. We will give money to strangers if it strikes us to do so.

Average:

Where most of us are at.

High:

We are concerned about our own personal safety. We have security systems for our home and automobile. We begin to save for our retirement the instant the thought enters our minds as adults. Money is on our minds a lot. We are upset if we have to pick up a dinner check we weren't planning to.

Ultra-high:

We not only have security systems for our home and auto, we have extra locks and devices, too. We never take chances with our lives. If we ski, we'll stay on the beginner slopes. We are obsessed with money. We never have enough and we are miserly with how we spend it.

Off-the-scale:

If we could afford to do it, we would make our home a prison fortress. We don't trust anyone. We'll wear gloves so that we avoid touching germs. We will do whatever we think necessary to accumulate hordes of money. Then we won't spend it.

Next, let's look at how these spindled programs might have evolved and how we should view them in ourselves, once we've recognized them.

26

Recognizing and Accepting
Our Spindled Programs

Most of us don't really know ourselves. What we see is the result of our own perceptions. It has been my experience in both the business and athletic worlds that most of us think of ourselves as at least one notch better than we really are. We appear to have the most difficulty in being honest with ourselves when we have high or ultra-high purpose, social, or power programs.

However, before you begin to strategize on how to trick your brain when circumstances necessitate it, you need to be as honest as possible with yourself in determining where you stand on the calibration of the six spindled brain programs. For example, here is how I see myself:

Purpose:	Average
Social:	Low
Power:	High
Territorial:	High
Sexual:	High
Security:	Average

Others might disagree, as they might with you. But only you are in touch with your rationality, which has to be the ultimate judge.

These positions, once established, are stubborn and difficult to change. But you can work to sidestep them when you know which programs are running, for example, in the midst of an emotional upset.

The CEO I spoke about before knew he had a problem with his tirades. I know he would have changed himself if he felt he had the capability to do so. He thought there was simply something wrong with him, that there was a glitch in his personality, as he once described it to me over dinner. If he had recognized that he was an "ultra-high" on the power scale, in a different world he could have made this known in advance to his employees. He could have said something like: "Look, I have this problem with my power program. Rationally I can see it, but I can't control it. But I promise you I am going to work on it with a psychiatrist. In the meantime, if I lash out at you, I will apologize as quickly thereafter as I can and we'll all attempt to move on from there."

While the positions on the program scales aren't carved in stone, they can take months or even years to change when you recognize and accept where you are and make a decision to attempt a change. To get another perspective on how difficult it is to make a change, let's look at what might happen if we tried to change the positions of others.

For instance, try talking to a fundamentalist Muslim, who is an ultra-high on the purpose program. Tell him that he is wrong in his beliefs, that we really don't know anything, and that he needs to take a second look at his beliefs. With his purpose program running at almost full speed, he'll think you're the one who is nuts.

Watch what happens when you tell a person who is ultra-high on the security program that she doesn't need all those locks on her doors or point out that she should be freer with the way she spends money, and that it's her position on the security program scale that is compelling her to do these things. It will go in one ear and out the other.

Mention to a person in prison, who has a barely discernible social program, that he should begin to cultivate the feelings of love and compassion; that this will make him a better person in the outside world; and that maybe he ought to buy a few books on the subject or undergo therapy, and he'll very likely call for the guard to escort you out.

If a publishing magnate who has an off-the-scale territorial program is told that it is ridiculous for him to have purchased a ranch of 100,000 acres because he'll never get to enjoy all of it, he'll think you're some kind of weirdo.

Pointing out to a woman with an ultra-high sexual program that she should stay home and do some knitting instead of making the rounds of every bar in town will elicit a blank stare.

Try telling a man with an ultra-high sexual program that it is ridiculous for him to be up at night consumed with jealousy because the girlfriend with whom he just broke up is spending the weekend somewhere with another man. He'll tell you to buzz off; he has enough problems.

These program positions are pretty well fixed, at least for the moment. So what we should do is view all six programs as records, mounted one on top of another on a spindle and set to turn at specific velocities when triggered. In essence, these spindled records make up our emotional outlook. They are the foundation of our basic personalities, our outlook on the world.

One result is that each time we encounter a situation where the programs are triggered, our reaction will be approximately the same. Whenever we are driving and someone cuts us off, if the combination of our involved programs makes us rant and rave, then that's what we'll do almost every time.

What fools us into thinking that we aren't robotic in our responses is that the speed of the programs might change slightly during any given day, along with the strength of our rationality, which is a seventh variable. But more often than not, we'll react to the same situations almost identically.

We might try to work at improving these responses. For example, if we are nervous and skittish for days before we are supposed to speak in public, we might try a number of things to change or get around this, including seeking the help of a licensed therapist in an effort to trick our brain into supporting rather than hurting us.

Something might work. But if not, we have to accept it. If we can't handle the emotional upset we are experiencing then our only course of action for the time being is to stop speaking in public.

We need to accept our positions on the program scales for what they are. We didn't walk into a brain store and order the spindled programs that made us nervous. A felon in prison didn't order the barely discernible position on the social program that left him without the capacity for love and compassion. The fundamentalist orthodox rabbi who loudly berates fellow Jews for driving a car on the Sabbath didn't walk into a store to order his off-the-scale purpose program. Nor did the female nymphomaniac with the off-the-scale sexual program, or my former neighbor who wanted pizza delivery men banned from our building.

We don't go to stores and order these programs with any premeditation. We are simply stuck with them at this moment and probably for some time beyond. We need to accept these facts about ourselves, regardless of where we or someone else might want to fix the blame. Our society is merciless when it comes to fixing blame. When a mistake is made in government, journalists and prosecutors will hound people to death to try to find culprits to blame. The investigation is as much a part of the story in the media as the event itself.

Typically we'll believe that the orthodox rabbi who is berating people on Saturdays is responsible for who he has become. But how responsible is he? If he came out of the womb in a home where the parents were atheists, how likely is it that he would be so off-the-scale with this purpose program? He might be the manager of a supermarket today. How responsible is the widow with the off-the-scale security program that keeps her indoors, away from dangers her brain is telling her lurk outdoors and are compelling her to wear gloves so she won't come in direct contact with germs?

This was actually the case with a grand-aunt of mine. If her husband hadn't died when he did and if she herself was positioned lower on the social scale, she wouldn't have undergone the trauma that within two years pushed her to off-the-scale on the security program.

How responsible is the convict in prison who was judged guilty of a serial killing? If he had been born with a different sperm cell and egg, a zygote with gentler genetic predispositions for his social and power programs and was raised by a kindly, religious family, would he have committed the killings?

While homosexuality is not part of the sexual program, the calibrated positions on it are without regard to sexual preference, and so the same concept of responsibility would apply.

A good friend of mine disagrees with this, as does a significant percentage of the world's population. They believe homosexuals actually choose this lifestyle, that given the choice, they would have walked into a brain store to order the homosexuality program.

Some of the latest brain and genetic research is confirming that homosexuality is another genetic aspect of the brain. But common sense also confirms it. A distant relative of mine has a homosexual son. This boy at the age of four would walk around in his mother's heels and he displayed feminine traits throughout his entire childhood. Now not every homosexual displays these traits in their early years, but enough do to indicate the genetic *predisposition.*

Were this a more accepting world, we would simply embrace my relative's son as he is. And my relative, who constantly talks about his heterosexual daughters, and has a high social program, would be less constrained to talk about his son.

But while we might not be to blame for what we have become, that doesn't let us off the hook. We need to accept the genetics and conditioning that was involved in establishing our positions on the scales of the six spindled programs. Then *we need to take the responsibility for them right now.*

We need to accept our program positions in the sense *that we need to manage who we've become.*

We cannot roam about hitting people with clubs and then simply blame the programs that are causing us to do so. While we might not have been responsible for our genetic predisposition, the father who deserted us at the age of six, or the other conditioning that impacted on us and caused our social program to be stuck at barely discernible, we need to be responsible for managing ourselves. If we feel an uncontrollable urge to hit people, we need to check in to see if it can be fixed. If it can't be fixed, we have to live where others will control the urge for us.

Psychiatrists would probably label persons at the extremes of the programs—barely discernible or off-the-scale—as psychotics. They are unable rationally to control the urges created by their program positions. A psychiatrist acquaintance of mine once told me that neurotics think about bad things, while psychotics actually do them. It was also his opinion that therapists do much better in treating psychotics and people with mental disease caused by physical defects than they do neurotics. At the end of any successful treatment of people with neuroses, like the person who is nervous before giving a speech, the psychiatrist would always call the patients back and ask them what the turning point in the treatment was. He was never sure himself.

What we do as a world in keeping psychotics—those people whose program positions impel them to do bad things—from committing such acts is threaten them with prison. This threat appeals to our reason. We might feel the urge to hit someone with a club, but reason also knows that if we do, we might end up in prison, which is a terrible place to be.

The system appears to be successful in borderline cases. If there is any way reason, which is responsible for managing our lives, can control an urge that will land us in prison, it will do so. But in the extreme cases it won't work at all.

A potential convict has the six programs in his head, each of them calibrated to move at fixed speeds when triggered. When he encounters a situation that triggers them, reason alone won't be enough to manage the situation. So off to prison he goes.

Some years ago, a black convict who was a university graduate and who was serving time for rape wrote a highly literate article for a Chicago magazine. In it, he talked about himself, the unpleasantness of prison life, and his hope that when he was released he wouldn't commit rape again. He was released, he raped again, and was sent back to prison. His ability to reason wasn't strong enough to control the urge to rape. The primary culprit was definitely an off-the-scale sexual program. It might even have included an ultra-high power program, as some contend. However, if he were born with the genetic predisposition for a barely discernible sexual program, he wouldn't be raping anyone, he wouldn't even care to have sex with anyone.

How the world will ultimately treat people whose positions on the program scale are at the extremes remains to be seen. One thing we can count on is that it will be far different 500 years from now than it is today.

In any event, once we accept responsibility for our spindled programs, with the exception of those of us who are not at the extremes, our next step is to work harder at managing them.

27

Our Seven Functional Programs

Before we begin to look at how we can best manage our six spindled, limbic-based programs, which create our emotions and our basic outlook, we need to quickly examine the nature of our hard-wired, functional programs. They are seven in number and the tools that Nature programmed into our brains, allowing us to move, communicate, remember, project, and differentiate ourselves.

Our functional programs allow us to perform. They are:

Physical dexterity:

Determines whether we are klutzes or scratch golfers. There is only so much we can do in expanding the limits of our physical dexterity.

Intelligence:

Determines whether we are master chess players or dolts. Each of us has the capacity for a great many vertical intelligences, which aptitude tests can help pinpoint. Some of us have more depth in these intelligences than others.

Memory:

Determines what we remember and has an "operator" of its own. Some of us have photographic memories, while others can't remember something that happened five minutes ago.

339

Language:

Some of us have excellent linguistic capability and can even learn several languages without much effort. Others of us have difficulty learning and coping with one language, which impacts on our ability to communicate.

Energy:

Some of us radiate it, while others are practically devoid of it. All of us are either energy givers or energy takers and we give and take with varying intensities. The most popular amusement parks only hire energy givers: wide smiles, enthusiasm, and chemistry.

Sensitivity:

Determines whether we can cultivate an appreciation for the arts. When combined with our physical dexterity, it determines if we can create or play the works as well as appreciate them.

Physique:

This isn't in the brain, but it is a functional absolute in our lives today. Some of us have better physiques than others. Some of us are more attractive or larger or taller or more shapely or more rugged.

Aside from physique, these are obviously genetic-based programs in our brains, all of which can be enhanced to some extent by conditioning. While we might work day in and day out to improve them, there is probably some upper limit beyond which we can't go. Otherwise, we would all be in sudden-death playoffs for chess and golf championships.

These functional programs probably deserve a book of their own. But in the context of brain tricks, we only need be aware of them because of their potential impact on our six spindled programs.

If one's spouse, for example, has a high sensitivity program and we don't, and she is tired of going to the ballet and art galleries alone while we watch Sunday football, this could trigger her power, social, or purpose programs to spin and cause her to make demeaning statements. "Is this all you want to do, watch that stupid football and drink beer? Don't you have any class at all?"

Now maybe the husband can work on his sensitivity program and sit through endless ballets and operas in the hopes that the artistry will hit him. This works for some people. It simply doesn't for others. His spouse has a higher sensitivity program than he does, something that was genetically based and then enhanced by conditioning. It is no great personal accomplishment. If her power program was low rather than high, she would simply accept the differences between them and forget the remarks. But someone with a high social, power, or purpose program who also has a higher functional program is usually nothing but trouble.

Perhaps her intelligence and linguistic levels are higher than his. She can do the *New York Times* crossword puzzle in an hour, while he has trouble winning in tic-tac-toe. If her power, purpose, or social programs are at high or above, the demeaning statements will sooner or later be directed at him.

The same with physical dexterity: she is a scratch golfer and he is a klutz. Regarding memory, she remembers everything, he can't remember what he did yesterday.

If we are at low or below on the purpose, social, or power scales, having superiority in a functional program doesn't mean very much. We have seen a number of great artists in public life with spouses who were almost peasant-like in outlook and who had a marvelous relationship. That's because these artists were at low or below on their spindled programs and understood that their gifts were the luck of the draw, nothing to become snobbish or arrogant about.

If we are low on the spindled programs, and a sports champion, we won't be carried away. We might come home one night and say: "Hi, honey, I just won the U.S. Open, what's for dinner?"

But if we are high on the purpose, power, or social scales, and have high functional programs, then it's time to watch out. We are Number Ones, perhaps at the most One-and-a-Halfs; the fact that we are functionally better at something will cause us to soar and separate from others. "Hey, I am a famous artist. My works sell for millions of dollars. If you want to talk to me, stand in line over there with the rest of my entourage and I'll get around to you." Or, "I am a beautiful movie star. Your looks repel me. I only talk to people like me. People like you bore me." Or, "I am a baseball player paid millions of dollars a year. You are some little punk kid. Don't bother me with your autograph requests and please don't get fingerprints on my BMW."

As this book has emphasized repeatedly, these hard-wired, functional programs are dependent on the breaks of life. They were coded into our thread in the minutes after our mother's egg was fertilized. The genes combined and they made us who we are. We weren't in the bleachers of the womb orchestrating anything. Everything was done for us. Therefore, if we are knock-outs to look at on the beach and we enjoy the experience, we should be grateful to our parents for having intercourse at the instant they did, with the genes that were involved. We didn't really do a damned thing. And all they did was maybe have some fun. If we are great pianists, then those genes gave us the combination of physical dexterity, intelligence, energy, and sensitivity that made our talent possible. It was blind luck. It was also blind luck that we had the early conditioning that brought the talent to fruition.

We need to accept these functional programs as givens, whether we lucked out with any of them or not. We need to be honest with ourselves in judging their strengths, while recognizing that they are not the big issues that most of us make them out to be.

If someone has the advantage over us with functional programming and is causing us unhappiness, it's vital that we understand why: they are high or above on the social, power, or purpose scales. Having this knowledge will allow us to use our rationality in strategizing how to trick their brains, or ours, so that we can avoid emotional upsets when our spindled programs are triggered.

28

Tricking Your Brain When Your Spindled Programs Are Acting Up

The objective in working with your brain should be to manage it so that it gives you as much peace and contentment as the nature of your life allows. If, for example, you are working at some high-powered job, who needs the extra aggravation that a brain with an ultra-high sexual program might give you? No matter how late you're at the office, you still stop at some singles bar, hoping to find a little action. Then again, you might be badgered by a brain with an ultra-high security program that constantly keeps you fretting about money and safety.

There will always be aggravation that you can never escape. Someone you love becomes very ill or dies. You couple with an alcoholic. Your kids get thrown out of school. No matter who or what you are, there are things waiting out there for you that are going to get you upset. Short of living your life on a mountain top, nothing is going to stop them. If it's not one thing, it will be another. Some of them will be serious upsets that might last months or even years; others will be minor and evaporate by the next morning, or sooner.

A business acquaintance of mine once described life's process in a very graphic, but relevant way. He said: "You have to picture yourself as being out in space sitting on a meteor. Flying at you are both plums and feces. The idea is to dodge so that you catch the plums and miss the feces. But now and then there is no way to avoid catching feces and some of them will be quite large."

If you were able to surround yourself with people who were average or low on the scale of spindled programs, you would find it much easier to have more time when your brain is giving you peace and contentment.

It's those who are above high on the scale, the Number Ones of the world, who will do their best to aggravate us. Or, if we ourselves are high on the scales, we'll do our best to aggravate ourselves. Our goal when this happens is to make the unhappiness, the upset, as short lived as we can. This is our job as managers of our brains, which we have to keep reminding ourselves are nothing more than electro-chemical, mechanical devices that need to be tricked because we don't have a keyboard we can punch.

When we experience such a deep upset that therapy is needed, one of the first things the therapist will do is to help us to begin to get in touch with our feelings. The idea is that if we can talk out our feelings and begin to see them rationally, we might be better able to recognize and resolve whatever it is in our present or past that is causing the upset.

A psychiatrist I knew years ago was always happier when I arrived emotionally upset. He could work with me while I was churning and help me draw out my feelings. The problem with this approach, however, is that there are hundreds of feelings and many of them are difficult to articulate. Some are so strong that they cloud our minds with physical manifestations such as dizziness, pain, nausea, and rashes. It is far easier to get in touch with the spindled programs responsible for the upsets, since there are only six of them.

For example, if we are sitting in a business meeting and someone openly criticizes our work, we will immediately begin to feel anger and embarrassment. Our immediate goal should be to get our brains back to the relative contentment they were feeling before our programs were triggered, to get them back into idle.

To do so, we need to quickly pinpoint which of the spindled programs are running. In this case, it's probably power and purpose. Our power is being demeaned as well as our knowledge of our job, one of the major purposes of our lives. Just the recognition that these programs are causing the upset will allow our rationality to function.

We are never fully rational when our spindled programs have been triggered. Many of the best executive secretaries hold letters written in anger for a day, even though the persons who wrote them insist they go out "this very minute." We look at those letters the next day and are usually grateful they weren't sent.

Once we can regain enough of our rationality, we can begin to strategize how to trick our brains to get rid of the upset all together.

The process might go like this. You have just completed presenting your marketing plan for the year. The new guy on the staff, seated at the end of the table, stands up and says: "That's quite interesting, but I've been doing some work on this myself." He then passes out his own version of the marketing plan.

You are boiling. This jerk has to be a Number One, if he's prepared something like this without telling you about it before the meeting so that you could offer comment. The other people in the room are avoiding your eyes. You think about walking out. But then you decide to get in touch with your programs. You realize right away that it is primarily your power program this louse has touched, and a little bit of your purpose program. You can see what your brain is doing to you. It is not your friend at all. You need it at this minute to be calm so that you can think, and all it wants to do is run your insufferable, high-intensity, spindled programs.

The mere recognition of this jolts some of your rationality back. You are now calm enough to think about what you can do to get yourself out of the situation. The thought hits you that it would be best not to appear defensive, but to be a team player. It's a no-lose way out. After looking at the paper, you say, "You have a few good ideas here. Let's talk about them." Then you start to review this jerk's paper. The rest of the group is so relieved not to be witnessing a tension match that they begin to help, melding what you were suggesting originally with those thoughts this guy came up with that had merit.

As soon as you feel you're back on the team, your spindled programs will slow almost to idle. At the end of the meeting, your brain might even make you feel better as a reward for calling its bluff.

Let's take another situation. Perhaps your spouse has an important assignment and needs to work late at night. He's been on the job for two weeks and now neglects to call you. Your spindled programs are triggered. Now you are beginning to imagine all sorts of things. Maybe he isn't working; maybe he is having sex with someone. Maybe he doesn't care about you anymore. Maybe this, maybe that. It's starting to drive you nuts.

The fact is, he may not be doing anything suspicious at all. He has a low social program and an average or high power program. He likes your relationship, feels in love with you, but you're not constantly on his mind. He feels independent and doesn't like to check in. He thinks you should trust him.

Then one night you simply say to him: "Look, my spindled programs can't take this. I don't care if you work late, but my sexual and power programs do. Do me a favor and help me trick my brain by calling me or leaving me a number to reach you. I'm going to feel a lot better, and our relationship should be worth this little sacrifice on your part."

If he won't do it, then the best way to trick your brain out of the situation is to break up the relationship. Who needs this kind of aggravation? The world is full of potential spouses who have some concern for your spindled programs.

A friend of mine claims that two of his divorces were caused primarily because he had to read something before he went to sleep. He didn't care what happened immediately before, even if it was sex with his wife. Before he could fall asleep he had to read for at least ten minutes. But neither wife could sleep with the light on: their spindled programs were such that they didn't like him leaving the bed and going into the other room. "If you're going to sleep in the other room, why should we be married!" Of course, there were more problems in the relationships than that, but before he started a relationship with anyone new, he always asked first: "By the way, can you sleep with the light on?"

The point is that when the spindled programs don't meld in a relationship, and you can't trick your brain or your spouse's brain into transcending the program, the ultimate trick is simply to break off the relationship.

On the other hand, my aunt Tillie and uncle Irving, even in their eighties could hardly be apart from one another. Every time I saw them over a period of more than fifty years, they were holding hands. But Tillie would sometimes drive him nuts, telling him to do this thing or that, when her power or social programs were running. I once asked my uncle, "Irving, how can you take that?" and he replied, "She's worth it."

However he did it, he was able to handle her spindled programs, her quirks. Maybe his own power and social programs were low and so things worked out. You don't always need to get divorced because your spouse can't sleep with the light on.

Maybe you find yourself annoyingly upset when your neighbor and friend starts his own business and begins hitting it big. All of a sudden a new room addition is being built, new appliances delivered, then one day there is a live-in maid. You want to feel happy for him: you have, after all, been friends for years. But deep down you feel envy and anger each time you look at his home as you pull in your driveway at night or when you think about it during the day.

Now you decide to get in touch with your programs. It's obvious your power program is running at full steam. Your purpose and social programs are also turning, but slower. You can now see quite clearly that before your friend became successful, you were equals in power: your homes cost the same, and you did primarily the same things. All of a sudden he comes into money and it turns out that he must be a high on the power scale, maybe even ultra-high. If he were average or low, he wouldn't be buying all these obvious, new symbols of his status. Every week, it seems, he does something with his money that aggravates you. A person who is low on the power scale wouldn't do this to his friends and neighbors. If he wanted all these new things, he would move to a new neighborhood, where most families would already have them.

Your purpose program is running as well because this fellow is doing better with his life's mission than you are. Your social program is being strained because you are no longer accepting and compassionate.

So what do you strategize to trick your brain? Recognition of the programs in this type of upset—something that is in the middle of the serious spectrum—will usually not give you very much relief. The only relief it offers is not blaming yourself for feeling so damned envious when you've tried to lead a calm, reasoned life. Now you can blame the detestable intensity of your spindled programs.

Maybe at first you decide just to block it out of your mind. But that didn't work for long. Your brain just builds up the pressure. Remember, your brain is usually not your friend when your spindled programs are above average on the scale and they are triggered.

Then you decide to take the offense and let it all hang out. You visit him and tell him that you are thinking about building a deck because your spindled programs are killing you. Now you are wondering how much more of this ostentation he is planning on so you can figure out with relative precision how long it will be before you go broke.

If your neighbor and friend actually turned out to be no higher than average on his own power scale, he didn't realize what he was doing to you and his other neighbors. After being confronted, he would stop it all right then. He might even offer to tear down the deck and get rid of the maid, risking serious injury from his wife, who he now confides to you is an ultra-high on the power scale and is the driving force behind the ostentation.

Knowing this would solve the problem. Your neighbor and friend is still your equal on the power scale. It's his wife who is the problem, and you can handle that. Your friend agreed that he will tell you about her latest ostentations in advance so that you can moan and groan about it together over a beer. Now the envy and anger is evaporating.

But if it turns out that it's your neighbor and friend himself who is the high or ultra-high, and doesn't care how you feel, the envy and anger will persist and probably get worse. The only brain trick available to you is to consider moving away. If your wife objects, tell her, "Look, my spindled programs cannot take this idiot next door. If you want our marriage to be a happy one, we have to get out of here. I checked with the guy and he doesn't plan to move. So we have to." Whether or not you actually move, just thinking about it can afford you a little relief.

Remember, your objective is to keep your spindled programs at idle, but with any upset in the middle of the serious spectrum or above, drastic steps are sometimes necessary. While you are seeking a solution, stop blaming yourself. There is nothing wrong with you. Your spindled programs are the real problem. You didn't walk into a brain store and order them. You have them and you are responsible for managing them; that's what you're trying to do, to the best of your ability.

Maybe you're a golfer and you know you can knock at least eight strokes off your scores if you could just stop choking up in pressure situations: in particular, when you have a three-foot putt to make. Every time you get the ball to that three-foot circle, something happens and eight times out of ten you miss the shot. You know it's not something physical, because on the practice green, things are just the reverse. You *make* the shot most of the time.

The next time you're on the course, you decide to get in touch with your spindled programs. You have to wait until you are on the sixth hole before you have a three-foot putt to make. You notice that as soon as you walk up to the ball, you become tight as a drum. You are feeling pressure, anxiety. Your practice strokes are rushed and stiff. Before you actually make the putt, you think about your spindled programs and you can see right away that your power program is probably the culprit here. You want to be better than you are. You don't want to be perceived by your partners as worse than you are. They are already joking about how you choke under pressure.

See the terrible contradiction we have to live with? Our brains should be our friends. In situations like this, they should be helping us. Why are they making us feel like we are in front of a firing squad? But we have a high-power program, maybe ultra-high, and when it's triggered, our brains are useless when it comes to lending a hand.

Knowing this, we hit the putt and we miss. Just pinpointing the program in a situation like this is usually not enough. But at least we know what the problem is and so it's time to strategize on ways to trick our brain to help us in the future.

The following week, you call a friend who knows some golf pros in the area. You ask him to recommend a pro who is good at dealing with the mental aspect of the game. He does. You contact the pro and go out for a round. You tell him: "Look, my spindled programs are causing me to miss these stupid, little putts. What can I do about this?"

After seeing you play, he suggests that you buy one of those carpeted practice putting greens for your basement and then each morning or night, hit at least 250 three-foot putts. He tells you that until you hit 10,000 putts (this is the number that many coaches actually use), that you won't be confident with the shot. Confidence is the key to overcoming pressure, he says. Until you *feel* you can do it, you're not going to have the confidence and will continue to choke up.

So you buy the practice putting set and start hitting those three-foot putts, 250 each day. In addition, you go to a bookstore and pick up three books dealing with the mental side of golf. You study the mind tricks suggested by the pros. For example, picture the exact line you want the ball to travel; imagine the entire event before you shoot, including visualizing the ball going in the hole.

Maybe the practice or the books helped. Maybe at least you're sinking more three-foot putts than you did before. Your confidence is up a little. Then again, maybe nothing you've tried works. If that's the case, then accept the fact that you choke up on three-foot putts, and confess it to your golf partners. "Men, I have a confession to make. My spindled programs, particularly my power program, are screwing up my putting game. If you want me to find another foursome, that is fine with me. Otherwise, you'll just have to bear with me."

If your partners are Number Ones they might ask you to leave the game. If they are Number Two-and-One-Halfs and above, they'll realize your problem and want you to stay. They might even needle you. "Oh, oh, it's a three-foot putt, there go his spindled programs." But so what, you're not out on the course to win the Masters. You're out there to enjoy yourself and have some fun with your friends. So accept your programs and have fun. Maybe next year, you'll move down a notch on your power scale and you can try it all over again.

Next let's look at an emotional upset that is higher up on the serious spectrum:

A man with children is in the middle of a divorce. Things just didn't work out. He met his wife on a blind date twelve years ago. She was gorgeous, he thought; her personality was absolutely great. They got along like two peas in a pod. Marriage was a natural evolution. Things were still great after the marriage. He loved his wife and she loved him; they both worked and couldn't wait to get home to be together.

Then the children arrived, three of them. Before long, the little problems that every couple has began to magnify. She loved company, but he was working so hard he couldn't stand the thought of going out. She liked to visit her family at least once a week, but he found the experience boring. With the kids going to Sunday School, she became religious again and wanted to go to church every Sunday.

He didn't mind going, but only on the major holidays. There were constant arguments and tension. The sex began to diminish and this just made the tensions worse. She began joking about his sexual abilities. Soon it was hopeless and they knew it was time to split.

No one was really at fault, except maybe the person who organized the blind date. But there he is in his own apartment, with his brain driving him absolutely crazy with guilt and remorse. He begins to think there is something fundamentally wrong with him.

One night he is so depressed he can hardly move. Here he is, trying to do the right thing to help himself through the rest of his life, and his brain isn't helping at all. Why isn't it supporting him, he says to himself. Who is up there directing things? Where is a keyboard he can punch? Finally, he puts the spindled program concept to work.

He looks at the problem and is sickened. *All six* of his spindled programs are moving at one time. His power program is running because he is no longer an official head of household. He is not sure where he is in the power rankings, even in relation to his kids. He can't discipline them, wield any power over them, because he's afraid they'll end up hating him.

His social program is running. He misses the love and compassion he felt when they were all in a family unit. His brain makes him remember primarily the good times. The bad times that would make him feel good about the impending divorce are conveniently forgotten. Some friend.

His sexual program is running. On the one hand, he needs to couple, but he is afraid of one-night stands because of AIDS. On the other, he avoids females who might be great future companions because he doesn't want another commitment so soon. To make matters worse, he hears that his about-to-be-ex-wife is going out with other men; his sexual jealousy is chugging full steam.

The husband's purpose program is spinning, but it's probably the slowest of all the programs on the spindle. He begins to question who he is, what he is supposed to be doing on this planet. He thought it was to have a nice family and enjoy his later years with his wife beside him and his grandkids at his feet.

Even his territorial program is running. The house he owned is no longer his. Worse, there are probably other men sitting in his favorite chair and walking around his house, which is no longer a home. In the meantime, he is renting! He thought this was behind him. He has a high territorial program.

Finally, his security program is running. Now he has to support two households. Money is tight. He has to watch every nickel. He worries that he might be losing his grip at work. If he gets laid off, what then?

With all six spindled programs running, he realizes why he is feeling as bad as he does. This is Nature throwing its couples separation syndrome at him full tilt, hoping the pain will force him back together with his wife.

Now he begins to strategize on how he might trick his brain into giving him the peace and contentment he is seeking. He wants to get the spindled programs slowed down and ultimately into idle.

The first thing he thinks of is to see a good therapist, someone who specializes in divorced couples, if there is such an animal. He had thought about seeing a therapist after his first two weeks in the apartment, when the misery began to really set in. He didn't like the idea. It assaulted his manhood.

However, now the husband sees that his brain is not his friend, that it has to be tricked. And he perceives the therapist as someone who can help him do just that.

But before he takes the plunge, he decides to scout the book stores to find books about how to endure divorce and still love himself. Maybe there is a trick or two he can pick up from these books. And so he reads every book he can find. Maybe they help him a little, maybe they don't.

If they don't, he decides to pursue the therapist. He has read that one of the things a therapist does to help is to draw out the story of the client's life leading to the marriage, and then the pertinent experiences of the marriage itself. He repeats this over and over and over again through the gentle guidance of the therapist until his spindled programs get the message that his rationality already knows . . . that this marriage was a no-fault mistake. He did the best he could, considering the nature of his spindled programs, which he didn't go to a store and buy. He is trying to achieve the all-important "insight," as many therapists call it.

Maybe six months to a year of this will help him slow his spindled programs down a little. If so, it will be quite a relief. If not, he will know for a fact that his brain doesn't want him off the hook.

It thought it had a sucker in him, to couple and nurture the young. This is something that Nature wants awfully bad. Now he is going against the grain, and his brain wants him to suffer for it. So he is going to have to live with the lousy feelings until his children have grown, or a new life just hits him over the head.

Maybe by sheer accident he'll bump into someone who can calm his spindled programs. Maybe she'll convince his brain that he's actually back with his wife.

He'll never know for sure what's really going to work when it comes to tricking his brain. He can only strategize and give it his best shot.

Now let's look at one more example that is up there on the spectrum of serious emotional upsets:

A woman can't get ahead in business life, even though reason tells her that she has the skills to do so. She would like to blame it all on being a female, but she sees many of her friends getting ahead. They don't seem to have a problem.

One night when she is with them, she decides to ask for a frank evaluation. What's wrong with me, she asks. They think about it and tell her that from their point of view, it appears she is suffering from low self-esteem and that this is frustrating her.

When she is with them, as she is tonight, she is just fine. But in business situations, she comes off as too abrasive, too obviously obsessed with moving ahead.

She thinks back and realizes that her early conditioning was no bed of roses. Her parents were rarely supportive. They never helped her through the early emotional problems that are part of every normal person's adolescence. They constantly nagged at her until she began to question her own abilities. She never realized then that her brain was not her friend. It didn't help her fight back when it saw that her parents were below reasonable minimums in parental ability.

And when she finally got out of the house to go to a university, the nagging continued by long distance. Her parents never let her alone. They would always compare her to this cousin or that one, who was doing so much better, or so they thought. She managed to graduate, half in a mope. When she went out in the business world, she found that her problems only compounded. She saw herself as absolutely luckless. She couldn't get a break no matter what she tried.

Now, however, she decides to apply the spindled program concept.

The first thing she sees is that all the hassle her parents gave her helped to generate a power program that was nearing ultra-high. Yet she couldn't get a foothold to exercise that power. Whenever she had an opportunity she would overdo it. She came off as abrasive and obsessed with herself. Her power program was definitely spinning.

Her purpose program was also going at full steam. She wanted to be somebody in life, to prove to her parents and others that she was worth something and had a destiny to fulfill. But she was doing nothing with her life of which her parents would approve. She was 27 and they still wouldn't leave her alone. They read Ilyich Barkeloff's chapter on the "Delusions of Maturity" and couldn't understand how a 110-year-old Russian could know anything. "What can an old dummy like him know," they said.

Her social program was running, although at a lower speed. She was lonely. She missed the love and acceptance that she saw the parents of her friends giving them.

The recognition of the programs gave her some relief, as did the conclusion that her brain was definitely not her friend. Where was it all these years, when she had to suffer the endless abuse of her parents? Why couldn't it help her sort through the awful emotions she was feeling and give her some comfort?

So why not trick this flawed organ of hers, she thinks to herself. Now she begins to strategize. She begins to think about what she can do to trick it.

She decides first to put herself through a whole battery of psychological testing. She would nail down how good her functional programs were, her vertical intelligences and memory in particular.

When the tests are complete, she learns that she is at least as good as she always thought she was. It is her running, spindled programs that have been confusing her.

Then she decides to attend seminars aimed at raising her self-esteem, the Dale Carnegie type of classes. She calls friends in training and human resources and locates the best outfit in the city. She goes through a week of intensive work. Among other things, she is videotaped giving canned presentations. Now she can see how she comes off. Then she attends other seminars and programs of the same type.

Maybe this begins to work for her, maybe it doesn't. All she knows is that she is going to keep at it in a relentless pursuit to get her spindled programs to slow down. She understands that it isn't she who has the problems, it's her brain, a flawed instrument that causes problems for everyone. Someday something might get a message through to it and it will finally start to help her. Or maybe it won't. If not, blame it on lousy luck because that's what she had. She did what she could.

*   *   *

When you have a problem involving your emotions or your thought processes, you no longer need to cope with them as if there is anything wrong with *you. You can now assume there is nothing wrong with you. You are the victim of the spindled programs in your brain.*

These programs were inputted either by your genetics or your conditioning and at this point in your life they exist as they are. It is useless to blame your parents, your friends, your relatives, employer, your luck, even the basic nature of your brain as it was formatted to be the day you came out of your mother's womb. That is all behind you now. The damage is done, and there isn't one of us who hasn't suffered from our genetics and our environment.

We are all damaged, we are all flawed. All of it is encoded chemically in our brains. Earlier, Dr. Roy Sanders put it properly when he said that we can make no real choices on our own. The choices we have made at any given time in our lives were choices that our brain programs were preordained to make for us. If we made bad choices, the only thing to blame were the brain programs that existed at the instant the choices were made.

The idea now is to look at your brain as if it were a computer sitting on your desk. View any problems you have as flaws in either its hardware, the basic genetic structure that you inherited from the genes of your parents, or its software, all the environmental inputting that was done as you grew up and proceeded through life.

As I am writing this I know that the word processing software I'm using has a flaw. Some of the command functions described in the operating manual are missing and occasionally the copy will drift off the right side of the screen. The software company agrees that these are flaws, a surprising acquiescence that came during a toll-free service telephone call. They are sending me a new disk. Regrettably, it is not so easy to fix the flaws in our brains.

We as yet cannot place a toll-free call to some group of Super Scientists to request that repairs be made. If we have a lousy memory, are unable to spell, want to rid ourselves of an excessive sex drive or biting jealousies or a compunction to steal things from department stores, we have to cope with the problem ourselves. That begins with an attitude that doesn't blame anyone, ourselves included, but focuses on the defects in our brains as they exist at the moment.

With this kind of attitude we can approach it in a more business-like manner. The question must always be: *What is my brain doing to trick me into feeling about myself the way I do and what can I do to trick it back?*

If you decide to go to a bookstore to purchase a self-help book of some kind, you don't need to look around embarrassed to see if someone is watching. You are doing it in an effort to trick your brain, to reprogram it in some way and there is no shame in that. If you can afford to work with a sports professional to improve your athletic ability, go ahead and do it. If you think that consulting a therapist, a psychiatrist, or psychologist who might trick your brain into solving a mental quirk or give you the peace and harmony you deserve, then do it.

You don't have to tiptoe around it. The psychiatrist has no more of the big answers to life than you do. He or she can't tell you the general idea behind the universe or whose idea it was. In terms of real life issues, you are equal to everyone. The difference between you and a therapist is that these professionals are trained to help you identify your problem and then help you resolve it. You might be trained as an accountant or baseball player or maybe you are good at parking cars, you never dent one. Whatever you do, you are just as good as the therapist.

However, therapists have the training you need at the moment to trick your brain into doing or undoing what needs to be done. As Art Meyer said, you might eventually be able to walk into a brain store and order brain cassette PSY48709 and in minutes become a fully trained psychiatrist yourself, ready to help others. Having such training is not a big deal under those circumstances.

You should realize as well that you may not be able to trick your brain into helping you resolve a problem, no matter what you try. If you hate your son-in-law because he is black and you are white, you might find there is nothing that will solve the problem for you, even after years of effort. You can simply blame it on the spindled power program given to you at birth that makes you distrust anyone who is different. That distrust can range from a mild annoyance to full-blown hatred. You got the full dose. You inwardly want to love this guy because he is making your daughter happy. It would improve the state of your family unit if you could make it happen. Some of the things you thought of trying, like camping with the man for two solid weeks, just you and him in the wilderness, might work. You could begin to see beyond the pigment of his skin. Then again, it might not work. You go camping, during which you genuinely begin to like the fellow; but then you get home, see him with your daughter, and the rage is automatically retriggered.

If this happens, live with it as you would if you only had one eye. It is a flaw. Do the best you can. Tell your son-in-law that this is just a lousy, spindled power program and you hope it will go away. In the meantime, work to mask your feelings.

Remember, there is no toll-free number to call to get your brain fixed, whatever your problem. You might be able to do something about it or you might not. If you can't, then consider it another handicap you have to live with, like a sore elbow or tendonitis in the knee.

Maybe you're the president of a small country, one of those in eastern Europe that recently became independent. Your people are howling and marching in the streets because the country adjacent to you just claimed four square miles of land you thought was yours. They want you to mobilize your small army and "liberate" the area. But now you see that the hysteria is caused by the territorial programs we have that make us want our own land and stake it out, protecting it at all costs.

You realize that the "motherland" your citizens are calling your country is nothing more than a manifestation of this lousy spindled program that makes us covet and protect the land. You sympathize with the arguments that this land has been occupied by the forefathers of your country's citizens for more than two thousand years. You can feel the emotional ties yourself. But you also know, as a student of history, that two thousand years is nothing but an eye blink in anthropological time. You also understand that at some point back in time, those forefathers uprooted another tribe to lay claim to the land, in what for most of the world has been an unending, relentless, and unthinking genetic process.

Your problem is to trick the brains of your countrymen into seeing that war is no answer. If the world had one recognized authority under which all nations had to exist, you could apply to it for a review and seek relief. But that option isn't open. You consider going on national television with a chart of the brain and explain to your citizens how they are the victims of a genetic, territorial program and to please relax while you try to work out a compromise with the country next door. But you discard that idea because your people will think you are crazy and throw you out of office.

Finally, you come up with an idea. You learn that two old generals, one from each country, are longtime friends. You approach them and they agree to set up a commission to work out a compromise plan. You get them both on television. They project a gentle and reasonable image. They recount the horrors of war. They bring their entire family groups with them. The families mingle and talk warmly to one another. Mothers parade their kids in front of the cameras, all wearing signs saying: "We trust our grandfathers to reach a satisfactory compromise."

That night you can hardly sleep hoping that what you did will work, that the brains of your citizens will be tricked into giving you the time you need. But you also know that it might not work. You are already thinking of other ideas. You know that the brains of your citizens are not their friends. They want war over a relatively trivial matter; you know they deserve peace, harmony, and contentment. You are determined to do anything civilized to trick their brains into doing the right things.

This has been the message of *Brain Tricks*. Your brain is not always your friend. If you are lucky, it will give you days and perhaps years of happiness and contentment. But at some point it will become your enemy. You will find yourself thinking or doing things that are not rational. When that happens, remember that your brain is tricking you. Realize it, cheer up, relax, and then work hard to trick it back.